Dissident Postmodernists

Penn Studies in Contemporary American Fiction

A Series Edited by Emory Elliott, University of California at Riverside

A complete listing of the books in this series appears at the back of this volume

Dissident Postmodernists Barthelme, Coover, Pynchon

Paul Maltby

UNIVERSITY OF PENNSYLVANIA PRESS   Philadelphia

Permission is acknowledged to reprint excerpts from published works. A complete listing can be found following the Index to this volume.

Copyright © 1991 by the University of Pennsylvania Press
Printed in the United States of America

Library of Congress Cataloging-in-Publication Data
Maltby, Paul.
  Dissident postmodernists : Barthelme, Coover, Pynchon / Paul Maltby.
    p.   cm. — (Penn studies in contemporary American fiction)
  Includes bibliographical references and index.
  ISBN 0-8122-3064-7
  1. American fiction—20th century—History and criticism.   2. Barthelme,
Donald—Criticism and interpretation.   3. Coover, Robert—Criticism and
interpretation.   4. Pynchon, Thomas—Criticism and interpretation.
5. Postmodernism (Literature)—United States.   6. Dissident arts—United States.
I. Title.   II. Series
PS374.P64M3   1991
813′.5409—dc20   91-25115
                                                                    CIP

For Shirley

Contents

Acknowledgments

Peter Nicholls of Sussex University supervised the doctoral thesis from which this book originated, and I am particularly grateful to him for the guidance and support he gave me during the years of research. Thanks are also due to Madan Sarup of London University, Peter Humm of Thames Polytechnic, and John Whitley of Sussex University for helpful suggestions on how to improve sections of the book. I alone take responsibility for any errors of judgment or interpretation. Finally, I wish to thank Shirley, my wife, for typing the manuscript and for patiently enduring the sacrifices made on behalf of this project.

Paul Maltby

Notes on the Text

Postmodernist writers make frequent use of ellipses. Therefore, when making cuts in quotations from their texts, I have distinguished my own ellipses by enclosing them in square brackets.

Works are cited by the year of publication of the edition I have used. Original dates of publication are included in the Bibliography.

Introduction

This study seeks to mark out and explore a dissident tendency within that body of fiction known only generally as "postmodernist." The conception of a dissident postmodernist fiction raises questions about what, in the postmodern culture of late capitalism, constitutes the political and what constitutes an oppositional mode of writing. A study of this fiction must accommodate a reconceptualization of the political, for notions of what may be said to be encompassed by politics were revised in the 1960s and 1970s, precisely the period in which nearly all the texts examined below were written. I shall discuss the prodigious enlargement of the notion of the political within the sphere of language during these years. I shall argue that developments specific to, or more advanced under, late capitalism have altered the forms of discourse and structures of communication in ways that have politicized perceptions of language and, in particular, raised consciousness of language as a medium of social integration. Principal among the developments considered are: the erosion of the "public sphere"; the diffusion of concept-poor discourses which limit social understanding; the enlargement of the state's propaganda apparatuses; the corporate management of mass communications; the ideological ascendancy of functionalist discourses.

It is this expanded notion of the political within the sphere of language and communications that will serve as a basis for distinguishing a dissident current of postmodernist fiction from an "introverted" current. I shall read the texts selected for the case studies as pursuing the political implications of language, with special reference to their heightened perception of the integrative powers of language in its prevailing late-capitalist forms. And I shall read the reflexivity of these texts and their disruptions of linguistic and narrative norms not just as a probing and demonstration of the textual production of meaning (the primary concerns of "introverted" postmodernist fiction). Rather, they will be grasped as, in the first instance, the tactics of writing which exposes and struggles against the ideologies and conceptual limits of language in its postmodern modes.

In a study of this kind it will be necessary to confront several influential constructions of postmodernism as a literary-critical concept. I shall question, among other things, the ahistoricity of accounts which miss, or at least under-theorize, the relevance of late-capitalist developments to the postmodernist writer's preoccupation with problems of language. Finally, any discussion of postmodernist fiction today must be situated in relation to recent debates about postmodernism as a general theory of aesthetics and culture. ("Postmodernism" as a category of literary criticism predates by about fifteen years "postmodernism" as a category of aesthetic and cultural theory, and despite their kindred perspectives these categories are, for present purposes, best discussed separately.) The debates about postmodern aesthetics have consequences for the ways we read postmodernist fiction. Of particular relevance to a study proposing a dissident current of postmodernist literature is the influential view, fostered by Fredric Jameson, Terry Eagleton, and others, that postmodernist art is essentially non-adversarial. It is a view I shall want to contest. First, however, a theoretically loaded term like "postmodernism" requires some introduction, and so I shall begin by briefly surveying the range of the concept in its current usage.

Chapter 1
Constructions of Postmodernism

Postmodernism—Overview of an Expanding Concept

Cultural studies in recent years have been invigorated by the debates about postmodernism. The concept, once confined to literary and architectural theory, has burst its bounds and now occupies a privileged position in cultural and social theory and has footholds in philosophy. The remarkable development of the concept has given currency to the idea of "postmodern culture" and even the epochal notion of a "postmodernity." The concept has become so firmly entrenched in contemporary thought that to dismiss it as merely an intellectual fad is an inadequate response; at the very least, irrespective of arguments about its meaning and legitimacy, the frenetic discussion of postmodernism is itself a cultural phenomenon worthy of attention: Why has the concept of postmodernism flourished?

We may begin by noting the charismatic appeal of a term which, at one and the same time, has the power to suggest a mutation in artistic practice, an epistemic shift in western thought, and an epochal transition to a new cultural order. It is an enormously pretentious concept, and yet its very pretensions provoke thoughts about cultural change. A command of the term seems to promise to situate us on the cutting edge of cultural analysis; it seems to promise to fulfill our distinctively *unpostmodern* desire for a totalistic concept through which we can gain intellectual purchase on a glut of radically new ideas and practices. Second, the concept of the postmodern is proving to be ideal ground for a multidisciplinary approach to cultural studies. We have quickly grown accustomed to analyses of postmodernist texts that mobilize concepts from a wide range of disciplines. The concept, as it has evolved in recent years, is, broadly speaking, a conjunction of three fields of thought: postmodernist aesthetics, post-structuralist philosophy and literary theory, and post-Marxist sociologies. Third, the extraordinary ascent of the concept must be seen as an ideological matter. The debate about postmodernism is a battleground of competing political visions. The terms in which postmodernist practices are celebrated or denounced imply, as Fredric Jameson has observed, ideological positions (Jameson 1984b). Take the case of art. For a disillusioned Marxist like Lyotard, who acclaims postmodernist art for being "not in principle governed by preestablished rules" (Lyotard 1984b, p. 81), postmodernism is welcomed as the expression of a norm-free, dynamic, neo-liberal pluralism. On the other hand, Eagleton's repudiation of postmodernism as "the dissolution of art into the prevailing forms of commodity production" (Eagleton 1985, p. 60) is premised on a negative evaluation of capitalism as a process of universal reification.

Postmodernism today is a hypertrophied and unstable term that is fought over and selectively appropriated on behalf of various theoretical projects. So many issues are now discussed in its name that it is almost impossible to determine the boundaries of the concept. It is an eddy of intellectual cross-currents. The perceived inadequacies of diverse disciplines from psychoanalysis (cf. Rustin 1989) to social theory (cf. Kellner 1988) are increasingly analyzed within the conceptual frameworks of the postmodernism debates. Here, I shall merely introduce, without comment and with a large measure of conceptual overlap, selected key issues which currently inform discussions about postmodern art, culture, and society. Not all the issues adumbrated below are relevant to this study; the purpose of the following lines is just to give the reader some idea of the *current scope of the concept* "postmodernism."

Populist Aesthetics

The cultural space of late capitalism is suffused with the representations of commodity aesthetics and mass-media entertainment. These are understood to supply the dominant forms of cognition and imagination. Hence the postmodernist preoccupation with artifice, spectacle, dreck and kitsch. These features of a "debased," commercial mass culture become the materials of an art whose relationship to (high) modernism is, in consequence, rendered ambivalent. On the one hand, it rejects the grounds for the latter's "élitist" faith in its own (suprasocial) transcendence. On the other hand, this art is animated by the distinctively *modernist* impulses to innovate and transgress formal conventions. Under these circumstances, it is said, the (high-modernist) distinction between art and mass culture has collapsed.

Programmatic Self-Reflexiveness

The distinction between aesthetic practice and theory has dissolved as the former has systematically and self-consciously incorporated some perspectives of the latter in order to examine its own nature as a signifying practice. At the expense of "story," postmodernist art "foregrounds" the act of narration as a signifying process by exposing the operation of its narrative codes or rhetorical strategies. By this means the artist seeks to demonstrate that reality as perceived does not speak for itself but is always signified. Insofar as postmodernist art reveals itself as a signifying practice, it renounces claims to any transcendental or absolute perspective on reality and points to its own provisionality. In a postmodern culture, art is no longer privileged as a source of truth; like all discourses, it is understood to *constitute* its object of study. Finally, the practice of eclecticism may be read as self-consciously pointing to a notion of the artist as a pasticheur (a trafficker in others' meanings) as opposed to an author (an originator of meanings).

The Limit-Text

Postmodern literary theory extols the text which dissolves the union of signifier and signified, that is, which frees the signifier from its enthrallment to representation; the text which "bringing itself to the limits of speech [. . .] undoes nomination," which "brings to a crisis [the reader's] relation with language" (Barthes [1973] 1975, pp. 45, 14); the text through which (it is said) the reader exits from the symbolic order and hence from the subjectivities that order supports.

The Decentered Subject and the Primacy of Discourse

The epistemological juncture of postmodernism is defined by a paradigm shift in which post-humanist philosophies of language have superseded Cartesian/phenomenological philosophies of consciousness. Hence, the subject is "decentered" in relation to meaning; he/she is not the source or author of (private) meaning but quite the reverse: the subject or, more precisely, subjectivities are "called up" by discourses which position the subject within the social order and construct his/her perspectives on reality.

Discourses construct differences which give meaning to a world that would otherwise be perceived as an amorphous, undifferentiated mass. It is this recognition of the primacy of discourse (as opposed to mind) in the constitution of meaning that leads postmodern theorists to see the subject as encountering the world, history, society, or identity in the form of "narratives" or "fictions"; they are not given to consciousness immediately as essences.

Différance vs. Logocentrism

In the work of Derrida, "différance" is the "play" of signifiers that produces the differences on which meaning depends; it is "the differing/deferring origin of differences." Because this play or sliding or instability of signifiers in their relation to signifieds is perpetual, meaning is forever "deferred" or postponed and, therefore, necessarily illusory. This has profound implications for the business of interpretation. Interpretation ceases to be seen as a matter of recovering some original or transcendent meaning that serves as the foundation of a system of thought, as if that foundation existed *outside* the play of linguistic differences (logocentrism). Instead, interpretation becomes a deconstructive process of revealing how *all* meanings or, better, meaning-effects, are produced by the play of differences.

Critique of Universal Knowledge

Hegelian/Marxist conceptions of "totality" and the "dialectic" have been rejected by neo-Nietzschean philosophies which argue for a pluralist conception of reality as a chaos of fragments; which argue for a conception of historical development as nothing more than the random occurrence of micro-events; which substitute "perspectivism" for Truth. Thus, Lyotard defines "postmodern" as "incredulity toward metanarratives," where metanarratives are understood as totalizing theories of history or society that serve to legitimate scientific practice and that, moreover, are identified with "totalitarian" repression of "differences." The multiplicity of "language games" that are incommensurable with each other precludes a universal or "consensual" language of science whereby the subject can achieve a totalizing perspective on reality. Instead, postmodern knowledge "refines our sensitivity to differences." Finally, postmodern science, says Lyotard, is a "paralogical" practice, which, instead of seeking to unify knowledge as a *grand récit*, "searches for instabilities" (e.g., paradoxes and ruptures) that subvert paradigms of knowledge (Lyotard 1984a, pp. xxiv, xxv, 53, 60).

Radical Democracy

One influential strain of "progressive" politics, at the postmodern conjuncture, seeks to supplant the "essentialist paradigms" of Marxism, notably the theory that society is founded on class struggle and the projection of the working class as the necessary agent of emancipation. Denying that the social formation can be grasped as a unified, coherent structure, a "radical democratic politics" identifies multiple sites of antagonism. It respects the autonomy of diverse political struggles and appeals "democratically" not only to subjects as workers but to a plurality of nonclassist subject-positions (e.g., ethnic or feminist) (Laclau and Mouffe 1985).

Politics of Information

Computerization and a decisive shift toward the commodity production of information have engendered an "information economy" where ownership of, and access to, data banks become a critical political issue (see Lyotard 1984a and Morris-Suzuki 1986). Herbert Schiller has emerged as a key theorist of the politics of information management. In the following observations, he states some of the main themes of this field of enquiry:

The definition and presentation of everyday reality, nationally and internationally, have been the prerogatives of a score of media conglomerates. The concentrated control of information by Western monopolies has created enormous difficulties for those seeking economic self-determination and political autonomy. By their information selection and control, the Western media . . . assist in providing the transnational corporate business system with diverted and disoriented domestic publics. (Schiller 1981, p. 2)

Media Society

In Baudrillard's account of the "media society," mass-communication channels have penetrated and colonized the formerly protective enclosure of domestic space. Henceforth, exposed to the absolute proximity and total instantaneity of communication, the individual becomes "a switching center for all the networks of influence" (Baudrillard 1983a, p. 133), a post-alienated consciousness responding "ecstatically" (rather than critically) to media transmissions. This new communicative order marks "the end of the social" whose perspectival space—"the scene of conflicts and historical contradictions"—has been replaced by "the space of simulation [which] confuses the real with the model" (Baudrillard 1983b, pp. 82–84). It is a situation where (media) models of "the real" *precede* and constitute "the real," whence simulation is understood to dedifferentiate (or "implode") basic binary distinctions like "true" and "false" or "real" and "imaginary" (Baudrillard 1983c, p. 5).

Jameson on Postmodernism

While, for reasons given later, I recognize that the critical effectivity of art in a late-capitalist society may be greatly diminished, I want to question constructions of postmodernist art as essentially non-adversarial. Habermas opens a brief but cogent essay on postmodernism by endorsing one critic's response to the postmodernist architecture at a Venice biennial: "It is a diagnosis of our times: 'Postmodernity definitely presents itself as Antimodernity'" (Habermas 1983, p. 3). He proceeds to denounce postmodernism as a "neo-conservative" offensive against the Enlightenment "project of modernity"—the latter upheld by him as that which "revolts against the normalizing functions of tradition; [which] lives on the experience of rebelling against all that is normative" (pp. 5–6). Richard Gott shares this assessment of postmodernism as a reactionary tendency:

> The revolution was Modernism. [. . .] The counter-revolution is Postmodernism. [. . .] It is not difficult to comprehend this cultural and aesthetic trend now known as Postmodernism—in art and architecture, music and film, drama and fiction—as a reflection of (or a comparable phenomenon to) the present wave of political reaction sweeping the Western world. (Gott 1986, p. 10)

Eagleton offers an alternative account of postmodernist art as non-adversarial based, like Jameson's, on a "logic-of-capital" analysis. He writes:

> In the commodified artefacts of postmodernism, the avantgardist dream of an integration of art and society returns in monstrously caricatured form. [. . .] The very autonomy and brute self-identity of the postmodernist artefact is the effect of its thorough *integration* into an economic system where such autonomy, in the form of the commodity fetish, is the order of the day. (Eagleton 1985, pp. 61–62)

However, it is in Fredric Jameson's "Postmodernism, or the Cultural Logic of Late Capitalism," arguably the *locus classicus* of the postmodernism debate, that we find the most developed and compelling account of postmodernist art as essentially non-adversarial (Jameson 1984a). First, consider his discussion of pastiche.

Jameson identifies pastiche as a defining formal feature of postmodernist aesthetics. He sees two factors as crucial in the emergence of the "well-nigh universal practice today" whereby texts speak in the "dead" language and forms of the past (pp. 64–65). He argues that the "decentering" of the formerly "sovereign" or autonomous subject undermines the high-modernist conception of style—the unique, distinctively individual style of the *auteur*. All that remains for the producers of culture is the "imitation of dead styles" (p. 65). Second, Jameson links the emergence of pastiche to the absence of a linguistic norm, the latter explained as a consequence of "the stupendous proliferation of social codes today" into discourses which affirm ethnicity, gender, class allegiance, or race; into occupational and disciplinary jargons. It is a situation in which pastiche supersedes parody:

Pastiche is, like parody, the imitation of a peculiar mask, speech in a dead language: but it is a neutral practice of such mimicry, without any of parody's ulterior motives, amputated of the satiric impulse, devoid of laughter and of any conviction that alongside the abnormal tongue you have momentarily borrowed, some healthy linguistic normality still exists. (p. 65)

This account of pastiche is strikingly illustrated in a discussion of postmodernist architecture. Jameson refers us to "what the architecture historians call 'historicism,' namely the random cannibalization of all the styles of the past, the play of random stylistic allusion . . ." (pp. 65–66). Historicism is dramatically visible in the eclectic designs of Robert Venturi, Michael Graves, Charles Moore, and others, in the fusions, for example, of "pop" and "classical," or high-modernist and antiquarian forms.

Jameson, whose own conception of postmodernism originated in the architectural debates (p. 54), privileges architecture as the paradigmatic expression of postmodernist aesthetics (p. 79). Indeed, it is largely through the terms in which he explains postmodernist architecture that he reads postmodernist art in general. Yet, from the standpoint of a conception of an adversarial postmodernism, this procedure appears unsound. The problem is that this account of pastiche as a characteristically postmodernist practice misses the possibility that past styles may be invoked *antagonistically.* Postmodernist fiction is well known for its exploitation of past literary styles, but often this practice, unlike architectural historicism, is neither "random" nor "neutral." Rather, it is strategically motivated. Earlier narrative paradigms—for example, realism, melodrama, gothic fantasy—are critically engaged as forces whose epistemologies or mythic stereotypes *remain active* in coding our perceptions of the present. These past paradigms are certainly not imitated as "dead styles" or spoken as "dead language." A programmatic statement of the need to engage earlier narrative forms on the assumption that they are far from dead is announced in Coover's *Pricksongs and Descants.* After applauding Cervantes for an art that "struggled against the *unconscious mythic residue* in human life" (Coover 1970, p. 77, my emphasis), Coover makes the following observation/prescription:

The novelist uses familiar mythic or historical forms to combat the content of those forms and to conduct the reader [. . .] to the real, away from mystification to clarification, away from magic to maturity, away from mystery to revelation. (p. 79)

However, the argument cannot rest here. It remains to be asked: On the basis of what linguistic norm are these "familiar mythic or historical forms" engaged? For Jameson argues that the practice of pastiche is a symptom of the "linguistic fragmentation of social life itself to the point where the norm itself is eclipsed" (1984a, p. 65). To be sure, those postmodernist texts that exploit pastiche for oppositional ends often operate without a normative discourse which could serve as a foundation, as a politically or philosophically assured standpoint, from which to mount a critique of earlier narrative forms. Accordingly, they almost read like decentered narratives—almost but not quite. For, as I argue in the case studies, many of these texts implicitly convey the criteria of something like an "ideal speech situation," criteria which ultimately redeem them from the neutrality or blankness of a narrative without a privileged center. Suffice to say here, the criteria in question serve to evaluate language-use (past and present); they are derived from ideals of a language which is truly intersubjective, non-agonistic, vital, free of the distortions of mystification and mythification.

In support of his account of pastiche, Jameson also writes:

If the ideas of a ruling class were once the dominant (or hegemonic) ideology of bourgeois society, the advanced capitalist countries today are now a field of stylistic and discursive heterogeneity without a norm. Faceless masters continue to inflect the economic strategies which constrain our existences, but no longer need to impose their speech (or are henceforth unable to). (1984a, p. 65)

These comments seem to be in accord with the views of critics who have assailed the "dominant ideology thesis," arguing, for example, that under late capitalism the "limited ideological unity of previous periods has collapsed" (quoted in Therborn 1984, p. 98). However, whether or not Jameson's comments are valid, we must ask: How do postmodernist writers view the matter? Three novelists whom Jameson identifies as postmodernist, namely, Burroughs, Pynchon, and Reed (Jameson 1984a, p. 54), would almost certainly take issue with him here. From *their* standpoint, writing for the most part in America since the 1960s, it is the discourses of the dominant social groups which are normative. Indeed, it would be difficult to read these authors as if they assumed that the ruling fractions "no longer need to impose their speech." The target of Burroughs' subversive "Operation Rewrite" is precisely "the words of the all-powerful boards and syndicates of the earth" (Burroughs 1968b, p. 10). Pynchon's "Counterforce" must struggle for orientation in the midst of Their (the "elite"/"Elect") "cooperative structure of lies" (Pynchon 1978, p. 728). And "Jes Grew," Reed's Osirian, Voodoo-inspired counterculture, is resisted by the knights of the "Atonist Path" (the regime of white, western values) who hold "its [Jes Grew's] words [. . .] in bondage," who "move in" wherever "the untampered word exists" (Reed [1972] 1988, pp. 211, 213).

Pastiche, then, is examined in terms that take no account of its significance as a practice within the framework of an adversarial post-modernism. And a similar criticism can be made of Jameson's observations on depthlessness—"perhaps the supreme formal feature of all the postmodernisms" (1984a, p. 60). (These observations merit individual attention although, to be sure, the practice of pastiche is understood *inter alia* as a consequence of the demise of the depth-model of subjectivity.) It is, above all, in his perception of the "emergence of a new kind of flatness or depthlessness, a new kind of superficiality in the most literal sense" (p. 60), that Jameson distinguishes postmodernist from modernist aesthetics. (See also Jameson 1971, p. 105.) The modernist explorations of alienation, anomie, and angst were premised on a depth-model of subjectivity, a notion of "expression." These concepts, however, are seen as irrelevant to postmodern consciousness, which inhabits a space suffused with "simulacra," that is, primarily the images of mass entertainment and commodity aesthetics, images of history, society, and nature which "bear no relation to any reality whatsoever" (Baudrillard 1983c, p. 11). For Jameson, the "culture of the simulacrum" emerges in the era of a globalized commodity fetishism whose logic penetrates the psyche and informs all cultural production.

Jameson illuminates his account of depthlessness in a fine analysis of Warhol's painting, perceiving the reifying logic of the commodity form in the cool, static, glitzy images devoid of expressiveness, emotion, and commitment. Similarly, it is "Warhol's shoes and soup cans" that serve as Eagleton's reference point for discussing the "depthlessness, [. . .] decathected surfaces," and "commodified artefacts" of postmodernist culture (Eagleton 1985, p. 61). This raises the question of whether Warhol's work should be taken as representative of postmodernist depthlessness. Depthlessness in postmodernist art may, from a neutral or even celebratory standpoint, signal a "waning of affect" or loss of psychic interiority. Yet it may also be the strategic effect of visual arts and writing which recode the stereotypes and clichés of the mass media in terms that, *inter alia,* expose the hollowness or poverty of our cultural representations, where the latter are understood to supply the dominant forms of cognition. (Here I have in mind the paintings and photo-text collages of artists like Walter Robinson, Sherry Levine, and

Silvia Kolbowski. Literary texts that exploit depthlessness in an adversarial capacity will be discussed later.) In short—and the point is hardly contentious—depthlessness may serve a critical function, a possibility excluded by the terms of Jameson's (and Eagleton's) argument.

Finally, I want to examine Jameson's views on the problems of critical effectivity and aesthetic distance under late capitalism. His logic-of-capital explanation of postmodernist art is a stronger version of a familiar argument about the neutralization of art in late-capitalist society. According to the latter, transgression and scandal, once exploited by the avant-garde as weapons with which to offend bourgeois norms, are now *economically* imperative; the sale of goods depends on innovations in commodity aesthetics (e.g., in advertising or product styling) which work precisely as sources of cultural shock. However, for Jameson, it is not simply a matter of the late-capitalist economy feeding off contemporary art. What, according to him, defines late capitalism is the globalization of commodity fetishism, a process that has destroyed the "'semi-autonomy' of the cultural sphere" (1984a, p. 87); a situation whereby the logic of exchange-value is understood to penetrate all cultural production, including aesthetic counter-practices. Yet, in the case of, say, a play by Brecht or a film with an ecological message, are we really unaffected by the specific nature of the use-values sold, use-values which are likely to raise anticapitalist consciousness? The logic of exchange-value cannot determine *how* we receive a text. We do not "consume" artworks to realize exchange-value but to fulfill subjective needs which are often subversive of the logic of the commodity form. Use-values may be mobilized from positions which contradict the interests of capital (cf. Lovell 1980, pp. 251–55). In the tradition of Frankfurt School *Kulturpessimismus,* Jameson tends to exaggerate the incorporative powers of the late-capitalist system, a matter I want to consider in a little more detail.

Jameson's inability to ascribe critical effectivity to postmodernist art must be understood, ultimately, in the context of his model of late-capitalist society as a fundamentally stable formation. Class struggle and other contradictions intrinsic to capitalism have no place in his account of postmodernity. It is an omission that prompts one to question the terms on which he appropriates Ernest Mandel's major study, *Late Capitalism.* Jameson adopts Mandel's thesis of three stages in the evolution of capitalism—its "market," "monopoly," and "late" moments—as a materialist framework in which to theorize his own "cultural periodization of the [corresponding] stages of realism, modernism and postmodernism" (1984a, p. 78). Yet Jameson's model of late capitalism is essentially inconsistent with Mandel's and, indeed, from the standpoint of the latter, surely questionable. Jameson defines late capitalism primarily in terms of its multinational disposition, a definition which overstates the significance of what is just one component of Mandel's analysis. We postmodern subjects are disoriented in the new world space of multinational capital; we are unable "to map the great global multinational and decentred communicational network in which we find ourselves caught as individual subjects" (p. 84); and our "capacity to act and struggle [has been] neutralized by our spatial as well as our social confusion" (p. 92). It is not just that Mandel would very likely reject as mystification this image of the late-capitalist world as a cognitively unmappable "hyperspace." Surprisingly for a Marxist theorist like Jameson, there is no dialectic at work in his model of the late-capitalist system (the prospect for political praxis is limited to the proposal of a "cognitive mapping" by means of which we can regain our orientation as political subjects). Mandel, in sharp contrast, seeks to "explain the post-war history of the capitalist mode of production in terms of the basic laws of motion of capitalism discovered by Marx in *Capital*" (Mandel 1978, p. 10). Hence he persistently focuses on the *instabilities* of late capitalism. Indeed, we need go no further than to note *his* comments on the contradictory character of multinational capital:

the pressure for an international capital and money market adequate to the needs of the increasing internationalization of capital *must* collide with economic programming on the national level, and thus [. . .] intensify the susceptibility of the late capitalist economy to crises. (p. 342)

Jameson's perception of the postmodern period of late capitalism as a static, not to say counterrevolutionary, conjuncture underpins his thesis about the "loss" or "abolition of critical distance" (1984a, p. 85). He questions the Leftist assumption that cultural resistance can still be positioned "outside the massive Being of capital." For our cultural space is now defined by "the prodigious new expansion of multinational capital [which] ends up penetrating and colonizing those very pre-capitalist enclaves (Nature and the Unconscious) which offered extraterritorial and Archimedean footholds for critical effectivity." Under the global sovereignty of capital, all forms of cultural resistance are "disarmed and reabsorbed by [the] system" from which they can achieve no distance (p. 87).

Perhaps the space for dissent and contestation is narrower than formerly. Yet, short of all the crises and conflicts of capitalism, that is, its *contradictions*, disappearing, it is difficult to see how critical distance may be altogether lost. A critical space is opened wherever social relations are fissured by contradictions of, say, class, racial, or sexual difference. (And we may note in passing how Jameson's unspecified postmodern subject seems to float above those contradictions as he/she wanders in hyperspaces like the Bonaventura Hotel.) Furthermore, so long as Jameson takes his aesthetic bearings from the Warhol-Venturi pole of postmodernist practice, the claim that critical distance has been abolished looks stronger than if his points of reference were taken from oppositional currents of postmodernism. I have in mind a host of thriving counter-practices—for example, adversarial uses of video, performance art, and photography (all ignored by Jameson, and Eagleton too)—whose raison d'être is to critique hegemonic representations. If Warhol's Marilyn is emblematic of postmodernism as commodified artifact—the silkscreened series of a Monroe portrait suggesting the post-auratic status of art as reproducible commodity, then Cindy Sherman's Marilyn may be seen as emblematic of adversarial postmodernism. On a cover photograph of *ZG* (No. 7, 1982), under the caption "Desire," Sherman impersonates Monroe in a simulated film still. It is a mode of address which aims to suggest how (one side of) femininity is constituted by media representations of male desire. Sherman's work belongs to a lively current of postmodernism that contests patriarchal, Eurocentric, and bourgeois representations and whose practice is evidence of precisely those contradictions which engender interstices, if not distances, that serve as critical vantage points.

I shall identify that current of writing I call dissident postmodernist as a species of adversarial postmodernism. Finally, to avoid confusion, I should add that, like Jameson, I also raise the issue of the loss of critical distance but from two very different standpoints which, for the moment, may be summarized as follows: (a) I read dissident postmodernist writers as raising this issue themselves, not so much as a problem *of* their work but as a general problem of late-capitalist society, which they make into a theme *in* their work; (b) the issue is discussed in the context of matters such as the disintegration of the public sphere and the diffusion of conceptually impoverished discourses.

Postmodernism as a Literary-Critical Concept

It was not until the late 1960s that "postmodernism" gained currency as a literary-critical term. However, then it was just one designation among others (e.g., "metafiction," "antirealist fiction") and did not achieve its status as the preeminent generic term for the fiction in question until the 1980s. The origins of the term have been sketched out by Ihab Hassan (Hassan 1980). Here, I shall attempt a brief account and critique of the principal constructions of postmodernism as a literary-critical concept.

There is a tendency in literary studies to speak of "modernism" and "postmodernism" *tout court*. Yet as rubrics they are a source of vagueness and ambiguity. It is a commonplace that the prefix "post-" in "postmodernism" may be read as denoting a relationship with modernism which is one either of succession or of supersession. But there is another problem of terminology which is less often noted. The use of modernism and postmodernism as monolithic categories conceals a process of discrimination which may frame our reading of a text. For there are, of course, *several* currents of modernist and postmodernist writing, and our perception of the political significance of a postmodernist text can depend on whichever current of writing has been selected to serve as the normative model of modernism. Thus, for Terry Eagleton, "It is as though postmodernism is [. . .] a sick joke at the expense of [. . .] revolutionary avant-gardism" insofar as it is the avant-garde practices of Mayakovsky (or Tzara or Breton) which are invoked as the normative model of modernism (Eagleton 1985, p. 60). Yet, for Leslie Fiedler, postmodernism is "subversive," a blow to the "elitism" or "concealed class bias" of a modernism he identifies with Eliot and Joyce—a current of writing sometimes referred to as "high" modernism (Fiedler [1968] 1975). And it is this latter, largely anglophone, modernism (which, typically, also includes Faulkner, Woolf, and Wallace Stevens) that critics most often invoke to signify modernism *in toto*.

The need to differentiate between currents of postmodernist fiction will be discussed later. Suffice to say here, a problem as fundamental to postmodernist writing as the "fictionality" of meaning (i.e., the perception that the "real," history, or nature can only be apprehended in narrative form, that is, as "stories") does not, as we shall see, have the same implications for, say, Barth, Nabokov, and Gass, as for Barthelme, Coover, and Pynchon. Yet, all too often, we find these names indiscriminately bracketed together.

Further problems arise from discussions of postmodernist fiction that automatically take modernism as their principal point of reference. In response to the perception that the "real" is fundamentally non-significant, postmodernist writers have developed an aesthetics of "self-reflexiveness," that is, a mode of fiction which investigates the very process of signification or meaning-production. In particular, literary-narrative conventions like plotting, use of metaphor, and omniscient narrator are parodied so as to expose their role in the fabrication of meaning; so as to present the text as a fiction-making apparatus. Narration (literary, historical, philosophical, etc.) and naming are revealed as inherently fictionalizing activities. Thus Malcolm Bradbury observes the postmodernist insistence on "the utter fictionality of *all* attempts at naming, structuring, and ordering experience" (Bradbury 1983, p. 159). And Mas'ud Zavarzadeh has remarked upon the emergence of "noninterpretive narrative forms" which embody "the contemporary writer's approach to the world-as-it-is, free from any imposed scheme of meaning or extracted pattern of significance" (Zavarzadeh 1976, p. 4).

It is the postmodernist preoccupation with the fictionality of meaning which inevitably invites contrasts with (if I may generalize) the high-modernist faith in totalizing meaning-systems, such as those founded on cultural tradition. (It is the basis for these contrasts that I take to be the principal rationale for speaking of a *post*-modernist fiction.) Recall Eliot's observations on *Ulysses*, whose "mythic method" he held up as an exemplary model for modern writing: "a way of controlling, of ordering, of giving a shape and significance to the immense panorama of futility and anarchy which is contemporary history" (quoted in Russell 1985, p. 11). Many commentaries are grounded in this fundamental contrast between "high" modernism's striving to impose a scheme of meaning on the world (e.g., Stevens' "Idea of Order," Eliot's Tradition, Joyce's Mythology) and postmodernism's ironic questioning of the very possibility of meaning. David Lodge provides a concise, graphic account of the matter:

> modernism, which for all its formal experiment and complexity held out to the reader the promise of meaning, if not of *a* meaning. "Where is the figure in the carpet?" asks a character in Donald Barthelme's *Snow White*, alluding to the title of a story by Henry James that has become proverbial among critics as an image of the goal of interpretation; "Where is the figure in the carpet? Or is it just . . . carpet?" A lot of postmodernist writing implies that experience is just carpet, and that whatever meaningful patterns we discern in it are wholly illusory, comforting fictions. (Lodge 1977, p. 43)

This is an illuminating comparison, yet it is also typical of the prevalent tendency to define postmodernist fiction primarily in terms of its relationship to modernism. The following statements, all by eminent critics, exhibit this tendency: "postmodernist fiction tends to attack, undermine, parody, or otherwise call into question certain characteristic assumptions of modernist fiction" (Hite 1983, p. 4); "Once we have identified the respective dominants of the modernist or postmodernist systems, we are in a good position to begin describing the dynamics of the change by which one system emerges from and supplants the other" (McHale 1987, pp. 10–11); "the world view of the Postmodernists is built [. . .] on a polemics against Modernism" (Fokkema 1986, p. 83). To be sure, postmodernist fiction embodies a critique of the formal conventions and epistemology of literary modernism (but then it also embodies a critique of literary realism, and there is a case to be made for speaking of an "antirealist" rather than a "postmodernist" fiction).[1] However, I want to question the invocation of modernism as the *principal point of reference* for situating and making sense of post-modernist fiction.

An approach to postmodernism which uses modernism, that is, the Anglo-American "high" modernism of, roughly, 1915–30, as the main point of reference tends inevitably to understand the critical thrust of this fiction as chiefly *retrospective*. That is to say, this approach explains postmodernist fiction as, primarily, a response (ironic, deconstructive) to the narrative forms and epistemology of an earlier, literary-cultural paradigm. But, while acknowledging this retrospectiveness as a feature of, perhaps, all postmodernist fiction, there is an oppositional current of this fiction which is best thought of as, in the first instance, "circum-spective." By this I mean a response to or, more accurately, a critical engagement with, surrounding or contemporaneous discourses (in-cluding literary narrative forms and the meaning-systems they em-body); precisely, the discourses of postmodern culture. "Postmodern-ism" need not only be read as an invitation to situate postmodernist fiction in relation to modernism; it may be read as an invitation to situate it in relation to *postmodernity*, to our experience of postmodern culture.

In the 1960s a number of critics, notably Leslie Fiedler, Ihab Hassan, and Susan Sontag, welcomed postmodernism as a species of subversive writing. It was understood as the literature of a "time of Endings" (Fiedler 1975, p. 365), challenging the social hierarchies and oppres-sive meaning-systems of a supposedly moribund bourgeois culture. Hassan sees postmodernist fiction as an "Antinomian" attack on "rea-son and history, science and society," as an expression of "Anarchy" and an impulse to "decreation" (Hassan 1971, pp. 27, 29). And for Sontag, with Burroughs and Beckett, among others, in mind, "contemporary artists [. . .] share the same disdain for the 'meanings' established by bourgeois-rationalist culture, indeed for culture itself in the familiar sense. [They proclaim . . .] a harsh despair and perverse vision of apocalypse. . . ." (Sontag 1983, p. 203). Fiedler situates postmod-ernist fiction in an era he defines as "apocalyptic, anti-rational, bla-tantly romantic and sentimental"; a time when "the Dream, the Vision, *ekstasis* [. . .] have again become the avowed goals of literature" (Fiedler 1975, pp. 345, 364). These critics were writing at an explosive moment of protest and dissent—the moment, that is, of an insurgent counter-culture. Perhaps their focus on the apocalyptic strain in postmodernist fiction reflected the belief, common at the time, in the exhaustion and imminent demise of "bourgeois-rationalist culture." In this respect, my reading of this fiction will be almost diametrically opposed to theirs. Suffice to say here, I shall read it (but for one or two texts) as a literature responsive not to a "time of Endings" but to a time marked by the *consolidation* of "bourgeois-rationalist culture."

In his landmark essay (from which I have just quoted), "Cross the Border—Close that Gap" (1968), Fiedler observes that the postmodernist writer has turned to popular art forms to draw on their "Mythical" and "Visionary" potential (p. 362). The art forms in question are those targeted for the mass market, typically forms like the "western," "science fiction," and "pornography." Fiedler contends that insofar as it exploits the motifs and conventions of these subgenres, postmodernism resists evaluation in the terms of the "class bias" inscribed in the literary Establishment's "high"/"low" criteria. The "Aristocratic conceptions of art" which have led critics to canonize "high" modernists like Eliot, Joyce, and Proust, have been superseded: "a closing of the gap between elite and mass culture is precisely the function of the novel now" (p. 351). Postmodernism subverts class-based norms:

The notion of one art for the "cultured," i.e., the favored few in any given society—in our own chiefly the university educated, and another sub-art for the "uncultured," i.e., an excluded majority [. . . is] an invidious distinction proper only to a class-structured community. [. . .] Pop Art is, whatever its overt politics, *subversive:* a threat to all hierarchies insofar as it is hostile to order and ordering in its own realm. (pp. 359–60)

How valid is the claim that (literary) postmodernism is democratizing, that it annuls the class-based distinction between "high" art and mass culture? One might ask of two of the writers cited by Fiedler, namely Barth and Nabokov, precisely *whom* do they address? Surely one has to be intellectually prepared for works like *Lost in the Funhouse* or *Pale Fire*, not to mention, say, *V*, *Snow White*, and *Pricksongs and Descants*. These are "self-reflexive" works which depend upon the reader's prior knowledge of the narrative conventions which they exploit, parody, and subvert. Whether or not these works sell well, they speak, first and foremost, to the minority sensibility of the college educated. Indeed, what Fiedler describes as the "academicism" of the "Age of T.S. Eliot" survives in the sense that many postmodernist writers are, or have been, university writers-in-residence or professors of literature: for example, Barth, Barthelme, Coover, Gass, Hawkes, Nabokov, Sukenick, and Vonnegut. The fact is, postmodernist fiction has an institutional base, an enclosed cultural milieu, which from Fiedler's standpoint looks positively élitist. However, to argue that this fiction addresses only an educationally privileged few is not to imply that it has little or no subversive value; rather, it is to recognize that the claim for its subversiveness cannot rest on the thesis that postmodernism "closes a class [. . .] gap" (p. 359).

Finally, Fiedler assumes that postmodernist fiction assimilates mass-market subgenres *uncritically* (nowhere in his essay does he suggest otherwise). This may be true of some early postmodernist writing. However, in many of the postmodernist texts discussed later, we shall see how subgenres are incorporated within an oppositional framework which exposes and contests their ideological content.

The formal complexity of postmodernist writing has given a new lease of life to formalist criticism. Unquestionably, some of the most distinguished and valuable studies of this fiction are formalist. Robert Scholes, David Lodge, Douwe Fokkema, Brian McHale, and Christine Brooke-Rose are among those who have theorized a poetics or rhetoric of postmodernism. McHale and Lodge, for example, have ingeniously exploited Jakobson's structuralist concepts in their constructions of postmodernism. McHale has built a "descriptive poetics" around the concept of the "shifting dominant," explaining the change from modernist to postmodernist fiction in terms of the periodic shift in the literary system's hierarchy of artistic devices (whereby dominant devices become subsidiary and vice versa) (McHale 1987, pp. 3–25). Lodge, perceiving literary history as a pendulum movement between what Jakobson has identified as the "metaphoric" and "metonymic" poles of language, explains postmodernism as a violation of Jakobson's "law" that "there is nowhere for discourse to go except between these two poles" (Lodge 1977, pp. 42–43). My concern here is to outline the problematic of what I have broadly defined as "neo-formalist" criticism and note the kind of questions it does not address (which is less to find fault with this criticism than to indicate its conceptual limits).

In *Fiction and the Figures of Life,* William Gass censures those who "continue to interpret novels as if they were philosophies themselves [. . .] middens from which may be scratched important messages for mankind; they have predictably looked for content, not form" (Gass 1980, p. 25). Interpretation is a misconceived goal and criticism must focus on the text's formal properties, its figures, syntax, and design. A preoccupation with form follows from Gass's conception of fiction as an autonomous "verbal world." We are enjoined to stop thinking of fiction as ancillary to the task of reflecting reality, for, as Gass puts it in a memorable aphorism, "There are no descriptions in fiction, there are only constructions" (p. 17). Scholes makes a similar point: "All writing, all composition is construction. We do not imitate the world, we construct versions of it. There is no mimesis, only poiesis. No recording. Only constructing" (Scholes 1975, p. 7). Literature which incorporates this critical perspective, that is, which self-consciously renounces any pretensions to mimesis and projects itself as a purely verbal fabrication, is called by Gass, Scholes, and others "metafiction." Many of the writers discussed under this rubric are also identified as postmodernist, for example, Barth, Barthelme, Coover, Gass, Nabokov, and Pynchon. However, "metafiction" has a much wider compass than "postmodernism" and is generally used to denote *any systematically self-reflexive* work of fiction, that is to say, fiction which investigates and exposes the processes of its own construction and, by implication, the codes and shifting parameters of "literature." Hence Cervantes, Sterne, Barth, and Barthelme may all be defined as metafictional but only the latter two are postmodernist.

Critics who adopt the term "metafiction" invariably take as their starting point Gass's definition, which labels as metafiction those literary texts "in which the forms of fiction serve as the material upon which further forms may be imposed" (Gass 1980, p. 25). It is a helpful and perceptive formulation but there is a problem in that it implies an intertextuality that is purely literary. To be sure, it is in this sense that the texts of, say, Barth, Nabokov, and Gass, which above all interact with other (usually earlier) literary forms, are metafictional. However, there is also a strain of postmodernist writing, which includes the work of Barthelme, Coover, and Pynchon, whose texts interact not only with literary but often with *nonliterary* forms of discourse. This kind of intertextuality tends to be oppositional in orientation; it works to lay bare and combat the ideologies inscribed in, for example, pop-cultural, scientific, and political discourse. For this type of postmodernism, "metafiction," as it is usually defined, is an inappropriate term. Furthermore, while postmodernism may be conceived as relating the fiction in question to a postmodern culture or postmodernity, metafiction, as a term, altogether lacks sociohistorical reference.

Around 1969–70, the neo-formalist approach to postmodernist fiction was invigorated by an input of structuralist ideas. There are, to be sure, striking correspondences between, for instance, Barthes's ideas on literature—for example, literature conceived as an interplay of codes rather than a medium of representation; the call for a mode of writing which privileges *discours* over *histoire*—and the thinking of Gass, Scholes, and other critics. (The concepts of structuralism/post-structuralism have undoubtedly been of value in articulating the linguistic-philosophical concerns of postmodernist writers, but we should not necessarily assume that these writers were structuralists/post-structuralists *avant la lettre*. The precise connections—theoretical and temporal—between post-Saussurean theory and postmodernism need to be researched.) However, the structuralist influence has also worked to reinforce the neo-formalist tendency to fetishize the text, to abstract the word from the world. The problem of the fictionality of meaning may serve to illustrate a limitation of this tendency. Thus, while this criticism may examine the formal implications of this problem, for example, the self-reflexive focus on the factitiousness and arbitrariness of the narrative conventions on which meaning is shown to rest, it does not address a question like: Why should the fictionality of meaning become a major issue at a particular time, in a particular place (i.e., in late-capitalist America)? The problem is that such a question cannot be adequately, if at all, posed by the discourses of neo-formalism. No coherent model of postmodern culture underpins neo-formalist studies of postmodernist fiction. In these studies, the fictionality of meaning is an issue rarely examined beyond its aesthetic and epistemological implications. And yet our very idea of fictionality has been enlarged and enriched by sociological inquiries into the nature of postmodern culture. For example, note the pervasive discourses of commodity aesthetics where the illusion (the false promises and fraudulent claims) of use-value becomes detached from use-value itself (Haug 1986, pp. 16–17); note the simulated realities of a media society, "the generation by models of a real without origin or reality: a hyperreal" (Baudrillard 1983c, p. 2). An explanation of the postmodernist writer's preoccupation with fictionality requires, *inter alia*, acknowledgment of his/her situation in a culture pervaded by illusory use-values and simulacra.

The dominant, neo-formalist strain of criticism generally precludes readings of postmodernist fiction as an oppositional current of writing. However, there are, of course, critics who have identified strands of postmodernist fiction as adversarial literature. Linda Hutcheon, for example, has proposed the category of "historiographic metafiction," instanced by such works as Reed's *Mumbo Jumbo* and Doctorow's *Ragtime*. This fiction operates through a subversive, highly self-reflexive use of parody. It ironically or paradoxically incorporates into its very structure the forms of historical narratives in order to destabilize them "from within"—exposing them as purely social constructs and contesting their ideological closures. "To adapt Barthes's general notion of the 'doxa' as public opinion or the 'Voice of Nature' and consensus, postmodernism works to 'de-doxify' our cultural representations and their undeniable political import" (Hutcheon 1987, pp. 12, 21; 1989, p. 3). And Charles Russell has discussed the "avant-garde strategies of aesthetic disruption" whereby Burroughs, Pynchon, Coover, and Sukenick, among others, attempt to demystify and deconstruct the social codes in which subjective identity is seen to be enfolded. It is a project which "shift[s] the previous social context of rebellion to the social text of ideology" (Russell 1985, p. 253).

Both Hutcheon and Russell, who have contributed much to the idea of an adversarial postmodernist fiction, are, like myself, interested in the latter as a critique and contestation of hegemonic discourse. However, their arguments lack an account, not to say a systematic analysis, of the conjuncture or moment (late capitalist? postindustrial?) at which this fiction is written. Hence, a fundamental question is not addressed: What developments, *historically specific* to our society, have given rise to a mode of fiction that is so preoccupied with language as a political issue? In the subsequent pages, I shall discuss a number of social changes—identified later as distinctively *late-capitalist* developments—which, I shall argue, have been instrumental in raising consciousness of the political implications of language.

Finally, "postmodernism" has become an overloaded and remarkably diffuse concept. A partial inventory of those lines of thought (mostly developed in the 1960s), which are discussed in the name of postmodernism, which are apprehended as postmodernist, would include: post-humanist theories of language that decenter the subject in relation to meaning; neo-Nietzschean critiques of the Enlightenment épistème; post-Marxist social theory and politics; theories of the globalization of commodity fetishism; populist aesthetics, and art which is systematically self-reflexive. (See above for explanations of these points.) The term "postmodernism" may be summoned to signify a mutation in artistic practice, an epistemic shift in western thought, or a mode of experience and perception specific to the late-capitalist subject immersed in a sign-saturated, consumer culture.

Enough has been said to indicate that "postmodernism" is a far from self-explanatory term; in any context *today,* one needs to say how and why it is being used. I shall start by giving reasons why I have chosen to work with this problematic and embattled term. First, in *literary-critical* discussions of American postmodernist fiction, we know, by force of convention, *who* are the postmodernists, for example, Barth, Barthelme, Coover, Vonnegut, or Pynchon; and who are not, for example, Bellow, Updike, Styron, Baldwin, or Salinger. There is broad agreement about the grounds for making this distinction: very simply, and at the level of a *preliminary* definition on which critics build in different ways, the fiction of Barth et al. is programmatically and preeminently self-reflexive and (largely as a consequence of which) radically transgressive of narrative conventions, while the fiction of Bellow et al. is not. (Suffice to say here, fiction is self-reflexive when it examines its own nature as a signifying practice and, by implication, points to its own provisionality as a meaning-system. Later, I shall explain why I find "self-reflexive" an unsatisfactory term and note how, as a concept, it is often appropriated in ways which foreclose on its adversarial implications.) "Postmodernism" is the term most often summoned to denote, in the first instance, the literary self-reflexiveness and transgressiveness of the postwar period. (See, for example, Fokkema and Bertens 1986; Bradbury 1983; Hutcheon 1989; Russell 1985.) Indeed, it has beaten off all rival contenders for the job, for example, terms such as "anti-realist fiction" (Guerard 1974), "new fiction" (Stevick 1977), and the chief rival "metafiction" (Gass 1980; McCaffery 1982; Scholes 1979). In recent years, postmodernism has become so deeply entrenched in the literary-critical vocabulary that, for the time being, no cognate term looks likely to supplant it; increasingly, alternative terms sound idiosyncratic. Thus, for most commentators today, it no longer seems a question of *whether* to use "postmodernist" as a generic term for postwar self-reflexive/transgressive fiction, so much as *how* to use it, for example, how to expand its range of reference or how to mobilize it politically.

Second, I favor the use of the term because of the historical inflection it has recently acquired. Its prefix "post-" is generally read as signaling a "break" in aesthetic practice that radically separates modernist from postmodernist art (a claim vigorously contested by some).[2] Clearly the legitimacy of postmodernism as, *inter alia*, a concept signifying a new order of aesthetic practice must rest on the identification of a new conjuncture which can assign that practice an historically specific meaning. And it has been Fredric Jameson's achievement to provide just this kind of conjunctural analysis, one which traces the mediations between late capitalism and postmodernist aesthetics (Jameson 1984a). His "periodizing hypothesis" has significantly broadened the historical dimensions of the concept "postmodernism." Now, more than formerly, the term has a marked historical orientation that rival literary terms like "metafiction" and "antirealist fiction" altogether lack. Henceforth, it is difficult to think of postmodernism without some notion of "postmodernity" or a new stage in the development of capitalism. Accordingly, the term is readily invoked here in a reading that situates postwar self-reflexive/transgressive texts in the context of developments specific to, or more advanced under, late capitalism which have transformed the field of language and communications.

Chapter 2
Language and Late Capitalism

Politics, Language, and Mass Communications

Politics, in postmodern society, has been radically reconceived by those who have come to see the culture-language sphere, rather than the sphere of production, as the primary locus of power and conflict. Marx is credited with the most compelling and developed account of the mode of production as the basis of power relations. According to this "productivist" model of politics, conflict arises when socialized labor, without a share in the ownership of the means of production, struggles over the distribution of the surplus product which, however, under capitalism, is privately appropriated. Moreover, social identity is chiefly defined in terms of economic class position, and it is understood that, by historical necessity, the working class will be the principal agency in the wholesale transformation of society. However, the experience of late capitalism has led to substantial revisions of ideas about the location of power, the constitution of identity, and the viable forms of oppositional practice; the experience has, in short, altered notions of what constitutes the political. In the late-capitalist period, there has been a prodigious enlargement of the notion of the political within the culture-language sphere.

There is no single term that encompasses this expanded conception of politics, but we might begin by noting the emergence of what could be called a neo-Gramscian cultural politics. Gramsci had argued that a revolutionary seizure of state power and the economy would lack "national-popular" consent (it would have no more authority than a coup d'état) unless hegemony, that is, intellectual and moral leadership, could be won on the terrain of "civil society." Civil society is the ensemble of private, voluntary institutions outside the sphere of the state and the economy; it includes trade unions, political parties, religious organizations, and community associations. A Bolshevik-style frontal assault on the state would have to be preceded by a "war of position" in the struggle for hegemony in the politico-cultural sphere. (See Gramsci 1971, pp. 57–58, 238–39.)

Postmodern consciousness is distinguished by this conception of politics in which power and struggle are understood to be diffused throughout the cultural domain and not simply located in the spheres of state and economic activity.[1] Hence, in the late-capitalist period, new patterns of dissent emerge; the language of protest changes; political objectives are typically redefined in terms of the ambitions of single-issue movements, the latter superseding global strategies to transform the mode of production. In America (to focus on the period of most of the texts discussed later, that is, the 1960s, early 1970s), this is the conjuncture of the Peace Movement, student power, and a growing conservationist lobby. The "counterculture" expressed its opposition to the system not in the "Old Left" language of class exploitation but in terms which challenged the *cultural supremacy* of the ruling bloc, its hegemonic values—technocratic, bureaucratic, militaristic, business-oriented. It was a refusal of the dominant categories of experience which Marcuse welcomed (though not uncritically) as the expression of a "new sensibility." He remarks on "a fundamental change in the situation" whereby political protest "assumes a *total* character," activating formerly "apolitical" dimensions of experience (Marcuse 1969, p. 30). Thus in the rebellion against "repressive rationality," the new sensibility insists that "the right and the truth of the imagination become the demands of political action" (p. 30); it insists on a "desublimation of culture" as a vital objective in the liberation of the id (p. 35); it expresses the "aesthetic need" for "a revolution in perception, for a new sensorium" (p. 37).

In France too, the focus of dissent is enlarged. Alongside the macro-political strategies of the Communist party (occupancy of state power, seizure of the commanding heights of the economy), there emerges a micropolitics of *everyday* practices. The focus of revolt of *les soixante-huitards* was not just factory life but all spheres of everyday life. Foucault identifies the most crucial sites of resistance to power in "local specific struggles." He observes:

One of the first things that has to be understood is that power isn't localised in the State apparatus and that nothing in society will be changed if the mechanisms of power that function outside, below and alongside the State apparatuses, on a much more minute and everyday level, are not also changed. (Foucault 1980, p. 60)

In his celebrated critique of late-capitalist society, *Everyday Life in the Modern World* (1968), Lefebvre calls for a "permanent cultural revolution," a "total revolution" which transforms life not only on the economic and political planes but on the cultural plane—an "avenue [which] has been blocked by economistic [. . .] interpretations of Marx's doctrine," by "productivist ideology" (Lefebvre 1971, pp. 197–99). And a little later there appears a plethora of studies by Bourdieu, de Certeau, and others into the nature of, precisely, *everyday* oppositional practices. Finally, it may be added that in tandem with this molecular focus on the processes of everyday life has gone an assault on the totalizing perspectives of conceptual systems (e.g., Hegelian or Marxist) that seek to embrace all phenomena, and a preference for "local knowledges" (Foucault 1980, p. 85) or *"petits récits"* (Lyotard 1984a, p. 60).

A cultural politics of the everyday explains the phenomenal enlargement of our notion of the political within the sphere of language and communications. Just for the moment, some familiar names and notions must suffice to give an impression of the scope of this enlargement. Barthes has analyzed the "mythification" of everyday, anonymous representations; it is an ideological process whereby historically and culturally determined meanings are appropriated by a metalanguage (myth) which "naturalizes" them such that "things appear to mean something by themselves" (Barthes 1973, p. 143). Foucault has drawn attention to the "order of discourse" or "regimes of truth"; these are institutionalized constraints which ensure that communication is contained within a socially permitted range of thought by, for example, authorizing *who* is qualified to speak or *what* may or may not be spoken (see Foucault 1981). Habermas has elaborated a communicative ethics giving currency to the concept of the "ideal speech situation." In one context, the concept serves as a critical standard for judging the degree to which the validity claims on which communication is premised (e.g., the claims to truth or sincerity) are compromised by ideology and other social modes of domination. Marcuse and Lefebvre (of whom more later) have examined the political implications of "one-dimensional language" (Marcuse 1966) and the "decline of referentials" (Lefebvre 1971). More generally, we should note the prodigious growth, within sociology, of communications studies that examine the nexus between power and the ownership/control/organization of communications systems, with eminent contributions from, among others, Herbert Schiller and Armand Mattelart. Lastly, this conjuncture is marked by the emergence of an "identity-politics" in which substantial numbers of society's marginal and disenfranchised (e.g., blacks, women, gays) have come to define themselves not in class terms, that is, in relation to their position within the sphere of production, but in relation to their position within society's hegemonic codes. These codes—ethnocentric, patriarchal, heterosexual, and so forth—are perceived as the primary source of oppression and hence become the principal sites of protest and resistance. Baudrillard says of these social groups:

> Their revolt thus aims at the abolition of this code, this strategy composed of distinction, separations, discriminations, oppositions that are structured and hierarchised.
> The Black revolt aims at race as a code, at a level much more radical than economic exploitation. The revolt of women aims at the code that makes the feminine a non-marked term. [. . .] This position of revolt is no longer that of the economically exploited; it aims less at the extortion of surplus value than at the imposition of the code, which inscribes the present strategy of social domination. (Baudrillard 1975, pp. 134–35)

The identity-politics which developed in the 1960s may, in part, have been fertilized by contemporaneous liberation movements in the Third World. The struggle for political autonomy went hand-in-hand with an assertion of cultural identity. The colonial powers had endeavored to construct an identity for the colonized; they employed a system of cultural representations—essentially a strategy of ethnocentric stereotyping—that aimed to "fix" the colonized subject in a position of "otherness" (see Bhabha 1986). Ngũgĩ wa Thiong'o has discussed the striving of Africans for "self-definition" as a struggle against the "linguistic encirclement" of Africa by "the languages of imperialist imposition." He observes:

> It is an ever-continuing struggle to seize back their creative initiative in history through a real control of all the means of communal self-definition in time and space. The choice of language and the use to which language is put are central to a people's definition of itself in relation to its natural and social environment, indeed in relation to the entire universe. (Ngũgĩ wa Thiong'o 1985, pp. 109–10)

Finally, a few words on quaternary production and questions of media power in the age of the communications revolution. The hyper-production and -consumption of signs are defining features of late-capitalist society. The quaternary sector of the economy has phenomenally expanded; work for nearly half the work force is a daily experience of producing, distributing, exchanging, and recording information. At an OECD conference on computer-telecommunications policy held in Paris in 1975, a four-sector analysis of production was proposed which is now widely recognized in the United States. Formerly, production had been analyzed on a three-sector basis: primary or extractive industries; secondary or manufacturing industries; tertiary or service industries. However, the exponential growth, in the late 1950s, of one department of the tertiary sector, that is, services involved with the *transfer of information,* called for the creation of a fourth or "quaternary" category of production. It was felt necessary to have a category that reflected a substantial recomposition of the labor force within the advanced economies, whereby between 1945 and 1970 the number of workers in information-based employment almost doubled to around 47 percent, a figure which remains roughly the same today (see Jones 1982, chap. 3). A revealing sign of the growth of the quaternary sector is that, by 1985, the cash flow of IBM had overtaken that of General Motors (Davis 1986, p. 244).

The revolution in communications technologies and the exponential increase in the number of mass-communications channels has led to an infinite multiplication of signs. The physical world seems to be remote from an environment saturated with signs. The world of the agricultural or industrial worker is essentially a tangible world of land, raw materials, and physical artifacts. The world of the late-capitalist producer/consumer is increasingly intangible—an environment of electronic signals and print where signs have more experiential immediacy than physical objects. (And as reality is experienced as, in the first instance, linguistic, symbolic systems and symbolization have become privileged and expansive areas of research; this is the age of linguistics, semiology, discourse theory, communications theory, and media studies.) Baudrillard argues that in advanced capitalist societies even tangible commodities tend to be consumed as "social signifiers," which code identity and behavior, instead of as material use-values. Moreover, this primacy of "sign-exchange value" is explained as a consequence of the development of mass-communication technologies (Baudrillard 1988). Our virtual addiction to signs has created a culture in which signs of the real have come to assume the authority of reality itself. The mass media, the most highly resourced forms of communication today, have played a leading role in this valorization of the sign.

In late-capitalist societies, mass-media discourses have colonized a substantial portion of our linguistic space; they are the principal purveyors of information (especially in "news" formats) and entertainment; they speak loudest of all, thanks to the broadcasting power of media corporations. Such prominence has drawn social scientists to research the influence and effects of the media, in particular their role in the organization of public opinion. Thus, Herbert Schiller and Armand Mattelart have undertaken extensive empirical studies that reveal the near-monopolistic control and management of around 90 percent of the West's information flows by a "score of media conglomerates" (see Schiller 1981; Mattelart 1980). And the researches of, among others, the University of Glasgow Media Group and the University of Birmingham's Centre for Contemporary Cultural Studies have consistently pointed to the ideological effectivity of media messages (especially in the news networks) and, in particular, to their persistence in the public mind (cf. Philo 1990). But it must be said that some theorists are skeptical about the power of the media to persuade and mobilize their audiences (see McQuail 1983). They argue that their campaigning potential is overestimated; "reaction effects" may be short-lived, the public not as suggestible as is commonly supposed. We must also reckon with counter-practices which, it is said, "subvert" media messages. Cultural theorists, for example, have discussed the phenomenon of *bricolage* where media representations that affirm the official culture are recoded by "subcultural" groups in order to affirm their own identity (cf. Hebdige 1979, pp. 104–5). However, in general, discussions of the mass media in the 1960s—when most of the texts discussed below were written—do not share this latter view of their limited powers. Rather, they are generally informed by a lexicon of "conspiratorial" terms: for example, "manipulation," "indoctrination," "brainwashing," "conditioning." This terminology is especially evident in the arguments of Frankfurt School theorists like Marcuse and Paul Lazarsfeld.[2] Thus, Marcuse asks: "Can one really distinguish between the mass media as instruments of information and entertainment, and as agents of manipulation and indoctrination?" (Marcuse 1966, p. 8. See also pp. 12, 57, 85). Similarly, Lazarsfeld observes:

Increasingly the chief power groups [. . .] have come to adopt techniques for manipulating mass publics through propaganda in place of more direct means of control. [. . .] Economic power [. . .] [has] turned to a subtler type of psychological exploitation, achieved largely by disseminating propaganda through the mass media of communication. [. . .] These media have taken on the job of rendering mass publics conformative to the social and economic status quo. (P.F. Lazarsfeld and R.K. Merton, cited in Miliband 1973, p. 197)

For these theorists, mass-media discourses are integrative precisely insofar as they are seen to promote and confirm prevailing norms and values, insofar as they are seen to contain thinking within the spectrum of a consensus that is predominantly conservative. Dissident postmodernist writers will be seen to share this view of the media as agencies of political conformity and socialization but, *inter alia,* on the basis of a more developed conception of their ideological effectivity.

Language as a Medium of Integration

A substantial body of theory from the 1960s and early 1970s (i.e., the years of most of the fiction in question) is marked by a heightened perception of language as a medium of social integration—language, that is, *in its prevailing late-capitalist forms.* (Here, as elsewhere in this discussion, "language" must be understood not as the abstract system of rules—*langue,* but as *discourse,* i.e., language as historically activated in forms appropriate to specific sociocultural contexts.) This perception informs the work of theorists who were received as gurus by the dissidents of the period, theorists like Marcuse or Lefebvre. Here I want to discuss some developments in the field of discourse and communications which, I shall argue, have been instrumental in raising consciousness of language as a medium of social integration. This calls for attention not only to the ideological inflection of everyday and socially privileged forms of language, but also to other components of the "discursive field" like the ensemble of institutions and apparatuses that regulate the use of language. The developments I want to review are the erosion of the public sphere; the enlargement of the state's propaganda agencies; the impact of technological rationality on language; and the spread of conceptually impoverished discourses that impede critical reflection on society. Here I would add that the communications revolution, the phenomenal enlargement of the state machine, the ideological ascendancy of technological rationality, and the erosion of the public sphere have all been explained in the context of the restructuring and growth of capitalist economies in their postwar phase; they have been identified as distinctively "late" or "advanced" capitalist phenomena.[3] Accordingly, these developments will be understood not as isolated phenomena but as *integral features* of late-capitalist social organization. Hence, "late-capitalist" will serve here both as a periodizing term and as a term of synthesis.

Erosion of the Public Sphere

In late-capitalist culture, a substantial proportion of communication is delivered by the media as "information"—information that the public seeks to make sense of political issues, to make its social situation intelligible. However, the structures and objectives of the principal communications channels work to degrade and distort the information on which political and social understanding depend. The problem is perhaps best discussed from the standpoint of the fate of the public sphere.

Habermas has defined the public sphere as "that realm of our social life in which something approaching public opinion can be formed" (Habermas 1974, p. 49). The public sphere, which, in its liberal-bourgeois mode, emerged in the eighteenth century, was idealized as a domain of rational discussion and free expression, a domain in which established forms of power and authority (ecclesiastical, aristocratic, etc.) could be subjected to the critical scrutiny and judgment of the public. In theory, all interests were to be represented there but, in practice, it proved to be a medium for the ideology of the rising bourgeoisie. Nevertheless, *as an ideal* it has been perceived as a progressive feature of the Enlightenment, an essential element in the project of universal emancipation.

Habermas has investigated the "structural changes" that have led to the dissolution of the public sphere. In an interview he has remarked:

I have the impression that the tendencies to disintegration of a public sphere of the liberal type—a formation of opinion in discursive style mediated by reading, reasoning, information—have intensified since the late fifties. The mode of functioning of electronic media testifies to this, above all the centralization of organizations which privilege vertical and one-way flows of second and third-hand information, privately consumed. We are witnessing an increasing substitution of images for words, and also that intermingling of categories such as advertising, politics, entertainment, information, which was already criticized by Adorno. (Habermas 1985, p. 97)

Today, the mass media are the main source of public information (McQuail 1983, p. 88). This in itself need not damage the health of the public sphere if media provision included critical inquiry and commentary from a standpoint outside the spectrum of the consensus. However, under the prevailing structure of monopolistic ownership and control, the presentation of events from genuinely alternative perspectives is a rare and marginal practice. Mass-media conglomerates are generally united on viewpoint and news values, with proprietors often exercising their prerogative of "private censorship" (Miliband 1973, p. 205) to affirm or exclude views as suits their own political prejudices (which are normally biased toward support of the established order). This means that in many American towns and cities, where the dominant media (daily paper, television, radio) are often under the same ownership, there is a one-way flow of "information"; there is, simply, no public sphere.

What counts as information may, of course, be of variable quality and use. If it is to serve as the material for "the formation of opinion in discursive style," it needs to be, *inter alia*, reliable and relevant. However, in postmodern culture, information is all too often devoid of these qualities and assumes such debased forms as "factoids," sound bites, and spectacle. Norman Mailer introduced the notion of the factoid: "That is, facts which have no existence before appearing in a magazine or newspaper, creations which are not so much lies as a product to manipulate emotion in the Silent Majority" (Mailer 1973, p. 18). Sound bites may be described as remarks expressly fashioned for easy quotation by the media, slick quotability taking precedence over substance. And spectacle—the pageants, disasters, sporting feats, and VIP conventions on which the news media obsessively focus—turns the "news" into a species of tourism, reifies reality as a series of spectator events.

The late-capitalist period is also marked by the extraordinary expansion of public relations—the term itself a PR euphemism for what amounts to the professional refinement of propaganda on behalf of big business and political organizations. Edward Bernays, the leading advocate of public relations in the U.S. business sector, has brazenly defined the industry's "engineering of consent" as the very essence of democracy (quoted in Chomsky 1988, p. 45).

Collectively, these manipulative practices significantly erode critical space; they degrade, pervert, or simply suppress the vital and relevant information on which a healthy public sphere of the liberal-bourgeois type depends.

State-Directed Communication

> ". . . when you hear the phrase 'our vital interests' do you stop to wonder whether you were invited to the den, Zen, Klan or coven meeting at which these were defined? Did you speak?"
> (Barthelme 1985, p. 43)

Regimes whose preservation does not, or cannot, depend chiefly on coercion endeavor to represent themselves as worthy of support. To this end, discourses are mobilized which justify the social system in the name of some accredited or hallowed principle (e.g., "productivity" or "freedom"). The unprecedented level of state intervention in the everyday life of late-capitalist societies has greatly increased this pressure for legitimation (see Habermas 1976, pp. 36–37, 68–72). Habermas has argued that in the "liberal" phase of capitalist development, when production operated under the "steering medium" of the market, the issue of the social system's legitimacy did not arise; the relations of production appeared to be governed by the purely objective and spontaneous functioning of the market. However, in the "late" phase of capitalist development, when production is largely regulated by the state (e.g., through fiscal policy or subventions to industry), the issue of the social system's legitimacy does arise. State administrators have to justify the way they manage the system; they are far more accountable to the public than formerly. This pressure to defend policies has led to a phenomenal enlargement of the state's propaganda apparatuses; the period is marked by a far greater "ideological discharge" than in previous phases of capitalism. Partisan definitions of problems are diffused, via governmental agencies and the media, throughout the cultural sphere with the aim of securing consent for the social order or, at least, reconciling the public to unpopular policies. (This is not to lose sight of the fact that the public may see through the legitimation process; that the process may be vulnerable to crisis. See Habermas 1976, pp. 68–75.)

The area of late-capitalist state policy that, perhaps, best illustrates how the pressure for legitimation increases directly in line with an increase in the level of state intervention is that of military budgeting. Policies of colossal military expenditure have given currency to such notions as the "permanent arms economy" (Mandel 1978, chap. 9) or "military Keynesianism" (Davis 1986, p. 202; Chomsky 1988, p. 53). These terms express the crucial role of exorbitant arms budgets in the preservation of late-capitalist economies, especially in respect to the United States. (See also Harman 1982 and Green 1985.) Until quite recently, U.S. administrations have justified the excessive costs, risks, and secrecy of its armaments program by deploying its primary propaganda strategy—the Cold War. To be sure, cold-war politics have served other purposes too, but suffice to note here that by deliberately raising the level of confrontation with the U.S.S.R. (see especially Chomsky 1984), successive U.S. administrations have mobilized public support for their high level of military expenditure. One cannot overestimate the extent to which cold-war propaganda has permeated public discourse in America (a matter examined in detail in Chapter 4).

State agencies seek to delimit the field of political debate in order to contain it within government-approved limits. It is a tendency which Mailer angrily confronts in *The Armies of the Night:*

That same newspaper story had quoted a Pentagon spokesman's reaction to charges of brutality by Pentagon marchers: "We feel," said the spokesman, "our action is consistent with objectives of security and control faced with varying levels of dissent." *Consistent with objectives of security and control! levels of dissent!* [. . .] The spokesman was speaking in totalitarianese, which is to say, technologese, which is to say any language which succeeds in stripping itself of any moral content. For if the spokesman had said, "We were trying to keep order against varying degrees of violence and insurrection," the speaker could have been asked, "What kind of violence? Insurrection in the name of what? and against which order?" (Mailer 1968, p. 315)

Finally, insofar as state agencies exploit the broadcasting power of mass-communications systems, it is possible to promote partisan versions of events as "official," to publicize and prioritize only those social problems which offer the opportunity for affirming consensual values.

Functionalist Language

In the 1960s and early 1970s, Marcuse and Lefebvre, Habermas and Mandel, among others, saw "technological rationality" as the ruling ideology of capitalism in its "late" or "state-regulated" phase—a capitalism promoted by its apologists as "organized capitalism." This view is discussed in more detail later (see Chapter 5). Suffice to say here, technological-rationalist ideology is understood to acclaim the benefits of systematization, "cybernetization" (Lefebvre) and global planning, the goal being the technical-bureaucratic organization of production and consumption. A reflection of this ideology is the functionalist tendency to think of all social practices in systemic terms—wholes to which all parts ("subsystems") must be adapted or adjusted in order to optimize the system's "performance." The system may be a bank, an industrial plant, or society itself ("the System"), and performance is a question of productivity, efficiency, or operativity. From this standpoint, a social order founded on commodity production is administered by the state (though not necessarily successfully) as if it was a "total system" to which the subject must be adapted (i.e., "systematized" or incorporated) as an efficient producer and ideal consumer. (Frankfurt School theorists did much to develop this notion of a total system, while overlooking the contradictory relationship between the "hedonism" of the ideal-consumer subject-position and the discipline of the efficient-producer subject-position.) In other words, practices oriented toward improving performance are informed by a logic of control that, with respect to the subject, demands (though may not achieve) his/her adaptation to the system.

Both Marcuse and Lefebvre have examined the impact of technological-rationalist ideology on language. Marcuse has discussed "the linguistic tendency 'to consider the names of things as being indicative at the same time of their manner of functioning . . .'"; this he explains as the effect of "technological reasoning, which tends 'to identify things and their functions'" (Marcuse 1966, pp. 86–87). Lefebvre, writing in 1968, has remarked on the increasing presence of functionalist terminology: "norms, compulsions, demands, imperatives, not to mention 'rigor,' and, of course, the word 'system.' These words *reflect* the limited rationalism of bureaucracy, of technocratic ideology, of industrial programming" (Lefebvre 1971, pp. 200–201). The prominence of functionalist terminology is, in part, a consequence of the prestige and growth of cybernetic, managerial, and other sciences in the service of practices governed by performance criteria. Consider, from Marcuse's standpoint of "The Research of Total Administration" (Marcuse 1966, p. 104f.), the examples of psychology and sociology. These disciplines, with their huge potential for industrial and commercial use, prove themselves to be eminently functionalist discourses. Theories of motivation are applied to problems of employee morale and personnel selection. Theories of conditioning (behaviorism) issue in techniques for stimulating incentive (e.g., bonus schemes) and stimulating demand (e.g., advertising). Sociology, in its industrial-commercial application, issues in management techniques (controlling unions, regimenting the labor process) and public relations skills, exploited, notably, by governments and big business.

The functionalist cast of so much language militates against critical, oppositional thought and divests social issues of their moral content. It embodies a mode of rationality which thinks in systemic terms of function/dysfunction, adjustment/maladjustment. In short, for a writer of the 1960s and 1970s, a discourse is functionalist insofar as it embodies a technological-rationalist logic of control.

Attenuated Language

Lefebvre sees language, at the late-capitalist stage of its evolution, as an attenuated medium. He has identified a substitution of "signals" for "signs," a process which, he argues, "eliminate[s] all other dimensions of language and meaning such as symbols and significant contrasts" and gives rise to "a general sense of meaninglessness" because the subject can no longer articulate or totalize his/her experiences. The shift from signs to signals has the effect of eliding mediating thought processes and so enhancing control over behavior: "signals provide practical systems for the *manipulation* of people . . ." (Lefebvre 1971, pp. 39, 62). And William Burroughs has commented on a specific aspect of language attenuation. In an interview, he has observed that: "An essential feature of the Western control machine is to make language as non-pictorial as possible, to separate words as far as possible from objects or observable processes" (Burroughs 1970, p. 98). And elsewhere, he remarks on "the feat of prose abstracted to a point where no image track occurs" (Burroughs 1968a, p. 27). For Burroughs, our intellectual purchase on reality is weakened when the language at our disposal chiefly comprises abstract, imageless words. Finally, Marcuse has argued that language forms have emerged which limit consciousness to nonantagonistic modes of understanding; which render language incapable of expressing negation. He identifies a public discourse notable for its use of "syntactical abridgment," as in the propensity for acronyms and catchphrases. It is a syntax which erodes the critical "space" between the parts of a sentence by condensing subject and predicate (Marcuse 1966, pp. 86–87). This results in propositions such as "the Free World" or "the clean bomb," which come across as "self-validating, hypnotic formulas." It is a mode of discourse which impedes conceptual thought; which "serves as a vehicle of coordination and subordination," an "irreconcilably anti-critical and anti-dialectical language" which "absorbs . . . the negative oppositional elements of Reason" (pp. 96–97). Evidently, for Marcuse, this (perceived) deadening of the critical impulse in language facilitates the integration of the subject into the social order. And while, to be sure, he has also identified points of resistance to the "established universe of discourse," noting the linguistic counter-practices of subcultural groups (Marcuse 1966, p. 86; 1969 pp. 34–36), his analysis of the prevailing state of language is overwhelmingly pessimistic.

Certainly, postmodern culture is marked by a preponderance of conceptually impoverished discourses that inhibit reflection and lack the perspectives necessary for critical analysis of the social order. Anyone can observe the impact on language of the phenomenal profit-motivated expansion of mass-media broadcasting and publishing. Fulfillment of the twin objectives of maximal marketability and rapid product-turnover demands the construction of easily consumable language forms like the pop lyric, the teen romance, or the tabloid story. Hence, much of the time, we receive discourse in the emaciated forms of catchphrases, clichés, and platitudes. There is a marked preference in television and radio shows for bland, frictionless talk, for conversation purged of critical and provocative content. Of much greater concern is the increasing tendency toward cosmeticized political discourse whereby issues are reduced to competing slogans inspired by the mesmerizing jingles of advertising.

All this is not to suggest that the prevalence of attenuated discourse *necessarily* renders the subject more susceptible to social incorporation (nor is it to suggest that in pre-postmodern times everyday language was animated by a critical impulse or was experienced as if endowed with a plenitude of meaning); my only concern here is to indicate certain changes in the field of discourse and to note how dissident thinkers have responded to them. However, I would add that we must not lose sight of the contradiction that although banalized and trivialized forms of language may have usurped much of our cultural space, at the same time, late-capitalist publics are information-conscious to a degree that is historically unprecedented. (One need only consider the insatiable demand for education and news or the phenomenal growth of the "knowledge industry.") The value placed on concept- or information-rich discourse would suggest that, in general, publics do not "consume" conceptually impoverished discourse unself-consciously or complacently. And, indeed, there is a growing awareness of the potential to develop media forms which promote knowledge, reflection, and critical debate. The necessary resources—for example, interactive communication technologies, data banks, media expertise—already exist in abundance and only await the conditions for their universal mobilization.

Dissident Postmodernist Fiction

I have argued that in the 1960s and early 1970s there was a prodigious enlargement of the notion of the political within the sphere of language. I noted, in particular, that a conception of language as a medium of social integration was a vital element in the dissident thought of this period. Furthermore, I sought to ground that conception of language in political, cultural, and other developments that have transformed the field of language and communications. And I have indicated that these developments are specific to, or more advanced under, late capitalism. These points will provide a framework for a discussion of the texts in the case studies which follow shortly—texts which I shall now identify as "dissident postmodernist."

Now, I want to distinguish between two tendencies in American postmodernist fiction: a "dissident" tendency, exemplified not only by the work of Barthelme, Coover, and Pynchon, but also by that of Burroughs, DeLillo, Acker, and Reed; and an "introverted" tendency, exemplified by the work of Nabokov, Gass, and, intermittently, Barth, among others. By way of a preliminary observation, I shall say that dissident postmodernist fiction embodies that enlarged notion of the political within the sphere of language as discussed above. And it is from this standpoint that I shall read the fiction of Nabokov and others as introverted—a literary tendency whose exploration of language barely registers its political dimensions. (Of course, from other standpoints, the work of Nabokov et al. may be evaluated without the negative undertone it has here.) This is not to propose hard and fast categories in which any postmodernist text can be instantly placed. Indeed, almost any literary text may be read as addressing, however marginally or obliquely, some political implications of language. Ultimately, the difference between these tendencies is best thought of as one of degree: the dissident tendency may be distinguished from the introverted by its *heightened perception* of the politics of language.

The problem of the "fictionality" of meaning will serve to highlight the above distinction. For the postmodernist writer, the "real" is essentially non-significant (it does not speak for itself), and the search for meaning, the endeavor to interpret the world, is perceived as a process of fictionalizing reality, of "storifying" it. It is understood that extra-discursive referents—historical events, social processes, natural phenomena—can only be apprehended in narrative form, never in their pure, naked state, that is, "as they really are." Postmodernist writers respond to the problem of the fictionality of meaning by, *inter alia,* composing texts which mock, interrogate, and subvert the "classical" realist-empiricist assumption that language can reflect or render "things as they really are." (I say *"classical* realist"; I do not suppose that all works classified as "realist" aim persistently at a faithful transcription of reality or are unconscious of the problem of meaning as outlined above.) Their primary strategy is to use language in a self-reflexive, as opposed to self-effacing, fashion in order to demonstrate the operation of narrative codes in the constitution of meaning. It is a strategy that often results in word games which work to parody reality as subject to uncontrollable textualization.

However, the problem of the fictionality of meaning does not in every respect have the same implications for all postmodernist writers. Consider some texts of introverted tendency. The narrator of Barth's "Lost in the Funhouse," one of a collection of stories about the inescapability of storytelling, observes: "The climax of the story must be its protagonist's discovery of a way to get through the funhouse. But he has found none, may have ceased to search" (Barth 1969, p. 96). We are all lost in the funhouse of fiction-making and there is no way out. Like Borges's Library, the funhouse is our textualized universe. In "Menelaiad," Menelaus exclaims in despair: " 'When will I reach my goal through its cloaks of story? How many veils to naked Helen?' " (Barth, p. 144). "Menelaiad" progresses as one story enframes a second which, in turn, enframes a third and so on, thereby suggesting, as the quotation marks multiply, that reality is but a framework of infinitely nesting narratives. Finally, "Pale Fire" is a poem, a patently literary artifact (meticulously constructed in rhyming pairs of iambic pentameters) that reflects self-consciously on the powers of linguistic invention: "playing a game of worlds," building "Empires of rhyme." This text, moreover, is the object of study of another text, an overblown "Commentary" of nearly two hundred pages by one Charles Kinbote. But this "apparatus criticus," against Kinbote's express intentions, becomes the "monstrous semblance of a novel" (Nabokov 1973, p. 71)—*Pale Fire* itself, but also Nabokov's parody of historical romance fiction. (Kinbote, who may be a king in exile or just a deranged émigré scholar, reads the poem as a coded biography of *his* escapades as king of "Zembla"—a mock-Ruritania of palace plots, secret passageways, and courtly love affairs.) In this way, Nabokov suggests that there is no direct passage from language to the real; rather, cognition is caught up in an interplay of texts.

These "introverted" instances of postmodernist writing explore the individual ego's experience of entrapment in webs of narrative fiction. Typically, in this strain of fiction, the narrator-subjects are scholars, recluses, or fantasists, remote from street level, meditating from within an enclosed, monadic environment. (This is also a notable feature of Gass's stories—see Gass 1981—and of course the *ficciones* of the master architect of hermetic spaces—Borges.) Here, the problem of the fictionality of meaning finds no grounding in social and historical conditions. On the other hand, for dissident postmodernist writers, the problem of meaning has a contextual dimension insofar as they perceive language as bearing the imprint of the institutions, projects, and conflicts in which it is imbricated. To be sure, these writers are acutely conscious of meaning as "narrative." But they are also conscious of meaning as imbued with the tensions of power-relations and conflicting value-systems. Thus Pynchon contextualizes the problem of the fictionality of meaning so that our "delusional systems" and "stories, all false, about who we are" cannot be understood without reference to a social order which "bring[s] the State to live in the muscles of your tongue" (Pynchon 1978, p. 384). Or consider this observation by Barthelme expressed in the form of an imaginary conversation: " 'Madelaine,' I say kindly to her over lunch, 'semiotics is in a position to claim that no phenomenon has any ontological status outside its place in the particular information system from which it draws its meaning, and therefore, all language is finally groundless [. . .]' 'Yes,' says Madelaine kindly [. . .], 'but some information systems are more enforceable than others.' Alas, she's right" (Barthelme 1985, p. 44). Dissident postmodernists, unlike the introverted ones, explore the political and ideological implications of the fictionality of meaning. Their writing illuminates the institutional parameters of meaning-systems; it reveals how the latter operate in force fields of power-relations; how, through the medium of ideology, meaning-systems are connected to established political structures. In short, while both introverted and dissident tendencies explore "the world within the word" (Gass 1978), as a rule, only the dissident tendency explores the word in the world.

The tendency to grasp the problem of the fictionality of meaning in political terms is one instance of what I have identified as a defining feature of dissident postmodernist fiction: its enlarged notion of the political within the sphere of language. A second instance of this, in which the first will be seen to be implied, is the focal point of this study: a *heightened perception of language as a medium of social integration.* This perception is not evident in all dissident postmodernist texts, but it is very much in the foreground of texts by, among others, Burroughs, DeLillo, Acker, and Reed, in addition to texts by Barthelme, Coover, and Pynchon. The dissident postmodernists' perception of language as a powerful medium of integration necessarily concerns them *qua* language-users; for, it need hardly be said, they are *implicated* in language both professionally as writers and generally as members of a speech community. The question then arises: Is an independent, critical standpoint within late-capitalist society possible? It is a question which haunts this fiction and which explains its self-conscious reflection on the limits of artistic autonomy.

Dissident modernists and postmodernists share the anxiety that communication is necessarily on terms established by the social order, such that to speak at all may be to surrender one's autonomy. Hence the problem of speaking in one's own voice becomes a theme in both currents of writing. Stephen Dedalus, the Irish protagonist of Joyce's *Portrait,* speaks for Joyce when, after an exchange with the dean of English studies, he reflects:

The language in which we are speaking is his before it is mine [. . .] His language, so familiar and so foreign, will always be for me an acquired speech. I have not made or accepted its words. My voice holds them at bay. My soul frets in the shadow of his language. (Joyce 1960, p. 189)

The passage expresses Joyce's unease at having to speak in the alien tongue of a colonial power (i.e., imperial Britain). And, a little later, the link between language and colonial subjection is made explicit: "—My ancestors threw off their language and took another, Stephen said. They allowed a handful of foreigners to subject them" (p. 202). But Joyce, in company with other literary (high) modernists, believed in a transhistorical plane of meaning, a judgmental standpoint *outside* of society's web of discourses, premised on the assumption that consciousness transcends language. Indeed, this faith in a transcendent consciousness is reflected in the novel's recurring image of flight, as in this famous passage: "When the soul of a man is born in this country there are nets flung at it to hold it back from flight. You talk to me of nationality, language, religion. I shall try to fly by those nets" (p. 203). For Joyce, there is a space beyond language to which the individual consciousness, privileged as the origin and legislator of meaning, can exile itself and "forge" a pure, non-alienating discourse. (And for modernists like Joyce, Stevens, and Yeats this is precisely the task of the artist—the artist exalted as a God-like "artificer.") In short, he affirmed the modernist view of consciousness as an autonomous source of meaning and hence upheld the possibility of speaking in one's own voice. Contrast this position with that of Burroughs, fifty years later:

That is the entry gimmick of The Death Dwarfs: supersonic imitation and playback so you think it is your own voice—(do you own a voice?) they invade The Right Centers which are The Speech Centers and they are in the right—in the right—in thee write—"Right"—"I'm in the right—in the right—You know I'm in the right so long as you hear me say inside your right centers 'I am in the right.'" (Burroughs 1968b, p. 75)

Clearly, for Burroughs, the subject is compelled to speak on alien terms. Language inscribes ("in thee write") a perspective on reality which is "right" both in the sense that it is approved by the social order and, by the latter's standards, in that it seems obviously correct. Consciousness, far from transcending language, is perceived to be enclosed by it: "What scared you all into time? into body? into shit? I will tell you: 'the word.' Alien Word 'the.' 'The' word of Alien Enemy imprisons 'thee' in Time. In Body. In Shit" (Burroughs 1968b, p. 10). Dissident postmodernists communicate the experience of entrapment in language with much greater insistence and desperation than is generally found in modernism. They are far less confident about the possibility of achieving an autonomous critical perspective in their work.

The forms a dissident literature may usefully assume cannot be divorced from prevailing conceptions of power. A rough contrast between turn-of-the-century naturalism and dissident postmodernism may serve to illustrate the point. Where writers like Sinclair and London saw power as concentrated in a property-owning class, it was possible to write fiction in a confrontational mode; the target was plainly objective. Such fiction, operating directly and overtly as an indictment of society, typically assumed a documentary/didactic form as in *The Jungle* (1906) or *The Iron Heel* (1907). In contrast, dissident postmodernists conceive of power as *diffused* through the cultural sphere, in particular, through language, the very material with which the writer works. Language is deeply distrusted, so that, for example, for Barthelme:

The question is, what is the complicity of language in the massive crimes of fascism, Stalinism, or (by implication) our own policies in Viet Nam? In the control of societies by the powerful and their busy functionaries? If these abominations are all in some sense facilitated by, made possible by, language, to what degree is that language ruinously contaminated? (Barthelme 1985, p. 42)

Given the dissident postmodernists' perception of language as a site of power, we can see why fiction in the confrontational mode seems to be of less strategic value than formerly, and we can begin to theorize, instead, the strategic value of the mode of writing itself.

Most critics identify postmodernist writing as typically "self-reflexive." The problem with this term is that it suggests no more than a mode of writing that examines and exposes the processes of its own composition, thereby revealing its meaning as the construct of so many (literary) codes and conventions. One might be forgiven, therefore, for thinking of self-reflexive writing as a rather sterile, cerebral kind of game, a tediously self-obsessed literature. However, as most critics who use the term would surely agree, self-reflexive fiction does not only reflect on the role of literature in the constitution of meaning. Rather, it suggests, sometimes using literature as a paradigm, that *any* sign-system constitutes meaning; it is understood that meaning is wholly or in part (depending on one's view) the "effect" of the system's rules and codes which order signifiers into narratives. For the sake of accuracy, then, I prefer to speak of a "sign-reflective" rather than "self-reflexive" fiction.

Sign-reflective techniques of writing divert our attention away from story to the processes of signification.[4] Typically, there is a focus on the textual play of forms, plots, and tropes, and the way they mediate our relationship to the "real" or, at least, to the signified. (Pynchon, for example, foregrounds authorial plotting as one such mediation.) This form of writing is a medium particularly suited to the complex task of probing the relationship between language and meaning. More-over, with specific reference to the current of postmodernist fiction identified here as dissident, we can now begin to think of *its* sign-reflectiveness as the very property which enables it to perform a con-testatory function within a substantially eroded critical space; as the very property which guarantees this fiction a measure of autonomy. We may think of sign-reflective writing as discourse to the second power or metadiscourse; discourse which, insofar as it lays bare the very processes of signification, permits a degree of disengagement from the sign-systems in which the writer is necessarily implicated. This disen-gagement is a desired objective when the prevailing discourses, includ-ing the conventions and motifs of established literary discourse, are perceived as fraudulent, mendacious, mystificatory, or hollow. Sign-reflectiveness is the strategy whereby lost critical distance is, albeit provisionally, redeemed.

Chapter 3
Donald Barthelme

Barthelme's Aesthetic

"The key to Barthelme's new aesthetic for fiction," writes Jerome Klinkowitz, "is that the work may stand for itself, that it need not yield to complete explication of something else in the world but may exist as an individual object . . ." (Klinkowitz 1980, p. 80). Ronald Sukenick makes a similar point:

Needless to say the Bossa Nova has no plot, no story, no character, no chronological sequence, no verisimilitude, no imitation, no allegory, no symbolism, no subject matter, no "meaning." It resists interpretation. [. . .] The Bossa Nova is nonrepresentational—it represents itself. [. . .] Donald Barthelme is a writer who is very bossanova. . . . (Sukenick 1972, pp. 586–87)

The view that a work by Barthelme "stand[s] for itself" or "represents itself," that we should approach it as an *autonomous art object,* is a common one, and a view with which I broadly agree (although it needs to be said that some of Barthelme's stories are also, if not exactly representational, then, at least, referential. Cf. Wilde 1987). However, the *oppositional thrust* of this aesthetic of nonrepresentation, its significance as a mode of political discourse, is barely registered in commentaries on Barthelme's fiction. Rather, the tendency is to explain this aesthetic as, in the first instance, a response to *epistemological* problems. We are referred to a condition of "epistemological uncertainty" (McCaffery 1982, p. 105; Couturier and Durand 1982, p. 38); to "epistemological skepticism" (McCaffery 1982, p. 110); to a "conventional epistemology [that] fails" (Klinkowitz 1980, p. 70). Barthelme's art, it is said, responds to epistemological uncertainty by exempting itself from the obligation to "know" the world or reflect social meanings and, instead, makes a virtue of simply "being," existing as an art-object, as a reality in its own right (e.g., see McCaffery 1982, pp. 105–6). To be sure, epistemological problems, that is, problems of knowledge and meaning,

have profound political implications. Yet, the possibility that Barthelme's interest in these problems may be understood in political
terms tends to be either ignored or, at best, not sufficiently theorized.
Critics see clearly enough that this work embodies a critique of the
meaningless "dreck" of mass culture. However, this perception is not
elaborated in terms which give due weight to the dissident impulse that
animates Barthelme's experiments with language. This error of appreciation is largely a consequence of the absence, in Barthelme studies, of
a developed, articulate conception of the writer's late-capitalist culture,
especially its politics and definitions of the political. (Klinkowitz's "irrational inconsecutive times" is fairly typical of impressionistic references
to the conjuncture of Barthelme's writing [Klinkowitz 1980, p. 76].)

In the light of the above remarks, it is revealing to begin this discussion with an examination of "The Balloon," a story which, insofar as it
is often read as a manifesto of Barthelme's aesthetic principle of nonrepresentation, enjoys the status of a paradigmatic text. Secretly, one
night, in Central Park, an unspecified narrator inflates a balloon which
expands to such immense proportions that it becomes a locality in its
own right. The New Yorkers explore it, go for strolls across it, children
treat it as a play area. Some people are concerned about the meaning of
the balloon but their concern is dismissed as an obsolete reaction:
"There was a certain amount of initial argumentation about the 'meaning' of the balloon; this subsided, because we have learned not to insist
on meanings. . . ." (Barthelme 1978, p. 23, hereafter UPUA). Inexplica-
ble, purposeless, proteiform (the balloon "was not limited or defined
[. . .]. This ability of the balloon to shift its shape, to change" UPUA
p. 28), the balloon eludes interpretation; "there was only *this balloon,*
concrete particular, hanging there" (UPUA p. 23). The balloon assumes a life of its own quite independently of its creator's intentions. Its
autonomous existence is suggested by the fact that the narrating "I"
(the balloon's creator) of the opening paragraph all but disappears
from the story as an active, self-conscious presence until the last paragraph when he/she assigns the balloon a fixed, definitive meaning—at
which point it is dismantled. (The work of art "deflated" by an exhaustive reading?)[1]

The point of the story, according to a neo-formalist reading, is that a
work of art should be respected as a "concrete particular," respected
for its quiddity, and that any attempt to appropriate it through the
process of interpretation is repressive or destructive—as if the imposition of meaning robs a work of art of its "intrinsic" power. The story is
seen as the expression of an aesthetic ideal: the art object which defies
meaning, which cannot be said to be "about" anything. This account is
correct but incomplete. To be sure, the story *does* express an aesthetic

ideal: the balloon as metaphor for the desirability of autonomous art. But this ideal can be adequately explained only within a broader socio-political framework. Take the issue of the balloon's purposelessness:

The apparent purposelessness of the balloon was vexing [. . .] Had we painted, in great letters, "LABORATORY TESTS PROVE" or "18% MORE EFFEC-TIVE" on the sides of the balloon, this difficulty would have been circum-vented. (UPUA p. 25)

In a society dominated by the logic of commodity production, it is appropriate that Barthelme should evoke advertising as a likely dis-course for making sense of the balloon. But such a "reading" would, of course, diminish the value of the balloon as a proteiform "text" and reify it. In this respect, the purposelessness of the autonomous work of art has value as a means of resisting incorporation through the media-tion of a culturally dominant discourse. (More generally, such pur-poselessness may be said to defy the technological rationality which extends from commodity production into most areas of social life.)

The balloon as autonomous art object also elicits commentary char-acteristic of the second-rate newspaper review. We read that "critical opinion was divided":

"inner joy"
"Has unity been sacrificed for a sprawling quality?"
"*quelle catastrophe!*" (UPUA p. 27)

These statements not only sound glib, they seem to be unimaginative and inept responses to an indefinable phenomenon like the balloon. Moreover, owing to irregular type-spacing that leaves them visibly detached from the rest of the text, these remarks *look* arbitrary: they resemble graffiti.

Thus far, we may say that the balloon as autonomous art object has aesthetic value by virtue of its capacity to resist cultural integration; it defies definition in the terms of established systems of meaning. Ac-cordingly, the prevailing view of "The Balloon" as a story that illus-trates Barthelme's desire for a form of art that eludes *meaning per se* stands in need of two qualifications. The story is typical of Barthelme's stories in general in that it exposes the inability of our established meaning-systems to impose meaning that is other than stultifying or superficial, and it seeks to resist and, ultimately, transcend the habitual modes of perception promoted by those meaning-systems. Further-more, in "The Balloon," as in so many of his other works, Barthelme takes care to illuminate the social context in which the problem of meaning arises. Consider the following passage:

This ability of the balloon to shift its shape, to change, was very pleasing, especially to people whose lives were rather rigidly patterned, persons to whom change, although desired, was not available. The balloon [. . .] offered the possibility, in its randomness, of mislocation of the self, in contradistinction to the grid of precise, rectangular pathways under our feet. The amount of specialized training currently needed, and the consequent desirability of long-term commitments, has been occasioned by the steadily growing importance of complex machinery, in virtually all kinds of operations; as this tendency increases, more and more people will turn, in bewildered inadequacy, to solutions for which the balloon may stand as a prototype, or "rough draft." (UPUA pp. 28–29)

The indefinability of the balloon (*qua* autonomous work of art) is "pleasing" because it hints at the liberating possibilities of a way of life *alternative* to a "rigidly patterned" social existence. Marcuse writes, "The autonomy of art contains the categorical imperative: 'things must change'" (Marcuse 1979, p. 13). (Note also that the language of the passage—dry, impassive, technically exact—is symptomatic of the regulated existence it describes.)

In short, we can assign three critical functions to a story like "The Balloon" in its capacity as an autonomous work of art: (1) An indictment of society mediated through a critical exposure of the deficiencies and distortions of its prevailing forms of language. (2) Resistance to the prevailing forms of language (and, by implication, the social way of life which creates them) by means of a discourse which defies assimilation to linguistic norms. (3) The projection of an image of liberation in an aesthetic which seeks to transcend the constraints of the "given universe of discourse" (cf. Marcuse 1979, p. 6). It is in the terms of these critical functions that I shall try to show how Barthelme's texts operate as a mode of political discourse.

Fraudulent Signs

"Me and Miss Mandible," Barthelme's first published story, looks at the problem of misreading signs. The problem is not explored from some "neutral" epistemological standpoint, as if it was just a matter of faulty interpretation. It is explored from a political standpoint, understood as a matter of fraudulent sign-systems deceiving the public in the interest of sustaining (what is perceived as) a highly questionable social order. The story is presented in the form of a journal kept by a thirty-five-year-old man who is "plucked from [his] unexamined life among other pleasant, desperate, money-making young Americans, thrown backward in space and time" to the sixth grade of elementary school (Barthelme 1964, p. 108, hereafter CBDC). This dramatic dislocation occurs after he has misread the motto of the company which employed him as an adjuster:

I myself, in my former existence, read the company motto ("Here to Help in Time of Need") as a description of the duty of the adjuster, drastically mislocating the company's deepest concerns. (CBDC p. 109)

Conscientious about obtaining satisfaction for an injured elderly claimant, he awards a settlement at huge cost to his employers. Putting welfare before profit is perceived to be such a fundamental error of judgment that Joseph, the narrator, is sent back to school for "reeducation." But, as an adult, the experience provides him with a critical vantage point for observing at first-hand the workings of late capitalism's key ideological apparatus—school as an "incubator of future citizens" (CBDC p. 109), school as an institution for integrating subjects into society.

In one entry in his journal, Joseph remarks, "Everything is promised my classmates and me, most of all the future. We accept the outrageous assurances without blinking" (CBDC p. 107). And in another entry, he comments:

It is the pledges that this place makes to me, pledges that cannot be redeemed, that will confuse me later and make me feel I am not *getting anywhere*. Everything is presented as the result of some knowable process; if I wish to arrive at four I get there by way of two and two [. . .] If I yearn for the wheel of the Lancia 2.4-litre coupé, I have only to go through the appropriate process, that is, get the money. And if it is money itself that I desire, I have only to make it. [. . .] Who points out that arrangements sometimes slip, that errors are made, that signs are misread?

Then quoting, for the third time, a line from a manual on teaching pupils fractions, Joseph concludes "'They have confidence in their ability to take the right steps and to obtain correct answers'" (CBDC p. 110). These observations expose a hidden curriculum; they reveal the precise function of the education system in its role as ideological apparatus: to mold the expectations and, to a large extent, the categories of experience of the embryonic citizens in its charge.

Sue Ann Brownly, an eleven-year-old in Joseph's class, is also shown to have made the mistake of reading signs as promises. She is an avid student of the Liz Taylor-Eddie Fisher-Debbie Reynolds love triangle as recounted in the titillating pages of *Movie-TV Secrets*. Joseph notes the title stories of the magazines Sue Ann carries in her satchel:

"Debbie's Kids Are Crying"
"Eddie Asks Debbie: Will You . . . ?"
"The Nightmares Liz Has About Eddie!"

"The Things Debbie Can Tell About Eddie"
"The Private Life of Eddie and Liz"
"Debbie Gets Her Man Back?" (CBDC pp. 105–6)

And so on. Seventeen titles are listed thus suggesting the mass scale production of what, after *Snow White,* we are invited to call "dreck." Pop-journalist accounts of the affairs of Debbie, Eddie, and Liz evidently fill the minds of Sue Ann and others in her class and induce expectations of glamour and excitement after school. Joseph remarks:

it is obvious that she has been studying their history as a guide to what she may expect when she is suddenly freed from this drab, flat classroom [. . .] She is not responsible, I know, for what she reads, for the models proposed to her by a venal publishing industry. (CBDC p. 106)

Sue Ann competes with her teacher, Miss Mandible, for Joseph's attention, and when she stumbles upon them having sex in the cloakroom Joseph observes, "She ran out of the room weeping [. . .] certain now which of us was Debbie, which Eddie, which Liz" (CBDC p. 110). Evidently trash literature plays an important part in defining the experience of reality of juveniles like Sue Ann. Her sexual consciousness is largely constructed by discourses of the likes of *Movie-TV Secrets.*

At school second-time around, Joseph questions one of society's most hallowed symbols, the national flag. In his first entry he notes that "the class [. . .] is launched every morning with the pledge of allegiance to the flag" (CBDC p. 97). Near the end he remarks:

All of us, Miss Mandible, Sue Ann, myself [. . .] still believe that the American flag betokens a kind of general righteousness. But I say, looking about me in this incubator of future citizens, that signs are signs, and some of them are lies. (CBDC p. 109)

Thus the problem of fraudulent signs is finally displaced from school into the larger context of the nation-state, of society as a whole. Joseph perceives how society's dominant sign-systems (academic, pop-cultural, nationalist) make pledges that cannot be redeemed. In the last but one entry he writes, "My enlightenment is proceeding wonderfully." His enlightenment is possible only insofar as he is estranged from the sign-systems around him; only insofar as he has achieved a critical distance from them.

" 'Everybody knows the language but me' " (CBDC p. 177) says the sculptor, Peterson, in "A Shower of Gold." The language that everybody is speaking (the story was published in 1963) is a debased existentialism. Peterson's barber has written four books entitled *The Decision to Be* and discusses Nietzsche while giving Peterson a short back and sides.

Some girls who call on Peterson quote Pascal while cooking "veal engagé." When Peterson auditions for a place as a contestant on a TV quiz show called *"Who Am I?,"* the program organizer asks him the following questions:

"Mr. Peterson, are you absurd? [. . .] Do you encounter your own existence as gratuitous? Do you feel *de trop*? Is there nausea? [. . .] People today, we feel, are hidden away inside themselves, alienated, desperate, living in anguish, despair and bad faith. Why have we been thrown here, and abandoned? [. . .]" (CBDC pp. 173–74)

But it is clear that the source of Peterson's angst is not existential but simply economic. The story begins, "Because he needed the money Peterson answered an ad that said *'We'll pay you* to be on TV if your opinions are strong enough. . . .'" (CBDC p. 173). And when his art dealer remarks, "'You read too much in the history of art. It estranges you from those possibilities for authentic selfhood. . . .'" Peterson's only reply is, "'I know, could you let me have twenty until the first?'" (CBDC p. 175).

Peterson seeks refuge from interminable talk of alienation in his studio but is persistently harassed by intruders who reproach him for his "inauthentic" existence. The story ironically deviates from the conventional theme of the artist-figure as estranged from a mindless, philistine community (cf. Bloomsbury's estrangement from Huber and Whittle in "For I'm the Boy" [CBDC pp. 53–63]) and represents him as estranged from a society characterized by a hypertrophied self-consciousness. It is not, of course, the thinking of Sartre or Heidegger which Barthelme parodies but its popularization and commercialization, the way in which philosophies of self-consciousness have been institutionalized by a narcissistic, hyper-individualist society.

On the night of the quiz show, sitting beneath an illuminated tote board which spells out "BAD FAITH" in huge white letters for opinions deemed "invalid," Peterson addresses the camera with views that are ideologically rather than philosophically unacceptable. The emcee, who "resembled the President," tries to silence him, but Peterson continues undeterred. He holds that alienation is not an unalterable, ontological condition; we should not pessimistically resign ourselves to the idea that human existence is flawed:

"In this kind of a world [. . .], absurd if you will, possibilities nevertheless proliferate and escalate all around us and there are opportunities for beginning again [. . .] Don't be reconciled. Turn off your television sets [. . .] cash in your life insurance, indulge in a mindless optimism [. . .] How can you be alienated without first having been connected? Think back and remember how it was." (CBDC p. 183)

And as if remembering how it was, Peterson concludes his talk, and Barthelme concludes the story, with these words (the first of which allude to Ovid's *Metamorphosis*):

"My mother was a royal virgin and my father a shower of gold. My childhood was pastoral and energetic and rich in experiences which developed my character. As a young man I was noble in reason, infinite in faculty, in form express and admirable, and in apprehension . . ." Peterson went on and on and although he was, in a sense, lying, in a sense he was not. (CBDC p. 183)

After all the obsessive introspection of those seduced by a pedestrianized existentialism, this abrupt switch to a pre-individualist, mythic discourse comes as a breath of fresh air. But, more importantly, Peterson's utopian invocation of the origins of man contrasts starkly with the image of man projected by Pascal in a remark quoted twice in the story: " 'The natural misfortune of our mortal and feeble condition is so wretched that when we consider it closely, nothing can console us' " (CBDC pp. 177, 180). Peterson's mythical discourse betrays a yearning for an affirmative image of man at a time too easily given over to pessimism.

Finally, there is a paradox in that the philosophy of authenticity is shown to have become so faddish (materializing ultimately in the form of a TV quiz) that it seems phony. On the other hand, Peterson's manifestly fabricated discourse (fabrication suggested not only by its mythical content but by a self-conscious use of diction and syntax) looks fresh against "the jargon of authenticity" (Adorno) and indeed, retrospectively, makes the latter look clichéd and banal. Placed strategically at the end of the collection, *Come Back, Dr. Caligari,* Peterson's concluding words remind us of the power of art to expose the reified condition of language when its use-value is diminished by fashion and/or ideological inflection.

Loss of Critical Distance

The diminution of the use-value of language has political implications which Barthelme explores in some of the stories in his second collection, *Unspeakable Practices, Unnatural Acts.* In the opening paragraph of "The President" (1964) we are told that " 'He is a *strange fellow,* all right. He has some magic charisma which makes people———' " (UPUA p. 150). The President's charisma makes people faint; his mere presence triggers uncontrollable applause. This inscrutable figure commands devotion and mystifies everyone, including his opponents, with his "darkness, strangeness, and complexity." Of the other candidate who contested the presidency, we read, "the handsome meliorist who ran against him, all zest and programs, was defeated by a fantastic margin" (UPUA p. 152). In this context, "fantastic margin" also means margin of fantasy. For nothing is known about the President; he cannot be situated in the real world. The narrator remarks:

Certain things about the new President are not clear. I can't make out what he is thinking. When he has finished speaking I can never remember what he has said. There remains only an impression of strangeness, darkness [. . .] One hears only cadences. Newspaper accounts of his speeches always say only that he "touched on a number of matters in the realm of . . ." (UPUA p. 152)

His policies are unknown; people can only guess at his plans. Statements about the President always stop short of revealing anything about him. " 'The look on his face——' "; " 'But if anybody——any *one* man . . .' " (UPUA pp. 152, 153). Thus, faced with the President's inscrutability, the narrator has only trivia on which to focus, telling us twice that he is "only forty-eight inches high at the shoulder" (UPUA pp. 150, 154) or telling us about the President's mother's journey to Tibet in 1919 (UPUA pp. 154–55).

The elusive thoughts of the President, his inscrutability, operate metaphorically to suggest the difficulty of "reading" political situations in late-capitalist America. Indeed, this difficulty is reflected in the vacuous language in which the narrator describes his period: " 'Our period will be characterized in future histories as a period of tentativeness and uncertainty. [. . .] A kind of parenthesis.' " And " 'Our period is perhaps not so choice as the previous period, still——' " (UPUA p. 151). He speaks only in bland generalizations or with caution ("I am not altogether sympathetic to the new President" [UPUA pp. 150, 152]). He lacks a critical discourse which can give him an intellectual purchase on political circumstances. And the need for such a discourse is all the more acute given the subtle forms in which totalitarian politics have materialized in late-capitalist America. Indeed, the story has undertones of an emerging fascism, only the new politics cannot be "read." A year earlier (1963), Mailer remarked in *The Presidential Papers:*

. . . totalitarianism has slipped into America with no specific political face. There are liberals who are totalitarian, and conservatives, radicals, rightists, fanatics, hordes of the well-adjusted. Totalitarianism has come to America with no concentration camps and no need for them, no political parties and no desire for new parties, no, totalitarianism has slipped into the body cells and psyche of each of us. (Mailer 1976, p. 200)

The charismatic figure of the President and the hysteria that his staged, showbiz-like rallies induce (UPUA p. 155) are suggestive of an emotionally charged fascist politics in an American setting; a Führer

cult characteristically exploiting the forms of mass entertainment. By
the end of the story, the narrator is enthusiastically cheering the President despite earlier having expressed doubts and feelings of unease
about him. The critical distance available to the central figures in *Come
Back, Dr. Caligari* (e.g., Joseph and Peterson) is not available to this
narrator nor, as we shall see, to others in *Unspeakable Practices, Unnatural Acts.*

A commercial bit like "Robert Kennedy Saved from Drowning" (a spoof of the
English Lord and Elizabeth Taylor lady-magazine interview . . .) is simply
cheap. Here Barthelme's method fails for the idea is to *use* dreck, not write
about it. (Gass 1980, p. 102)

With these words Gass summarily dismisses the best known piece in
Barthelme's second collection of stories. But Barthelme does more
than spoof a lady-magazine interview; as we shall see, he uses the dreck
of pop journalism to make a political point. Couturier and Durand also
miss the political significance of the story when they observe that,
"What is problematized [is] . . . the activity of reference itself, the
possibility of situating any referent of a discourse" (Couturier and
Durand 1982, p. 38). But they overgeneralize; what is at issue in the
text does not concern "the activity of reference itself" but, specifically,
the activity of *political* reference.

Recall the date of the story's publication, April 1968, when Senator
Robert Kennedy was a presidential candidate in the primaries. He is
indeed a "hypothetical Robert Kennedy" (p. 38), the shifting, unstable
signified of the narrative. Yet Barthelme's choice of such a prominent
political figure for a subject cannot be without political significance.
Given his family background and political status, together with the
gathering momentum of his campaign juggernaut early in 1968, Kennedy was inevitably in the public eye. The story illustrates a problem
that has become acute in the media society: the perception of politicians and, by implication, the perception of politics itself is mediated
through channels of public information which are unreliable, superficial, and trivializing. The story is a montage of individually titled
paragraphs ("K. at His Desk," "Gallery-going," etc.) most of which read
like pop-journalistic tidbits: accounts of Kennedy at a party, his visit to
a restaurant or art gallery. (The very syntax and catchwords of the
story's title—"Robert Kennedy Saved from Drowning"—are suggestive of a newspaper's eye-catching headline.) No significant information ever emerges from these accounts, even when we are led to
expect some kind of revelation, as in the paragraph titled "A Friend
Comments: K.'s Aloneness." Kennedy's friend recounts the following
incident:

"He has surprising facets. I remember once we were out in a small boat. K. of course was the captain. Some rough weather came up and we began to head back in. I began worrying about picking up a landing and I said to him that I didn't think the anchor would hold, with the wind and all. He just looked at me. Then he said: 'Of course it will hold. That's what it's for.'" (UPUA p. 46)

In one paragraph, "Karsh of Ottawa," a photographer of celebrities talks of "the key shot, the right one" (UPUA p. 45) from among the many pictures taken at a sitting. This encourages us to think of each paragraph describing a different aspect of Kennedy's daily life as a duff snapshot, and that taken together they yield no insight into his psyche. It may be with this point in mind that critics have concluded that the story illustrates the breakdown of conventional epistemology, seeing in the disjunctive paragraphs fragments of empirical data from which no inference can be drawn (e.g., Klinkowitz 1980, pp. 69–71; McCaffery 1982, p. 112). Or it may be the narrator's admission that he is "a notoriously poor observer" which has led them to this conclusion. But it is worth noting in full the context which prompts this admission:

K. turns to the mother [his wife] of these children who is standing nearby wearing hip-huggers which appear to be made of linked marshmallows studded with diamonds but then I am a notoriously poor observer. (UPUA pp. 47–48)

Surely the poor observation has less to do with the unreliable account of Mrs. Kennedy's hip-huggers than with the fact that the narrator's focus should have strayed in that direction in the first place. And, of course, poor observation is not just the narrator's problem; it is *our* problem. The terms of social seeing inscribed in our everyday discourses, including those of lady-magazines and political speeches, limit, not to say mislead, our understanding. We cannot "see" or "read" the political figure "Robert Kennedy" because the prevailing discourses cannot see or read politics. What we should know about a politician are his policies, not the restaurants he visits or what his wife wears. Ultimately, all we get is Kennedy-as-Public-Image, public images which are often contradictory and which seem, insofar as they appear to float free of their referent, abstract, phantasmal; Robert Kennedy reduced to a hyperrealist construct.

The story also exposes the lost use-value of politicians' discourse. A notable feature of late-capitalist politics is the tendency for politicians to be nonspecific and noncommittal in their speeches. Hence the instantly forgettable non-statements in which their opinions and proposals are often formulated:

"It's an expedient in terms of how not to destroy a situation which has been a long time gestating, or, again, how *to* break it up if it appears that the situation has changed, during the gestation period, into one whose implications are not quite what they were at the beginning." (UPUA p. 50)

Or:

"Obsolete facilities and growing demands have created seemingly insoluble difficulties and present methods of dealing with these difficulties offer little prospect of relief." (UPUA p. 44)

Written in 1968, at the climax of American involvement in Vietnam, "Report" is a piece of antiwar fiction, "propagandistic" as Barthelme remarked in an interview (Ziegler and Bigsby 1982, p. 44). The catalog of sadistic weaponry is reminiscent of the grotesque fantasies of William Burroughs: testicle-destroying telegrams; a hut-shrinking chemical which causes the hut to strangle its occupants; hypodermic darts which piebald the enemy's pigmentation, and so on. These are science-fictional ideas, of course, but not so far removed from the actuality of napalm and defoliation. The question Barthelme poses is: what kind of logic overrides the moral sense in the production of such hideous forms of warfare?

The story begins, "Our group is against the war. But the war goes on. I was sent to Cleveland to talk to the engineers [. . .] They were friendly. They were full of love and information" (UPUA pp. 56–57). The incongruous coupling of love and information immediately weakens our belief in the engineers' amiability. The narrator then addresses the chief engineer:

I am here representing a small group of interested parties. We are interested in your thing which seems to be functioning. In the midst of so much dysfunction, function is interesting. Other people's things don't seem to be working. The State Department's thing doesn't seem to be working. The UN's thing doesn't seem to be working. (UPUA p. 57)

And the engineer confirms the narrator's impression: "Function is the cry and our thing is functioning like crazy" (UPUA p. 60). The "thing" turns out to be a secret weapon which I shall identify shortly. But, for the moment, I want to look at the theme of functionality.

The late-capitalist system is governed by the technological-rationalist criteria of efficiency, performance, and systematization (see Chapter 2, under "Functionalist Language"). In a society organized on the basis of maintaining and improving the conditions of commodity production, these criteria have priority over all other criteria—environmental, aesthetic, and, significantly here, ethical. Under these circumstances, functionalist discourses flourish: ergonomics, behaviorism, management sciences, and, most characteristic of our information age, cybernetics. Daily language is now infused with functionalist logic. The narrator, for example, objects to the war but speaks only of "errors": "I said that the government had made a series of errors [. . .] I said that ten thousand of our soldiers had already been killed in pursuit of the government's errors" (UPUA p. 58). With the diffusion of computer technology, the term "error" has acquired fresh currency. And note the functionalist language in which the engineer replies to the narrator's objections: "'. . . but we can't possibly *lose* the war, can we? And stopping is losing, isn't it? The war regarded as a process, stopping regarded as an abort? We don't know *how* to lose a war. That skill is not among our skills'" (UPUA pp. 58–59). Moreover, the engineer defends the development of the secret weapon (in words that parody Terence) thus: "'Nothing mechanical is alien to me [. . .] because I am human, in a sense, and if I think it up, then "it" is human too, whatever "it" may be'" (UPUA p. 60). The awkwardness of the remark suggests the engineer's difficulty in containing the reifying logic of functionalism.

He concludes his discussion with the narrator informing him:

". . . we have a *moral sense*. It is on punched cards, perhaps the most advanced and sensitive moral sense the world has ever known [. . .] With this great new moral tool, how can we go wrong? I confidently predict that, although we *could* employ all this splendid new weaponry [. . .] *we're not going to do it*." (UPUA p. 62)

Here Barthelme not only mocks the AI dream of computer simulation of moral judgment, but also, more seriously, suggests the triumph of functionalist logic in *absorbing* moral issues.

It seems that there is no discourse which can adequately represent the moral standpoint. Even the narrator's credibility as an antiwar protester is compromised insofar as his work in "software" (his nickname is "Software Man") associates him with the engineers and their faith in cybernetics. Indeed, by the end of the story, it appear that he has switched allegiance from his antiwar group to the engineers. The "we" = antiwar group/"They" = engineers distinction which obtained at the start of the story is reversed in the last paragraph: "I made my report to the group. I stressed the friendliness of the engineers. I said, It's all right. I said, We have a moral sense. I said, *we're not going to do it*. They didn't believe me" (UPUA p. 62).

The report lacks credibility; its claim to truth seems impotent against the prevailing logic whose only truth is functionality. Finally, as if to emphasize the extent to which this logic has infiltrated language, we learn that the unnamed weapon is "a secret word" which produces multiple fractures within a large radius of its utterance.

Language and Subjectivity

We can identify a significant difference between the stories selected from *Come Back, Dr. Caligari* and those selected from *Unspeakable Practices, Unnatural Acts* on the question of the relationship between language and consciousness. We saw how the protagonists in "Me and Miss Mandible" and "A Shower of Gold" are able to maintain a critical distance from their culture's dominant discourses. That is to say, the consciousness of each is not bounded by those discourses; Joseph and Peterson can make sense of the world without them. On the other hand, the narrators in "The President," "Robert Kennedy Saved from Drowning," and "Report" are unable to maintain a critical distance from the terms of seeing inscribed in the socially dominant discourses. The loss of critical distance and the susceptibility to social incorporation which follows from that loss are themes Barthelme examines in depth in *Snow White* and later works of fiction. These themes are explored through the relationship between language and subjectivity.

I remarked earlier that one of Barthelme's aims is to expose the limits that language, in its prevailing *late-capitalist forms,* imposes on consciousness. In his fiction, as in that of other dissident postmodernist writers, the limits of consciousness are revealed as corresponding to the limits of language; the forms of intelligibility are shown to be derived from the dominant discourses. This is not necessarily to say that Barthelme, like post-structuralist theorists, asserts the primacy of the "Symbolic Order" in the constitution of consciousness. But what we can say is that in his fiction the limits of language are focused through the consciousness of the subject, and that deformations of language issue in a deformed subjectivity.

What I want to emphasize is Barthelme's interest in what I have already referred to as the diminished use-value of language: the proliferation of dreck and other forms of language which lack critical potential. Much of his best fiction illustrates a thinning out of language in late-capitalist society, a process shown to lead to a loss of critical distance and hence increased susceptibility to social integration (or, as Barthelme might have it, "embourgeoisment"). What emerges is an image of an attenuated subjectivity: a consciousness, in the final stage of alienation, characterized by inertia; a consciousness at times "flipping" into a post-alienated state, ecstatically immersed in the instantaneous present.

"'Oh I wish there were some words in the world that were not the words I always hear!'" (Barthelme 1982, p. 6, hereafter SW). Snow White's first words express her desire to transcend the limits of understanding imposed by society's prevailing discourses. But, unfortunately, she lacks a transcendent language. In this respect, education was no help to her. The lengthy description of her curriculum at "Beaver College" is a parody of the irrelevance and experimental excesses of a "progressive" arts education (SW pp. 25–26). She has no intellectual purchase on her reality. When asked by the dwarves why she remains with them she replies,

"It must be laid, I suppose, to a failure of the imagination. I have not been able to imagine anything better." *I have not been able to imagine anything better.* (SW p. 59)

And near the end of the novel one of the dwarves raises these questions:

TRYING to break out of this bag that we are in. What gave us the idea that there was something better? How does the concept, "something better," arise? What does it look like, this *something better*? (SW p. 179)

The problem of Snow White and the dwarves is not simply, as Klinkowitz remarks, "lack of imagination" or "lack of knowledge" (Klinkowitz 1980, pp. 66–68). Once again, the issue is not epistemological but ideological. Their mental horizons are fixed by discourses that preclude conceptions of an alternative way of life, of "something better." They have at their disposal only debased meaning-systems or dreck with which to make sense of their predicament, their society, their selves.

Since Gass's essay "The Leading Edge of the Trash Phenomenon" (Gass 1980, pp. 97–103), critics have emphasized that "dreck" (not "excrement" as in its civil German usage but "crap" or "trash" as in its vulgar Yiddish usage) provides the linguistic material for much of Barthelme's fiction. This is correct but what has not been emphasized is, precisely, the *late-capitalist* significance of Barthelme's preoccupation with dreck. Thus one character proposes a "relation" between the high level of redundancy or "stuffing" or "blanketing" effect of ordinary language (SW p. 96):

"and what we're doing here at the plant with these plastic buffalo humps. Now you're probably familiar with the fact that the per-capita production of trash in this country is up from 2.75 pounds per day in 1920 to 4.5 pounds per day in 1965 [. . .] and is increasing at the rate of about four percent a year. Now that rate will probably go up, because it's *been* going up, and I hazard that we may very well soon reach a point where it's 100 percent. Now at such a point [. . .] the question turns from a question of disposing of this 'trash' to a question of appreciating its qualities, because, after all, it's 100 percent, right? And there can no longer be any question of 'disposing' of it, because it's all there is, and we will simply have to learn how to 'dig' it [. . .] So that's why we're in humps, right now [. . .] They are 'trash,' and what in fact could be more useless or trashlike? It's that we want to be on the leading edge of this trash phenomenon, the everted sphere of the future, *and that's why we pay particular attention, too, to those aspects of language that may be seen as a model of the trash phenomenon.*" (SW pp. 97– 98. My emphasis)

We find that Barthelme discusses dreck, that is, trashy language, in the context of production and consumption. The talk is given by Dan, the most entrepreneurial of the dwarves, at a plant engaged in the production of plastic buffalo humps, and the statistics describing quantities of trash should be read as an index of rising levels of production and consumption. But it is not only a question of the fact that hyperproduction and hyperconsumption are characteristic features of late capitalism. One of the most distinctive features of late capitalism, as observed by Fredric Jameson, is "a society where exchange-value has been generalized to the point at which the very memory of use-value is effaced . . ." (Jameson 1984a, p. 66). Indeed, the plastic buffalo humps exist as pure exchange-value; they fulfill absolutely no need: " 'They are trash, and what in fact could be more useless or trashlike?' " And insofar as Barthelme presents language in terms of the contemporary mode of production, we are encouraged to perceive it as devoid of use-value, that is, devoid of meaning, expressiveness, critical potential. Loss of use-value turns language into dreck.

In his discussion of the circulation of commodities, Marx remarks on the "metamorphosis" of the commodity which, once it enters the exchange process, is divested of its "natural and original use-value" (Marx [1867] 1976, pp. 203–4); it loses its substance, as it were, and becomes abstract and light. Similarly, when language is infused with the logic of exchange-value, it becomes attenuated; it takes the form of catchphrases, clichés, empty phraseology (see Chapter 2, under "Attenuated Language"). Dissident postmodernist writers, recognizing the role of attenuated language in the constitution of consciousness, reveal subjectivity in the forms of banalised feelings, stock fantasies, platitudes. Consciousness is seen to have lost its "depth." This thinnedout consciousness also finds its fictional expression in abstract characterization. The reader cannot fail to notice that *all* the characters in the novel are drawn diagrammatically as "abstract notions" (SW p. 180) or principles. The dwarves are principles of bourgeois complacency and Snow White is a principle of contemporary disaffectedness. Indeed, it is probable that in view of the popularity of the Walt Disney production of *Snow White,* Barthelme has capitalized on our primary image of the heroine as a cartoon figure which, like many cartoon figures, embodies not an individual self but an abstract notion. Furthermore, on the last page, Snow White is dissolved by a few quick strokes of the pen:

THE FAILURE OF SNOW WHITE'S ARSE
REVIRGINIZATION OF SNOW WHITE
APOTHEOSIS OF SNOW WHITE
SNOW WHITE RISES INTO THE SKY
THE HEROES DEPART IN SEARCH OF
  A NEW PRINCIPLE
HEIGH-HO

(SW p. 181)

The ostentatious ease with which Barthelme disposes of Snow White reinforces our impression of her as merely a malleable abstract notion, a subject, that is, who is not to be credited with an authentic self or unique identity.

The mental states of Snow White and the dwarves are revealed as the products of debased discourses: "educationese," faddish philosophies, commercials, pornography. These supply the dominant forms of their understanding. Accordingly, the possibility of intellectual insight and self-understanding is, for them, necessarily limited. There is an important ideological dimension to this condition. The discourses which provide the materials of consciousness (i.e., which make possible the forms of social seeing and self-perception) play a key part in the maintenance of a stratified social order. In Barthelme's society that order is bourgeois and the dominant discourses serve to affirm bourgeois hegemony. The Seven Dwarves are parodic embodiments of bourgeois values and thinking. But these are thrown into question when they encounter the discontented Snow White:

Before we found Snow White wandering in the forest we lived lives stuffed with equanimity. There was equanimity for all. We washed the buildings, tended the vats [. . .] We were simple bourgeois [. . .] Now we are complex bourgeois who are at a loss. We do not like this complexity. We circle it wearily, prodding it from time to time with a shopkeeper's forefinger: What is it? Is it, perhaps, *bad for business*? (SW pp. 87–88)

Moreover, when Bill, their angst-ridden leader, also disturbs their equanimity, they hang him and make the entrepreneurial Dan their leader. Under him they can safely continue their bourgeois way of life: acquisitive, complacent, hardworking, house-proud, and, above all, supportive of the capitalist social order with the production of pure exchange-values in the forms of plastic buffalo humps and exotic Chinese baby foods.

It is only with the help of a mind-altering chemical that one of the dwarves can momentarily transcend bourgeois categories of experience: " 'But it is worth it to have a blown mind. To stop being a filthy bourgeois for a space, even a short space. To gain access to everything in a new way' " (SW p. 142). Barthelme also seeks to gain access to everything in a new way, to find his way out of established systems of representation by experimenting with the forms of literary discourse. I shall return to this point later but for the moment we should note that at the level of the story or *histoire* (as opposed to the way it is narrated or plotted) transcendence is not given as a possibility. Bourgeois hegemony limits the dwarves' and Snow White's horizon of experience.

Snow White invests her hope in "princeliness," a kind of redemption which she expects from her relationship with Paul. " 'Someday my prince will come' ", " '. . . waiting for a prince, packed with grace' " (SW pp. 70, 77). She sits at a window and lets her hair down into the street, an invitation to be "saved" by any man who dares to climb it. But after a long wait she pulls in her hair:

"No one has come to climb up. That says it all. This time is the wrong time for me [. . .] There is something wrong [. . .] with the very world itself, for not being able to supply a prince." (SW pp. 131–32)

And later we read, " '. . . no one responded to Snow White's hair initiative [. . .] It suggests that Americans will not or cannot see themselves as princely' " (SW p. 141). American society cannot provide a prince-figure; " 'Paul's princeliness has somehow fallen away [. . . He] is just another complacent bourgeois' " (SW p. 157). The absence of a prince-figure reflects the felt absence of revolutionary hope in late-capitalist America; salvation is not thought a possibility in Barthelme's America.[2] Hogo, a friend of the dwarves, though speaking of his relationship with a girlfriend, expresses the inertia and acquiescence of disaffected Americans like Snow White:

"Nothing is to become of us [. . .] Our becoming is done. We are what we are. Now it is just a question of rocking along with things as they are until we are dead." (SW p. 128)

The void in Snow White's life—her " 'longing, boredom, ennui and pain' " (SW p. 102)—is a consequence of her social existence, of living in a society where the logic of exchange-value has effaced all other values. Yet in a sense it would be misleading to speak of Snow White's predicament as one of "alienation." Insofar as she is caricatured as an abstract notion, and insofar as her utterances are just clichés and banalities, Barthelme suggests her lack of depth and authenticity, the very preconditions of alienated experience. There are simply no grounds for comparing Snow White's thin approximation of anguish with the anguish of some of literary modernism's alienated figures: the angst of Kafka's K, the anomie of Joyce's Stephen Dedalus, the abysmal visions of Lowry's Geoffrey Firmin. The difference reflects a radical change in our perception of the human subject, a matter that calls for attention here.

Leading theorists of late-capitalist consumer society like Marcuse and Lefebvre have identified the emergence of a new type of subject. Marcuse has observed that:

the extent to which this civilization transforms the object world into an extension of man's mind and body makes the very notion of alienation questionable. The people recognize themselves in their commodities; they find their soul in their automobile, hi-fi set, split-level home, kitchen equipment. (Marcuse 1966, p. 9)

And Lefebvre observes, "We would suggest that alienation is spreading and becoming so powerful that it obliterates all traces or consciousness of alienation" (Lefebvre 1971, p. 94). Both Marcuse and Lefebvre have commented on the process of embourgeoisement whereby in consuming commodities the subject consumes bourgeois values.[3] Consumption, under conditions of capitalist production, guarantees bourgeois hegemony—the internalization of the values and forms of intelligibility which sustain the bourgeois social order. Accordingly, the subject is seen to be so deeply implicated in that order that the opportunities for establishing a critical distance from it have dramatically decreased.

Much modernist literature portrayed individuals striving to create personal meaning from a life experienced as contingent, disjunctive, and shapeless. This literature was preoccupied with the plight of the alienated subject, the "outsider" rejecting or rejected by bourgeois society. But from a postmodern perspective, alienation almost looks like a privileged condition. It suggests the possibility of a self-determining subject establishing a critical distance (albeit from the transhistorical perspectives of mysticism or myth) from society. That possibility is rarely open to the subjects of Barthelme's fiction.

Quotidian Consciousness

Critics have observed that many of Barthelme's works explore *la vie quotidienne,* that they conduct "a relentless investigation of the humdrum" (Wilde 1976, p. 49). I agree, but an important question has not been adequately posed: What perception of sociocultural change has induced Barthelme to focus on the quotidian? Invariably missing from studies of Barthelme are informed conjunctural accounts of what is specific to the culture of the postmodernist writer. I would argue that Barthelme's preoccupation with the quotidian is a consequence of that enlargement of the notion of the political within the culture-language sphere (see Chapter 2). In particular, this expanded conception of politics reflects the impression that the logic of late capitalism has penetrated the mundane, routine, and most intimate levels of our existence: consumption, the perception of space (see Jameson 1984a) and, central to this inquiry, language; a process whose end result is perceived to be an impoverished, attenuated subjectivity.

Quotidian experience in late-capitalist culture is communicated in Barthelme's fiction, first and foremost, through a use of language in its degraded forms of dreck, "stuffing," and "noise." These language forms lack depth and emotional resonance and are frequently marked by irrelevance and incoherence. They are often expressive of confinement to the instantaneous present: they suggest a consciousness englobed by immediacy, lacking a sense of history and a sense of life as a project. Strings of unrelated signifiers in works like "Brain Damage" and "Bone Bubbles" suggest a world of evanescent meanings, a quotidian consciousness entrenched in the particular, unable to generalize and hence to achieve a critical purchase on reality. In "Brain Damage" we read that, "The Wapituil are like us to an extraordinary degree": they have a limited span of attention ("they lose interest very quickly") and "have one disease, mononucleosis"—where "one" should be read as a noun (Barthelme [1970] 1976 p. 142, hereafter CL). They apprehend reality in the form of singular instants. And, as if to illustrate the point, on the adjoining page, beneath a picture of a distressed woman, there is a list (one of several in the story) of boldly capitalized words whose meanings do not interlock and thus cannot be generalized (or totalized) to yield some coherent perspective:

WRITHING
HOWLING
MOANS
WHAT RECOURSE?
RHYTHMIC HANDCLAPPING
SHOUTING
SEXUAL ACTIVITY
CONSUMPTION OF FOOD

(CL p. 143)

The list or inventory, one of Barthelme's favorite forms, serves ingeniously as a symptom of the attenuation of language. Words coded by their place in a list often have a low order of significance; they exist as mere items, shorn of semantic power. The list—the shopping list, the laundry list, the directory—is language at its most mundane, the quotidian form of language *par excellence*.

Another feature of Barthelme's prose which suggests the poverty of everyday experience is the conspicuous absence of mise-en-scène; details of landscape, architecture, and décor are, with few exceptions, virtually nonexistent. Mise-en-scène or ambience implies a mode of experiencing the world, namely, where the subject exists in a *meaningful* relation to his/her environment; it implies subjective depth. However, in accord with his conception of a thinned out, quotidian consciousness, Barthelme's fiction is devoid of ambience.

On the face of it, "Critique de la Vie Quotidienne," the lead story in the collection *Sadness* (1972), is a conventional, amusing piece about the breakup of a middle class American family; it satirizes the bourgeois ideals of domesticity and The Good Life. The discrepancy between reality and ideal is suggested by the narrator's apathy, which is evident from the start. His first words inform us that he reads the *"Journal of Sensory Deprivation."* He continues:

Our evenings lacked promise. The world in the evening seems fraught with the absence of promise, if you are a married man. There is nothing to do but go home and drink your nine drinks and forget about it.
  Slumped there in your favorite chair, with your nine drinks lined up on the side table [. . .], a tiny tendril of contempt—strike that, *content*—might [. . .] reach into your softened brain and take hold there. . . . (Barthelme 1981, pp. 183–84: Hereafter SS)

And, indeed, the narrator remains dependent on his J & B Scotch for its numbing effects throughout the story.

Yet, as the images of discontent accumulate, we sense that the story involves more than the unfulfilled promise of domesticity and affluence. This impression is confirmed by mention of a study by Lefebvre in the closing paragraph:

Wanda [the estranged wife of the narrator] is happier now, I think. She has taken herself off to Nanterre, where she is studying Marxist sociology with Lefebvre (not impertinently, the author of the *Critique de la Vie Quotidienne*) . . . (SS p. 190)

The suggestion that the story we have just read has been coauthored by Henri Lefebvre (albeit *qua* presiding intellectual spirit) enlarges its frame of reference. As mentioned above, in his studies of everyday life, Lefebvre has identified a new type of bourgeois subject. This subject, a product of the "bureaucratic society of controlled consumption," lacks the self-assurance, purpose, and will-power characteristic of the bourgeoisie at an earlier stage of capitalism. The bourgeois subject of late capitalism has become, under the pressures of enhanced privatized consumption, passive and atomized (see Lefebvre 1971, pp. 56, 115). Lefebvre sees consumption as a process of social integration, but here we should add it is a process which includes the integration of dissident or critical discourses:

> Has not this society, glutted with aestheticism, already integrated former romanticisms, surrealism, existentialism and even Marxism to a point? It has indeed, through trade, in the form of commodities! That which yesterday was reviled today becomes cultural consumer-goods; consumption thus engulfs what was intended to *give meaning and direction*. (Lefebvre 1971, p. 95, Lefebvre's emphasis)

Rereading Barthelme's story in the light of Lefebvre's observations, one notices an irony: in spite of its title, the story does *not* perform a critique of "la vie quotidienne." "Critique," *in Lefebvre's sense* of "a philosophical inventory and analysis of everyday life that will expose its ambiguities" (Lefebvre 1971, p. 13), requires a "critical distancing" from the quotidian (p. 27). However, the mundane focus of the narrative suggests a consciousness sunk in the quotidian; no transcendent horizon comes into view. The narrator—frustrated, isolated, profoundly discontented—drinks heavily, abuses his wife, hits his child; his wife throws the dinner on the floor, leaves him, returns, and tries to shoot him. Nevertheless, the possibility of some critique, some demystifying analysis of everyday bourgeois life, is not quite ruled out; at the end we find that the wife has progressed from being a devoted reader of *Elle* (organ of bourgeois Lifestyle) to a student of the author of *Critique de la Vie Quotidienne*.

Placed strategically at the beginning of the collection, "Critique de la Vie Quotidienne" announces the interrelated themes of the stories which follow: the impoverished order of quotidian experience; apathy; the atomistic, self-obsessed subject (see especially "Daumier"); the absence of a totalistic perspective and critical discourse. Consider, for example, the neglected story "The Rise of Capitalism" (originally published in 1970). It begins with the narrator confessing, "I thought I had understood capitalism, but what I had done was assume an attitude——melancholy sadness——toward it. This attitude is not correct" (SS p. 204). Yet in subsequent paragraphs it seems as if the narrator, Rupert, *does* have an adequate understanding of capitalism. For example, he observes,

> Each man is valued at what he will bring in the marketplace. Meaning has been drained from work and assigned instead to remuneration. Unemployment obliterates the world of the unemployed individual. Cultural underdevelop-

ment of the worker, as a technique of domination, is found everywhere under late capitalism. (SS p. 207)

But this account of capitalism (like earlier accounts of it), delivered as a string of aphorisms, has a routine air about it, like facts dutifully recited. We are left with the impression that understanding capitalism at this level will not overcome Rupert's "incorrect" attitude toward it, that is, his "melancholy sadness." Precisely what, then, confines him to this attitude to capitalism? In the third paragraph we read:

I scan the list of the fifteen Most Loved Stocks:
    Occident Pet 983, 100 20 5/8 + 3 3/4
    Natomas   912, 300 58 3/8 + 18½
What chagrin! Why wasn't I into Natomas, as into a fine garment, that will win you social credit when you wear it to the ball? I am not rich again this morning! I put my head between Marta's breasts, to hide my shame. (SS pp. 205–6)

Rupert has a thoroughly bourgeois mentality: he covets "social credit" and successful investments; he is ashamed of not being rich. Later, Marta tells him, "'the embourgeoisment of all classes of men has reached a disgusting nadir in your case'" (SS p. 208). A captive to bourgeois hegemony, Rupert has been integrated into the capitalist social order to the extent that, as noted above, the language in which he indicts the system lacks conviction and to the extent that the possibility of taking up a position toward capitalism "less equivocal" than that of "melancholy sadness" is precluded. Barthelme seems to be saying that even a discourse as uncompromisingly and sharply critical as Marxism has been neutralized, incorporated into the bourgeois social order. Its appeal to revolution cannot rouse Rupert to action.

    "Sadness" (symbolized by the weeping which pervades several stories) seems to be Barthelme's impressionistic term for feelings of impotence, for the feeling that all one can do at present is acquiesce in oppressive circumstances, for a general sense of paralysis in the face of overpowering forces. He unearths the obsolete word "abulia" which refers to a loss of will power, a pathological inability to act: "Smoke, rain, abulia. What can the concerned citizen do to fight the rise of capitalism, in his own community?" (SS p. 208). The narrator is certain of only one answer with which, thoroughly demoralized, he concludes the narrative: "Fear is the great mover, in the end" (SS p. 208). Appropriately, in view of these remarks, "The Rise of Capitalism" is a remarkably static piece of fiction. Written in nine short disjunctive paragraphs, there is no accumulation of action, no plot to galvanize the story. The only active entity is all-powerful Capitalism itself: "Capitalism arose and took off its pajamas. Another day, another dollar" (SS p. 207). The contrast is a stark one: a buoyant, dynamic capitalism and the human subject in the grip of inertia.

The story is titled not "Late Capitalism" or "New Capitalism" but "The *Rise* of Capitalism." In pursuing the implications of the choice of title, we arrive at a perspective counter to that of Rupert's. The fourth paragraph begins:

> Honoré de Balzac went to the movies. He was watching his favorite flick, *The Rise of Capitalism,* with Simone Simon and Raymond Radiguet. When he had finished viewing the film, he went out and bought a printing plant, for fifty thousand francs. "Henceforth," he said, "I will publish myself, in handsome expensive de-luxe editions, cheap editions. . . ." (SS p. 206)

It was Balzac, of course, who in the celebrated and massive *La Comédie Humaine* chronicled the rise of French capitalism. This was Engels's tribute to Balzac's magnum opus:

> Balzac, whom I consider a far greater master of realism than all the Zolas *passés, présents et à venir,* in *La Comédie Humaine* gives us a most wonderfully realistic history of French "Society," describing, chronicle-fashion, almost year by year from 1816 to 1848 the progressive inroads of the rising bourgeoisie upon the society of nobles, that reconstituted itself after 1815 [. . . A] complete history of French Society from which, even in economic details [. . .] I have learned more than from all the professed historians, economists and statisticians of the period together. (Engels [1888] 1977, pp. 270–71)

Barthelme's allusion to *La Comédie Humaine* is, in one sense, comical when we think of Balzac's multivolume project alongside Barthelme's treatment of capitalism in nine paragraphs. But the ironic juxtaposition has a more important implication. The scale and sweep of Balzac's study is testimony to the author's supremely confident focus on his subject. On the other hand, Barthelme's nine disjunctive paragraphs suggest a difficulty in achieving any kind of coherent perspective on capitalism in its advanced phase. The narrator is repeatedly frustrated in his efforts to obtain a hard critical focus on capitalism in his period:

> Always mindful that the critic must "*studiare da un punto di vista formalistico e semiologico il rapporto fra lingua di un testo e codificazione di un*—" But here a big thumb smudges the text—the thumb of capitalism, which we are all under. Darkness falls. (SS p. 204)

Indeed, the story abounds with references to obscurity: "mystification," "unfocusedness," "smoke," and so on. The issue is clear: Barthelme sees the late-capitalist subject as so thoroughly incorporated into the socioeconomic system ("embourgeoisment") that no critical perception is possible as instanced by the reduction of Marxist discourse to a parrotlike invocation of maxims. Moreover, we may recall Lefebvre's observation that the new bourgeois type to emerge in the society of privatized consumption—a society of "atomized" individuals amidst a "floating stock of meaningless signifiers" (Lefebvre 1971, p. 119)—is less able to totalize his/her experiences, less able to achieve a transcendent perspective on reality. Balzac could write from a critical vantage point *outside* of bourgeois society; he wrote from the marginal position of a "Legitimist," clinging to the ideal of the Ancien Régime. But Rupert has no critical vantage point; he is integrated into bourgeois society; his focus bound to the mundane, the quotidian. There is no ideal to which he can cling and, at the end, that includes religion: "'The Word of God,'" as expressed by the saints, is dismissed: "Alas! It is the same old message" (SS p. 208)—the otherworldliness of religion leaves capitalism undisturbed.

Dreck Transmuted

Barthelme's disquiet over the devaluation of language is not evident at the lexical level of his work. Quite the opposite, in fact. His language ecstatically feeds off the "noise" and dreck that bombard the sensorium of the late-capitalist subject. It is frequently modulated toward a high pitch of excitement. His prose is galvanized by an irreverent impulse that celebrates an aesthetics of trash: "'It's that we want to be on the leading edge of this trash phenomenon'" (SW p. 97); "'We like books that have a lot of *dreck* in them. . . .'" (SW p. 106). Indeed, the temper of Barthelme's language seems anything but oppositional—a paradoxical observation given that my purpose here is to draw attention to the critical thrust of his writing. Accordingly, it has to be shown how his *use* of dreck and "noise" (in this context, unintelligible or redundant language) performs a critical function.

What pressures compel Barthelme to communicate with debased forms of language? First, as we approach the point, not inconceivable to Barthelme, when dreck monopolizes all channels of communication, we must find ways to capitalize on its aesthetic qualities:

"I hazard that we may very well soon reach a point where [the per-capita production of trash] is 100 percent. Now at such a point, you will agree, the question turns from a question of disposing of this 'trash' to a question of appreciating its qualities, because, after all, it's 100 percent, right? And there can no longer be any question of 'disposing' of it, because it's all there is and we will simply have to learn how to 'dig' it [. . .] And that's why we pay particular attention [. . .] to those aspects of language that may be seen as a model of the trash phenomenon." (SW pp. 97–98)

In other words, seize the initiative and speak dreck. Dreck is emerging as the culturally dominant language. The writer in the postmodern age who aspires to an unadulterated, noise-free language risks being left behind in the slow lane while the faster traffic streaks by.

Second, language increasingly seems to obey the same laws as capital. In late-capitalist society, language, like capital, has a fast turnover time. The mass-communications industries, under pressure of competition, are geared to the express circulation of their commodities. In theory, this need not accelerate the decline of language into catchphrases and clichés (we could be blitzed with enhanced messages just as easily as with degraded ones). But, in practice, because the criterion governing the production of so much language is instant consumability, there is a tendency to an attenuation of its potential for any but the most nugatory meaning. Moreover, the communications revolution has exponentially increased the number of channels through which language, purged of its critical and analytical content, is relayed. Messages are endlessly replicated but, at least in the major communications networks, they are mostly low-grade "information," information in excess of meaning. Inflation of information, deflation of meaning: language has never been at such a discount.

Third, our impression of the physical character of language has changed. In his discussion of the circulation of commodities, Marx observed how the product, on entering the exchange process, becomes abstract and assumes a kind of phantom weightlessness. I would suggest that language, under late capitalism, embodies this property of commodification. Accelerated circulation and infinite reproduction seem to have robbed language of its material density. Words seem less heavy with meaning, more volatile.

These are some of the reasons why, in late-capitalist society, the idea of a privileged discourse, one pregnant with meaning, one which aspires to a universal perspective, has, for some, lost credibility. Thus Barthelme, with qualifications to be elaborated later, tends to use the forms of language through which contemporary experience is generally articulated: dreck and noise (the former in its extreme shading into the latter); the forms which "speak" the logic of late capitalism. His texts are enmeshed in the debased sign-systems that define and entrap consciousness. The very texture of his prose reflects the postmodern experience of language as a flux of signals, as an ephemeral phenomenon: it is a prose of coruscating surfaces and instantaneous effects. Consider this extract from "The Falling Dog" in which a sculptor finds inspiration in the image of a dog jumping from a high window:

But now I had the Falling Dog, what happiness.
(flights? sheets?)
of falling dogs, flat falling dogs like sails
Day-Glo dogs falling

am I being sufficiently skeptical?
try it out

die like a
dog-eat-dog
proud as a dog in shoes
dogfight
doggerel
dogmatic

am I being over-impressed by the
circumstances
suddenness
pain
but it's a gift. thank you

love me love my

styrofoam?

(CL pp. 47–48)

Barthelme is clearly enjoying himself. He is immersed in dreck without betraying a hint of displeasure. Yet the effervescent language amounts to more than pure verbal play. The falling-dog images are conceived by the story's artist with a sense of liberation. He has broken free of another kind of image, one that had formerly possessed his imagination:

My old image, the Yawning Man, was played out. I had done upward of two thousand Yawning Men in every known material, and I was tired of it. Images fray, tatter, empty themselves. (CL p. 47)

The montage of falling-dog images is counterposed to the static image of the Yawning Man. The contrasting images (it is, of course, an exaggerated contrast; both images are caricatures of artistic tendencies) belong to distinct discourses. The Yawning Man sculpture, ". . . faceless (except for a gap where the mouth was, the yawn itself)" (CL p. 47), seems to belong to a discourse of alienation; an image of ennui and anonymity. The sight of the falling dog excites images for sculptures that belong to a discourse of post-alienation: a euphoric, celebratory mode of discourse; an expression of the drifting "intensities" (Lyotard) of the decentered subject:

>   Cloth falling dogs, the
> gingham dog and the etc., etc. Pieces
> of cloth dogs falling. Or quarter-inch
> plywood in layers, the layers separated
> by an inch or two of airspace. Like old
> triple-wing aircraft
> dog-ear (pages falling with corners bent back)
> Tray: cafeteria trays of some obnoxious
>   brown plastic
> But enough puns
>
> Group of tiny hummingbird-sized falling dogs
> Massed in upper corners of a room with high
>   ceilings,
> 14–17 foot
> in rows, in ranks, on their backs. (CL pp. 46–47)

Against the lifeless image of the Yawning Man, this phantasmagoria of falling-dog images appears as an inspired advance. Yet the latter are fabricated from nothing but fragments of dreck, recycled scraps of language. I shall expand on this point later at a more general level. Here I want to note only that "The Falling Dog" typifies a common tendency in Barthelme's fiction: an animated discourse shatters the petrified form of consciousness embodied in a reified discourse. Let's see this tendency at work in another story.

"Eugénie Grandet" (originally published in 1968) is introduced by the following epigraph:

> Balzac's novel *Eugénie Grandet* was published in 1833. Grandet, a rich miser, has an only child, Eugénie. She falls in love with her young cousin, Charles. When she learns he is financially ruined, she lends him her savings. Charles goes to the West Indies, secretly engaged to marry Eugénie on his return. Years go by. Grandet dies and Eugénie becomes an heiress. But Charles, ignorant of her wealth, writes to ask her for his freedom: he wants to marry a rich girl. Eugénie releases him, pays his father's debts, and marries without love an old friend of the family, Judge de Bonfons.
> *The Thesaurus of Book Digests* (SS p. 236)

This is a triumph of banalization; Balzac's masterpiece made to read like a *Woman's Weekly* romance. It is this thinned out version of the novel, not the original, which serves as the *starting point* for Barthelme's own version of *Eugénie Grandet*. For Barthelme recognizes that there is no question of going back to Balzac, of attempting to restore the artistic integrity of *Eugénie Grandet* on Balzac's terms. He knows that in late-capitalist society our appreciation of writers is mediated through commercial enterprises like the *Thesaurus* (Masters of the Novel: Their

Lives, Works and Inspiration); that, for many, the *Thesaurus*'s account of Balzac's novel has more reality than the original.[4] The point is that Balzac's language cannot be recovered for it cannot address the post-modern sensibility that is attuned to the transitory signal and shifting surface; that consumes language in the emaciated forms of slogans and clichés. Accordingly, Barthelme's strategy is not to dispel dreck but, in a sense, to *amplify* it. Resistance to the reified language of commodification takes the form not of anti-dreck but hyper-dreck. Indeed, Barthelme engages enthusiastically in the production of dreck; the activity is experienced as (to invoke the title of the volume in which "Eugénie Grandet" is collected) a "guilty pleasure." Yet his dreck is not an exact imitation of the dreck of the *Thesaurus*. Dreck forms the building blocks of Barthelme's language, but the blocks are imaginatively assembled in such a way as to animate the language, not reify it.

Thus Balzac's text, having already been vulgarized by the *Thesaurus*, undergoes further distortions. Barthelme's "Eugénie Grandet" is a gaudy collage of tenuously related fragments, images and cheap jokes:

A great many people are interested in the question: Who will obtain Eugénie Grandet's hand?

Eugénie Grandet's hand:

(SS p. 237)

Part of a letter:

. . . And now he's ruined a
friends will desert him, and

humiliation. Oh, I wish I ha
straight to heaven, where his
but this is madness . . . I re
that of Charles.

(SS p. 238)

Photograph of Charles in the Indies:

(SS p. 243)

Clearly the text is energized by its self-consciously ironic relation to
Balzac's text. Balzac had seen himself as "secretary to Society" (Heath
1972, p. 15), one who would faithfully transcribe what he observed
around him. Barthelme's "Eugénie Grandet" ostentatiously flouts fi-
delity to reality of any kind (past or present), not to mention to Balzac's
original text. After all, we no longer share Balzac's confidence in the
mimetic powers of language; the postmodern experience of language
as dissonance, as a blitz of volatile signals, as low-grade information, as
dreck, disqualifies it as an instrument for transcribing reality. In particular, language which pretends to a totalizing, juridical perspective
suddenly seems idealistic, metaphysical. Yet it was language of this
privileged order that enabled Balzac to organize his writing into an
(apparently) organic narrative. For the postmodern author, however,
no such privileged language exists which can dictate the form a narrative should take. In "Eugénie Grandet," Barthelme exploits this absence for comic effect. The narrative progresses in flagrant disregard
of relevance or a sense of proportion. Thus in one of the twenty-five
disjointed sections which constitute the text, Charles's operations in the
Indies are simply recounted in a list of five words:

Charles in the Indies. He sold:

Chinese
Negroes
swallows' nests
children
artists
(SS p. 242)

while another section consists of nothing but the word "butter," written
87 times (SS p. 241).

In yet another section, the reader is bombarded with redundant
information about the coinage current in Grandet's time:

Charles. Take the money and use it for worthy purposes. Please. See, here is a
ducat, minted in 1756 and still bright as day. And here are some doubloons,
worth two escudos each. And here are some shiny quadroons, of inestimable
value. And here in this bag are thalers and bobs, and silver quids and copper
bawbees. Altogether, nearly six thousand francs. (SS p. 241)

These sections humorously capitalize on the absence of a controlling
(realist) perspective which could provide criteria that are not merely
arbitrary for distinguishing relevant from irrelevant material and for
maintaining a sense of balance. The nearest thing to such a perspective
is derived from the *Thesaurus* digest of Balzac's novel. As I indicated
earlier, it is this text, not the original, from which Barthelme proceeds.
"Eugénie Grandet" is the digest regurgitated in brilliant colors. Barthelme's subversive and comic use of language—principally, interplay
between fragments of dreck—develops an animated discourse from
one that embodies the reifying logic of commodification.

It would be a vain exercise to seek a "meaning" in the scenes, events,
or characters of "Eugénie Grandet," that is, to understand the text as if
it were a story illustrating a moral or teaching us something about life.
Similarly, the rash of capricious images which enliven the narrative of
"The Falling Dog" do not yield an insight or imply a moral judgment of
any sort. The sculptor reflects, "I had to wonder about what it meant,
the Falling Dog, but I didn't have to wonder about it now, I could
wonder later" (CL p. 48). But this reflection concludes the story; there
is no "later." Plainly, the search for "meaning"—the reader's expectation of philosophical or moral illumination—is rendered futile in these
texts as, indeed, it is in most of Barthelme's work.

The question of the absence of "meaning" (for the moment, quotes
will denote meaning in the above sense) has two sides to it. First, as
discussed earlier, Barthelme's work suggests that we cannot make substantial statements about, or "read," reality within the modes in which

language prevails in late-capitalist society, that is, as dreck or noise. Thus the absence of "meaning" or "depth" in his fiction is to be understood as a critical exposure of, in the first instance, a *social* problem, and then a philosophical one. The problem, as we have seen, arises from the material existence of language: the volatile condition of language in an age of floating signifiers that freely couple with signifieds; the poor condition of language in a society whose channels of communication are saturated with degraded messages. "The Falling Dog" and "Eugénie Grandet" illustrate that when a text is composed of dreck it is pointless delving for "meaning." Consider this well-known passage from *Snow White*:

> We like books that have a lot of *dreck* in them, matter which presents itself as not wholly relevant (or indeed, at all relevant) but which, carefully attended to, can supply a kind of "sense" of what is going on. This "sense" is not to be obtained by reading between the lines (for there is nothing there, in those white spaces) but by reading the lines themselves. (SW p. 106)

Here the reader is discouraged from probing for depths in books that have a lot of dreck in them.

Second, the absence of "meaning" in Barthelme's fiction has strategic purposes. He seeks an autonomous discourse, one whose narratives resist appropriation (and hence recuperation) in terms of society's prevailing meaning-systems and, more importantly, one which aspires to transcend those meaning-systems. Yet, insofar as meaning, in late-capitalist society, is largely mediated through debased and reified forms of language, this strategy may seem self-defeating, for Barthelme's texts are frequently assembled from scraps of dreck and snatches of noise. However, Barthelme does not use dreck or noise pure and simple. It was observed that in "The Falling Dog" and "Eugénie Grandet" he *manipulates* language in fragments or "blocks." On this point it is illuminating to quote remarks Barthelme has made in an interview, remarks which, while pertaining to two early stories, clearly seem applicable to much of his fiction:

> I might point out that both stories . . . ["Florence Green is 81" and "The Viennese Opera Ball"] are, from the aesthetic point of view, about noise [. . .], noise in the sense of that which is not signal [. . .] What I tried to do in both of those fictions in different ways was to make music out of noise.
>
> Now we must talk about what kind of noise this noise is. It has to do with sensory assault; it has to do with bombardment [. . .] I must have felt, when I wrote those stories [. . .] a high noise level. And that's a structural concept because that's the way the pieces were put together——in a mosaic fashion, by adding one little piece of noise to another little piece of noise [. . .] They were rather carefully built up of interesting bits [. . .] But as in collage, you select [. . .] The aesthetic idea being what it would be like if we had all of this noise

pulled together and then turned up very high——increase the volume. (Ziegler and Bigsby 1982, pp. 43–44)

Barthelme would like "to make music out of noise," that is, to make language "mean" in the indefinable way that music "means."[5] His method is to take the raw material most readily at his disposal, that is, noise (by which term I understand both the garbled and debased language by which we are daily "assaulted" or "bombarded") and reassemble its fragments ("bits") in the form of a "mosaic" or "collage." The aim is to *transcend* the degraded condition of language by investing it with fresh signifying power; to seek emancipation from the prevailing (reified) forms of language by fragmenting them into novel configurations.

Up to a point, this strategy invites comparison with the function of William Burroughs' "cut-ups." " 'Shift linguals——cut word lines' " is the refrain of the partisans in Burroughs' trilogy (Burroughs 1968a, p. 104; 1968b, p. 60). Hence, "operation rewrite": language is "silenced" using the cut-up method that disrupts the syntactical and semantic rules which normally govern the process of signification. Barthelme's fragments perform the same function. (In "Bone Bubbles," "Alice," and parts of *Snow White*, Barthelme uses the cut-up method himself.)[6] Fragments and cut-ups alike are assembled into collages in which signifiers enter into new "ungrammatical" relationships, yielding meanings which cannot be accommodated within the prevailing meaning-systems. Both writers seek to transcend the *verbal* limits of language. Burroughs wants to "rub out the word forever" (Burroughs 1968b, p. 10) and hopes that the "juxtaposition statements" generated by the cut-up method will trigger subliminal or "dream" images (Plimpton 1977, p. 149). Barthelme wants "to reach a realm of knowing that cannot be put precisely into words, but must be gotten as music is gotten" (see note 5, Chap. 3). That is to say, he aspires to a form of writing modeled on music insofar as its meaning would elude verbalization. It must be left to the reader to decide whether cut-ups or fragments achieve the transcendent ends intended for them; experimental forms like these are not bound to succeed.

To be sure, there is an important difference between Burroughs and Barthelme that centers on the former's overt distrust of language as primarily an instrument of direct domination and clandestine power. Accordingly, Burroughs' writing is distinguished by its adversarial temper; it is executed in a spirit of resistance.[7] However, in some ways, "resistance" seems too militant a term to apply to Barthelme's writing, a writing characterized by its playfulness and euphoria. His art is, nevertheless, one of resistance, but it is in a sportive rather than combative spirit that he struggles against the established forms of language.

"Fragments are the only forms I trust," declares the narrator in "See the Moon?" (UPUA pp. 160, 172), lamenting the fact that the disparate, contingent episodes of his life have refused to "cohere" into a meaning. Critics have fastened onto this line, using it to interpret Barthelme's fragmentary style of writing exclusively in epistemological terms. This style has been generally understood as a response to the impression that there is no structure or "coherent" pattern to "reality." On the other hand, arguing from the standpoint that Barthelme's fiction belongs to a dissident postmodernism, I have drawn attention to the *critical function* of his fragmentary discourse. This is not to deny that this discourse may have epistemological significance but, if the argument so far is valid, priority must be given to the critical intent behind Barthelme's disarticulation of language.

Several points have been raised in the foregoing pages and it will be helpful to draw on a third text in order to bring them together. An eminently sign-reflective piece like "Paraguay" can throw light on the usual methods by which Barthelme checks the production of meaning in the *prevailing* forms of dreck and noise. "Paraguay" is a satirical vision of a utopia where most activities are programmed and rationalized. (It is, in part, a reflection on the present cultural ascendancy of technological rationality, a rationality consummated, under late capitalism, in the cybernetic sciences.) Consider this account of the production of art in Paraguay:

Rationalization

The problems of art. New artists have been obtained. These do not object to, and indeed argue enthusiastically for, the rationalization process. Production is up. Quality-control devices have been installed at those points where the interests of artists and audience intersect [. . .] The rationalized art is dispatched from central art dumps to regional art dumps, and from there into the lifestreams of cities. Each citizen is given as much art as his system can tolerate [. . .] Rationalization produces simpler circuits and, therefore, a saving in hardware. Each artist's product is translated into a statement in symbolic logic. The statement is then "minimized" by various clever **methods**. The simpler statement is translated back into the design of a simpler circuit [. . .] Flip-flop switches control its further development. (CL pp. 33–34)

Here we have the ultimate culture industry where people are force-fed on a diet of mass-produced art. Moreover, the production of this art is part of a general condition in Barthelme's Paraguay, that is, "the proliferation of surfaces and stimuli" (CL p. 36). Paraguayans are continually exposed to bombardment by the degraded messages, the thin meanings, of mass-produced dreck. Resistance to this condition depends on the generation of "silence," especially in the form of "white noise":

In the larger stores silence (damping materials) is sold in paper sacks like cement. Similarly, the softening of language usually lamented as a falling off from former practice is in fact a clear response to the proliferation of surfaces and stimuli. Imprecise sentences lessen the strain of close tolerances. Silence is also available in the form of white noise. The extension of white noise to the home by means of leased wire from a central generating point has been useful, Herko says. (CL p. 36)

This passage has a sign-reflective function: it comments on the characteristic features of the text itself: "softened language," "imprecise sentences," and "white noise." In information theory, white noise occurs when an incoherent mix of frequencies renders signals unintelligible. By analogy, we may say that Barthelme produces white noise by mixing verbal frequencies or fusing fragments of incommensurable discourses, thereby refusing words their conventional significance. For example:

A skelp of questions and answers is fused at high temperature (1400°) and then passed through a series of protracted caresses. (CL p. 33)

We rushed down to the ends of the waves, apertures through which threatening lines might be seen. Arbiters registered serial numbers of the (complex of threats) with ticks on a great, brown board. (CL p. 37)

Creation of new categories of anxiety which must be bandaged or "patched." The expression "put a patch on it." There are "hot" and "cold" patches and specialists in the application of each. (CL p. 37)

These passages violate the rules which govern the combination of words ("the softening of language"). In each of the above cases we note Barthelme's deliberate use of a category-mistake: incorporating an abstract entity into a material process. Whatever these passages suggest to the reader, they defy significance in the terms of our established meaning-systems.

"Paraguay," like so many of Barthelme's stories, is a collage of disjointed, individually titled paragraphs. This fragmentary method of composition impedes accumulation of meaning (i.e., "depth"). Each paragraph reads more like an addition to, rather than a development of, the one that precedes it. " 'We try to keep everything open, go forward avoiding the final explanation,' " (CL p. 37) says Herko's wife, in a statement which summarizes Barthelme's narrative strategy. And when, in the penultimate paragraph, the narrator walks in a field of red snow, we read:

The snow re-arranged itself into a smooth red surface without footprints. It had a red glow, as if lighted from beneath. It seemed to proclaim itself a mystery, but one there was no point in solving—an ongoing low-grade mystery. (CL p. 39)

The low-grade mystery which there is no point in solving is an apt description of "Paraguay" and indeed several other stories ("Views of My Father Weeping" and "Robert Kennedy Saved from Drowning" among others). The reader's habit of seeking meaning or "final explanations" is explicitly repudiated in statements that read like authorial interventions. (Recall similar interventions in "The Balloon," "The Falling Dog," and *Snow White*.) In general, Barthelme responds to the proliferation of debased forms of discourse by impeding their production of meaning; he appropriates them in ways that "silence" or resist their conventional sense.

Barthelme's Linguistic Uprising

The last work of fiction I want to discuss, one which offers a dramatic illustration of the preceding points, is "The Indian Uprising," one of Barthelme's best-known stories. In his influential essay, "Cross the Border—Close that Gap: Postmodernism," Leslie Fiedler discusses, among other subgenres adopted by postmodernist writers, the western. He observes that, "The new novelists have taken a clear stand with the Red Man. [. . .] The violence celebrated in the anti-White Western is guerrilla violence: the sneak attack on 'civilization' as practised first by Geronimo and Cochise and other Indian warrior chiefs." (Fiedler [1968] 1975, p. 353). Fiedler does not include "The Indian Uprising" in his discussion, but his remarks may, nevertheless, serve as an introduction to it.

The story opens with the following paragraph:

We defended the city as best we could. The arrows of the Comanches came in clouds. The war clubs of the Comanches clattered on the soft, yellow pavements. There were earthworks along the Boulevard Mark Clark and the hedges had been laced with sparkling wire. People were trying to understand. I spoke to Sylvia. "Do you think this is a good life?" The table held apples, books, long-playing records. She looked up. "No." (UPUA p. 10)

The inclusion, in this paragraph, of the narrator's exchange with Sylvia suggests that it is not simply the city that is under attack but the "good life," the bourgeois "civilization" that extols consumerism as the chief good. (Significantly, the barricades, which have been erected against the incursions of the "Red men," are composed of commodities connotative of the "good life": silk, wine in demijohns, ceramic crockery, cognac, Fad #6 sherry, and so on.)

Barthelme's Comanches are not drawn from history but from the western; they are television Indians with their clouds of arrows and war clubs. In the thin guise of a dreckish, updated western, "The Indian Uprising" is really a linguistic uprising. In spite of all the confusion and uncertainty surrounding the events of the story (an inevitability given that the insurrection described is essentially an insurrection against accepted forms of language) two opposing discourses can be clearly identified. One of these is, albeit nominally, represented by Korzybski, of whom more in a moment. The other is represented by the sinister, authoritarian figure of a Miss R., "a teacher, unorthodox they say, excellent they said, successful with difficult cases, steel shutters on the windows made the house safe" (UPUA p. 12). In appropriately prim, starchy language, Miss R. declares her allegiance to one mode of discourse:

"The only form of discourse of which I approve," Miss R. said in her dry, tense voice, "is the litany. I believe our masters and teachers as well as plain citizens should confine themselves to what can safely be said. Thus when I hear the words *pewter, snake, tea, Fad # 6 sherry, serviette, fenestration, crown, blue* coming from the mouth of some public official or some raw youth, I am not disappointed. Vertical organization is also possible," Miss R. said, "as in
> pewter
> snake
> tea
> Fad #6 sherry
> serviette
> fenestration
> crown
> blue . . ."
". . . Some people," Miss R. said, "run to conceits or wisdom but I hold to the hard, brown, nutlike word." (UPUA p. 16)

Against the ossified forms of the list and litany, Barthelme counterposes another mode of discourse in, at least initially, the name of Korzybski. (Korzybski's ideas are far more in evidence in Burroughs' fiction.[8]) "I non-evaluated [Miss R.'s] remarks as Korzybski instructed" (UPUA p. 12). Crudely speaking, Korzybski, believing in "semantogenic" illness, argued that language must be freed from the socially and psychologically harmful effects of its "Aristotelian" logic. Accordingly, large portions of Barthelme's text take the form of clusters of inconsequent statements. For example:

I opened a letter but inside was a Comanche flint arrowhead played by Frank Wedekind in an elegant gold chain and congratulations. Your earring rattled against my spectacles when I leaned forward to touch the soft, ruined place where the hearing aid had been. "Pack it in! Pack it in!" I urged, but the men in charge of the Uprising refused to listen to reason or to understand that it was real and that our water supply had evaporated and that our credit was no longer what it had been, once. (UPUA p. 17)

Barthelme refuses to confine himself "to what can safely be said." In this text, "the hard, brown, nutlike word" is exploded into "strings of language [which, says the narrator] extend in every direction to bind the world into a rushing, ribald whole" (UPUA p. 18). Everything is fluid. There is a confluence of characters, occurrences, and surroundings. The battle is borne along on a flood of words. "'What is the situation?' I asked. 'The situation is liquid,' he said" (UPUA p. 14). Situations flow into each other:

Once I caught Kenneth's coat going down the stairs by itself but the coat was a trap and inside a Comanche who made a thrust with his short, ugly knife at my leg which buckled and tossed me over the balustrade through a window and into another situation. Not believing that your body brilliant as it was and your fat, liquid spirit distinguished and angry as it was were stable quantities to which one could return on wires more than once, twice, or another number of times I said: "See the table?" (UPUA pp. 14–15)

That Barthelme should figure his linguistic insurrection in the imagery of an *Indian* uprising is no mere caprice. In America's mythical imagination, the Indian stands for the antithesis of white "civilization"; he/she represents the values which obtain on the other side of the Frontier. Furthermore, that other side—the wilderness side—of the Frontier has a psychological dimension. It is the site of that which *cannot* safely be said; the site of language which threatens to fracture the ossified forms of discourse advocated by Miss R. The uprising may be read as a repressed language erupting into consciousness, a surprise attack on those areas of the psyche colonized by white, bourgeois meaning-systems. Hence, "The rolling *consensus* of the Comanche nation smashed our inner defenses on three sides" (UPUA p. 18, my emphasis); "Dusky warriors padded with their forest tread into the mouth of the mayor" (UPUA p. 18) (an infiltration of subversive speech?).

In the final paragraph, the narrator who, unlike the women in the story, has remained loyal to the white vigilantes, assisting in the brutal torture of Comanches, is captured by the enemy and brought before the "Clemency Committee" for interrogation. The closing lines read:

I removed my belt and shoelaces and looked (rain shattering from a great height the prospects of silence and clear, neat rows of houses in the subdivisions) into their savage black eyes, paint, feathers, beads. (UPUA p. 19)

This concluding image—the candid encounter with the Other against a background of "shattering" rain—seems to intimate impending liberation; the narrator on the verge of crossing the Frontier. Recall the words of the dwarf, Edward, in *Snow White*: "'But it is worth it to have a blown mind. To stop being a filthy bourgeois for a space, even a short space. To gain access to everything in a new way'" (SW p. 142). Barthelme also seeks to gain access to everything in a new way, to break out of established meaning-systems and enlarge the bounds of the signifiable. His works of fiction are an endeavor to transcend "for a space" debased and reified forms of language.

Chapter 4
Robert Coover

Policing the Bounds of Discourse

"Panel Game" is the first of Coover's "Seven Exemplary Fictions," the showcase of "apprentice" exercises in postmodernist writing at the heart of *Pricksongs and Descants* (Coover 1970, hereafter PD). In this story, the format of the TV quiz game—clues lead to tense anticipation of audience, followed by answers—serves as the analogue for the process of enigma, suspense, and disclosure which governs much conventional fiction. This process rests on the understanding that a chain of enigmatic signifiers will, ultimately, relay the reader to a conclusive signified or interpretation. Expressed in terms of the TV quiz, clues (signifiers) should be interpreted so as to yield an answer. However, Coover's "Unwilling Participant"—dragooned from the audience onto the panel—cannot arrive at an answer. His problem, on his own admission, is that he is ignorant of "the precepts and procedures" of the game (PD p. 82). He lacks a code which might enable him to extract significance from (what may be) clue-words. For example:

"Reminds me of the old story of the three-spined stickleback!" Clown cackles [. . .] So think. Stickleback. Freshwater fish: green seaman. Seaman: semen. Yes, but green: raw? spoiled? vigorous? Stickle: stubble. Or maybe scruple. Back: Bach: Bacchus: baccate: berry. Raw berry? Strawberry? Maybe. Sticky berry in the raw? In the raw: bare. Bare berry: beriberi. (PD p. 80)

Here the participant frenetically switches from code to code (e.g., homophony or synonymity as sources of signification) in an effort to generate meaning. Yet, the process of signifiers appears interminable; there is no natural or self-evident endpoint at which a definitive meaning emerges.

Coover's wordplay implicates the reader who, given his/her conventional reading habits, may well be an "unwilling participant" in an unfamiliar game of meaning: "And the Bad Sport, you ask, who is he?

fool! thou art!" (PD p. 80). Typically, the reader seeks the information that will tell him/her what the participant does not know—a futile exercise in view of how Coover positions the reader; he/she is just as ignorant of the rules of the game. The reader *expects* that the clue-words will eliminate the possibilities of meaning in the passage to the disclosure of a final meaning. Instead, those possibilities proliferate as Coover conspicuously manipulates the rules of language. It is a situation which compels the reader to reflect on the demands of conventional fiction. " '*Why are you here*,' the Moderator explodes, losing all patience, 'if not to endeavor to disentangle this entanglement?' " (PD p. 85)—it's a question *we* have to answer. But Coover's purpose is not simply to induce a questioning of the *literary* process of signification. Rather, he subverts literary-narrative conventions within the framework of a story so as to induce a questioning of signification as a sociopolitical process. To see this, we must, first, probe the Moderator-Audience metaphor.

A contriver of riddles and flashy lexiphant (e.g., " 'THE SAGA OF SAGACITY IS THE PURSE OF PERSPICACITY' "), the "Merry Moderator" is, in one respect, Coover's alter ego, a surrogate artist. He delights in playing word-games with Participant and Audience, just as Coover delights in playing word-games with his reader. Both are skillful manipulators of meaning. The Audience, "same as ever, docile, responsive, good-natured, terrifying" (PD pp. 79–80), whose members laugh, howl, and jeer *una voce*, is a caricature of a cohesive, conformist public. A defining feature of this audience is its susceptibility to manipulation. Its behavior is steered either by cue-words—"the Audience, cued to Thunderous Response, responds thunderingly" (PD p. 80)—or, more often, by the Moderator's mock-erudite eloquence. The latter, a bogus Shakespearean diction, never fails to elicit "wild applause" or "uncontrollable uproar." The Moderator, who can whip up his audience to a frenzy, is like a revivalist preacher "riding on waves of grand hosannas" (PD p. 84). Audience involvement seems like a displaced form of religious expression; applause, laughter, chanting, and stamping appear highly ritualized. (And one may think of the panelists as the icons of the TV age: Lovely Lady, Aged Clown, and Mr. America.)

It is from such an audience that "Unwilling Participant" is "dragged protesting" to serve on the panel and advised: "resign yourself to pass the test in peace" (PD p. 80). The test is to comprehend "*the lex of the game*" (PD p. 84), a discourse or language-game which apparently unites Audience, Moderator, and panelists into a tightly bound community. Language, then, is the touchstone which will establish whether "Unwilling Participant" is inside or outside this community. And he is sternly warned by the Moderator: " 'Muteness is mutinous' " (PD p. 84).

The situation is emblematic of a society where silence is no longer an option, where participation in the ruling order of meaning is enforced. In the event, the Unwilling Participant, with no purchase on the rules of the language-game, fails the test and, as a penalty, is to be hanged by his co-panelists. As the noose is fitted, he remarks naively: "'I thought it was all for fun'" (PD p. 87), never having grasped that the quiz was an in*qui*sition, a severe test, in this instance, of cultural affiliation. Hence, in the final analysis, the problem of meaning turns on the power, invested in the Moderator, to uphold the rules of cultural intercourse. Coover's Moderator, presiding over *"the lex of the game,"* polices the bounds of discourse against "unwilling participants."

"The Wayfarer" is the last of the "Seven Exemplary Fictions." A traffic cop narrates an encounter with a vagrant:

> I came upon him on the road. I pulled over, stepped out, walked directly over to him where he sat. On an old milestone. His long tangled beard was a yellowish gray, his eyes dull with the dust of the road. His clothes were all of a colour and smelled of mildew. He was not a sympathetic figure, but what could I do? [. . .] It was silent except for the traffic. (PD p. 120)

The old milestone, an obsolete sign in a space reorganized for the traffic age, metaphorically locates the wayfarer in another (archaic) cultural space. This cultural gulf between the two men is also suggested by repeated indications that the wayfarer fails to register the officer's presence: "he stared obliviously. Vacantly"; "His gaze floated unimpeded down the [rifle] barrel through my chest and out into indeterminate space" (PD pp. 120, 121). The officer interprets this and the wayfarer's silence as a refusal to acknowledge his authority, as a sign of *"contempt."* He comments: "The thought, unwonted, jolted me. I sat back in the dust. I felt peculiarly light, baseless. I studied my memo-book. It was blank! my God! *it* was blank!" (PD p. 121). Here he suffers a momentary loss of identity as the wayfarer, speechless, stares through him, and the blank page of the memo-book denies him the words in which he might find himself, the discourse that might call up his social role. He must cancel this vacuum of meaning which leaves him "peculiarly light, baseless." Hence he makes an entry in his book: "Urgently, I wrote something in it. There! Not so bad now. I began to recover" (PD p. 121). But the recovery is not complete; the wayfarer's silence persists as a source of anxiety, a disconfirmation of the officer's authority and, by implication, of the culture which assigns the latter his identity. Accordingly, with increasing violence, the officer tries to provoke an utterance from the wayfarer, but in vain. Only when he shoots him does the latter speak, but in a language altogether alien to the officer:

He spoke rapidly, desperately, with neither punctuation nor sentence structure. Just a ceaseless eruption of obtuse language. He spoke of constellations, bone structures, mythologies, and love. He spoke of belief and lymph nodes, of excavations, categories and prophecies. (PD p. 124)

Anther bullet silences the wayfarer for good, but that proves no consolation to the officer. After returning to his patrol car, he remarks: "My mind was not yet entirely free of the old man. At times, he would loom in my inner eye larger than the landscape" (PD p. 124). The encounter (but not the shooting) has proved profoundly unsettling. An older and despised universe of discourse—mythic, fantastic, occult—has collided with a contemporary, established one. The latter, as embodied in the language of the officer's narration, is pervaded by a functionalist logic. This is suggested both by the importance the officer attaches to concepts like "function," "duty," and "precision" (PD pp. 120, 121, 124) and by the formal, punctilious style of his account, punctuated and structured in contradistinction to the wayfarer's "ceaseless eruption of obtuse language."

Eventually, the officer regains his composure, and he concludes his account as follows:

I watched the traffic. Gradually, I became absorbed in it. Uniformly it flowed, quietly, possessed of its own unbroken grace and precision. There was a variety in detail, but the stream itself was one. One. The thought warmed me. It flowed away and away and the unpleasant images that had troubled my mind flowed away with it. At last, I sat up, started the motor, and entered the flow itself. I felt calm and happy. *A participant.* I enjoy my work. (PD p. 124. My emphasis)

Here, as the formerly exact language slackens and turns a little hazy, the suggestion is that it is not only the traffic that is flowing away but the traffic cop's mind. His absorption into the "flow" is conditional upon a state of unreflectiveness, a state he enters with relief after expunging an alien order of meaning that threatened the credibility or truth-claims of his own culture. (The "commendatory nods" with which those in the passing traffic endorse the execution of the vagrant reinforce the suggestion that the latter is perceived as a threat to the ruling culture.) Moreover, "traffic" proves a rich metaphor in this context. It suggests, in contrast to the footloose ramblings of the wayfarer, a road-system where movement is routed (i.e., determined); it suggests the commerce of a business culture and the mainstream of social life; above all, it suggests hyperconformity and maximum integration: "Uniformly it flowed"; "the stream itself was one. One." Indeed, here, as in "Panel Game," Coover projects an image of an ultra-cohesive social order.

This order sanctions the death of "unwilling" or nonparticipants; these defined by their silence, by their exteriority to the established system of discourse.

"Morris in Chains," another story from *Pricksongs and Descants*, admits of a reading very much like that of the above "exemplary fictions." Morris is a pipe-playing, priapic faun who illicitly herds sheep in a nature reserve. His "simple songs" appeal to some residue of Arcadian myth deep in the psyche: "Morris trod old paths, forced a suffering of the inveterate green visions, a merciless hacking through the damp growths of our historic hebephrenia" (PD pp. 46–47). These "green visions" are considered a threat to a cybernetized, hyper-urbanized culture. It is feared that Morris's piping may awaken some unsocialized part of the self. As the narrator remarks: "We can nearly admit notes of savagery in our parks, have not yet stifled the wild optimistic call" (PD p. 49). One Dr. Peloris is assigned to run to ground this incarnation of Pan before his corrupting influence spreads. Morris's capture is confidently anticipated: "it was merest Morris versus the infallibility of our computers" (PD p. 48). Eventually Morris is tracked down and subjected, like a zoological specimen, to a humiliating battery of tests. The examination culminates in the coercive extraction of a semen sample that leaves Morris "limp in the arms of two men," signifying, perhaps, that a technocratic-positivist order of knowledge has robbed myth of its potency.

Coover, it must be said, is not basing his critique of a technocratic culture on a retrospective idealization of rustic life. Indeed, there are moments when he debunks Arcadian themes. In one passage, he has Morris recall a romp with a goosegirl with an outcome that comically overturns clichéd ideas of pastoral lovemaking:

(. . . unbuttoned the flowered bodice whitebright breasts slud out of shadows my tremblin lips bent to the nubbins——foul taste! reared back! *goosebit by damn*! scarred and bloodied one blue pap flappin free and crudded under with some mucusy gop like to made me retch right there in her poor silly face it did!) (PD p. 51)

In another passage, Morris's sheep stage an insurrection in which they try to kill him after he has castrated the head ram. Yet, if Coover is not invoking some myth of bucolic tranquility, neither is he wholly rejecting that myth which has lost much of its efficacy. Rather, his practice, at least as it is announced in *Pricksongs and Descants,* is to rework and reinvigorate those elements of an exhausted narrative form that remain vital and relevant to some current perception of the world.[1] Thus, in "Morris in Chains," Coover develops the Pan-figure as a source of imaginative and lyrical energy. The latter is conceived as an artist whose poetic language serves as an alternative vision of nature and society, a vision that stands as an indictment of the prevailing positivistic worldview. It is "simple song against our science" (PD p. 47), "the old legends [against] conceivable realities" (PD p. 49).

The text regularly alternates between these two meaning systems. One is embodied in a narrator's "report to the nation," the other in Morris's monologues. The positivistic cast of the narrator's report is evident from its preoccupation with details of data gathering, "fact-finding," "recording," and examining. (This relentlessly empirical focus may be read as a parody of literary naturalism: while Coover has called for the "use of the fabulous to probe beyond the phenomenological" [PD p. 78], here we have the fabulous, as represented by the faun Morris, assimilated into the terms of the phenomenological.) In the language of the report, Coover parodies public-address bombast—"All praise to Dr. Peloris! Her wisdom is the State's blessing!" (PD p. 47)— and the sterility of cybernetic discourse: "systems analysts made octal and symbolic corrections to the operational program, broke down all software systems and reassembled the data under new descriptors" (PD p. 49). In contrast, Morris's language—racy, poetic, inventive—is marked by its vitality:

(. . . I efforted a parched kiss her sweet breath reekin of pogonias broad crescent smile starchy folds of springfrock listin over limbcurves and heftin in flushed breezes her toes to the sun old ganders circlin as if in sacred pieties lilywhite fingers fondlin my loose leatherns and grabbin hold like of a she-goat's milkswoln udder her eyes glittery brown beckonin me and me composin mad poetries in the back of my agitated skull. . . .) (PD p. 51)

Morris's monologues are inserted in parentheses which suggests his words are a furtive intervention, a proscribed mode of address. The "mad poetries" of this Pan-figure are judged subversive. Hence Dr. Peloris: " 'All possible cause for panic [recall the derivation of this word] will be eradicated [. . .] We shall put an end to idylatry' " (PD p. 48). It is in "idylatry," in an imaginative and lyrical use of language, that an unsocialized ("barbarian") Morris affirms his independence from an imperialist technocratic culture. Thus, in the closing lines, when the narrator expresses hope for Morris's "reintegration" and "rehabilitation" (PD p. 59), the latter, though in chains and "losin the old [poet's] touch," persists in his versifying:

(Doris Peloris the chorus and Morris sonorous canorous Horace scores Boris——should be able to make *somethin* outa that by juniper then there's bore us and whore us and up the old torus [. . .]) (PD p. 60)

There is something frenetic, *desperate,* about this wordplay. Morris's language, it seems, is a striving to sustain an alternative consciousness, an anxious assertion of personal autonomy.

Commentators, remarking this kind of animated wordplay, rightly identify fun and playfulness as defining features of postmodernist writing (e.g., Scholes 1979, p. 213). But there is an earnest underside to these lexical games too, at least in some dissident postmodernist fiction. We can, for example, appreciate the *writer's* energetic wordplay as an enclave of linguistic vitality in the midst of society's reified language forms. Moreover, insofar as the wordplay is often comic, we can also appreciate it as a means of relieving the pessimism ingrained in some of this fiction.

Pattern Power

In an essay on Coover's second novel, *The Universal Baseball Association, Inc., J. Henry Waugh, Prop.* (1968), a commentator observes:

> The remarkable richness and vitality of Henry Waugh's Association mark it as a self-enclosed world. Indeed, the ascription "Universal Baseball Association" forewarns the reader that nothing as petty or parochial as "American" or "National" is intended. The Association has its own metaphysics and must be seen as the product of a godlike creative act. Henry's initials—J.H.W.—identify him with the Hebrew god Yahweh. (Berman 1978, p. 211)

These observations are fairly representative of readings which, while perceptively commenting on the metafictional and metaphysical elements of the text, nevertheless strip them of their political and historical significance (cf. Heckard 1976 and Hume 1979). Therefore, first— to make a point that seems hardly contentious—far from being a "self-enclosed world," Henry's Association shows every sign of being an extension of the culture and society in which he lives, namely, contemporary America. Indeed, as I shall argue, the political and cultural dynamics of Henry's society are reproduced in his fabricated world. Second, there is nothing "petty or parochial" in identifying "Universal" with "American"; after all, as a global power, the United States commands the resources (e.g., communications technologies, exporting capacity) to universalize her culture. Still more to the point, "Universal," in the context of Henry's Association, is best read as connoting the power of some meaning-systems to *universalize* their claims (for Henry's baseball game is not just a game with dice and charts but a model universe of culture in which diverse discourses compete for ascendancy). Third, the view that "The Association . . . must be seen as the product of a godlike creative act" misses the element of parody implied by the representation of Henry as a Yahweh-figure. Seen from one viewpoint, the parody takes as its target that current of literary modernism which sees the artist as a godlike "artificer" (e.g., Stevens, Joyce, Yeats) standing in a transcendent relation to his/her creation— an idealist model of consciousness as supernal, detached, outside history and culture. Seen from another, broader, viewpoint (one that may be said to incorporate the first), the parody takes as its target the humanist assumption/presumption of the subject as *individual* guarantor or author of meaning. For Coover illustrates how meanings are constituted by society's ruling narratives—its myths, histories, and philosophies—and unconsciously reproduced by individuals who then, like J. Henry Waugh, *Prop.*, make proprietary claims to them.

Henry entertains the idea of writing a history of the first fifty-six years of his Association, the objective being "the exposure of some pattern or other" (Coover 1971, p. 211, hereafter UBA), an expression of what is later referred to as "the immortal lust for pattern" (UBA p. 230). Coover's characters, as critics have observed, seek pattern in words and numbers and sequences of events. The Brunists, Richard Nixon, Martin in "The Elevator," and Paul in "A Pedestrian Accident" (Coover 1970) are among those who are largely represented, and often caricatured, as pattern seekers.[2] It is the perception of pattern that gives experience form and significance. Indeed, for Coover, patterning is the quintessential mental process, one character referring to "the power of pattern over mere mind-activity" (Coover 1970, p. 55). This view may be seen as deriving from the Kantian model of the mind as an essentially structuring agency, imposing its "categories" on the raw flux of experience. However, it is the linguistic model of cognition as a process of "textualization," of knowing the world in the form of "narratives" or "stories," that seems more appropriate to a discussion of Coover's work.

It is important to stress that the patterns or "fictions" in which Coover's characters find meaning and, typically, become entangled, are not presented simply as the arbitrary constructs of hermetically sealed minds, the issue of pure, unconstrained Fancy, but are nearly always grounded in the social domain of politics and culture. Consider the derivation of the very first pattern "exposed" by Henry:

"THE GREAT AMERICAN GAME" [. . .] Well, it was. American baseball [. . .] had struck on an almost perfect balance between offense and defense, and it was that balance, in fact, that and the accountability [. . .] that had led Henry to baseball as his final great project. (UBA p. 19)

This perception of baseball as a "perfect balance between offense and defense" (repeated verbatim UBA p. 45)—in conjunction with Henry's interest in war games (UBA pp. 44–45) and his reflections on war as a ritual tonic for each generation (UBA pp. 130–31)—belongs to a militaristic culture which, characteristically, produces military modes of understanding. War, Coover seems to say, is "The Great American Game" and, indeed, a "universal" game, one whose geopolitics of "offense and defense" had, at the time of the novel (1968), embroiled the United States in Southeast Asia.

Another "exposed" pattern, which roots Henry's invented world in an historically specific culture, materializes in the form of a business accounting whose rationality pervades late-capitalist America. The "Inc." and "Prop." of the book's title imply this connection, linking the Association to a society whose cultural products are generally inscribed with the logic of corporate business and proprietorship. Furthermore, even though Henry, as an accountant by profession, may speak of his record-keeping for the UBA in the language of accountancy—"box scores to be audited, trial balances of averages" (UBA p. 27)—the rationality of business accounting is installed in his Association at a deeper, unconscious level:

Or like that guy who's discovered that the whole damn structure [of the Universal Baseball Association] from the inning organization up and double entry bookkeeping are virtually identical: just multiply it by twenty-one, like the guy claims, and you've got it all. (UBA p. 219)

There are also those patterns which are expressive of "all the mythic residue hidden away in daily life" (UBA p. 222). The thesis that animates much of Coover's work, and which is explicitly raised in his "Dedicatory Prologue to Cervantes" (Coover 1970, pp. 76–79), proposes that the abiding influence of the "unconscious mythic residue in human life" serves to mystify our perceptions and block understanding. Mythical narratives—for example, Bible stories, legends, fairy tales—though embedded in the unconscious in fragmentary form, remain active in encoding our contemporary experience; they exist as "deep structures" of communal meaning that enable us to conceptualize our world. Coover illustrates how this mythic residue is exploited in politics. The political parties of the UBA (which by the final chapter have become rival theological sects) compete in advancing mythical interpretations (i.e., "disclosing" mythical patterns) of the Association's history. "Turn it into folklore" (UBA p. 102) is the strategy favored by the machiavellian UBA Chancellor, Fenn McCaffree, when confronting any issue whose political implications threaten the integrity of "the social construct" (UBA p. 101). It is he who exploits the myth of the hero by creating "Brock Rutherford Day" for the UBA calendar in order to improve the electoral chances of his incumbent Legalist Party

(UBA p. 104, cf. UBA p. 221: "Centennial of everything these days").[3] In respect of its political use of myth, the UBA may be seen as a microcosm of the United States, where political questions are often represented in terms derived from the images and motifs of myth (e.g., Christian and pre-Christian myths. For instances of this point see below).

By year CLVII of the Association, the mythic patternings that have invested UBA history with meaning seem to be losing their efficacy.[4] Participants in "the Damonsday reenactment of the Parable of the Duel" (UBA p. 220) are haunted by a sense of "the collapse of the familiar patterns and emotions aroused" (UBA p. 224). The leading players in the Parable—Hardy Ingram (UBA pp. 224–25) and Paul Trench—experience the terror of a vacuum of meaning. Consider the case of Trench:

Beyond each game, he sees another, and yet another, in endless and hopeless succession. He hits a ground ball to third, is thrown out. Or he beats the throw. What difference, in the terror of eternity, does it make? He stares at the sky, beyond which is more sky, overwhelming in its enormity. He, Paul Trench, is utterly absorbed in it, entirely disappears, is Paul Trench no longer, is nothing at all: So [. . .] Why does he swing? Why does he run? [. . .] Why is it better to win than to lose? Each day: the dread. (UBA p. 238)

Trench's dread arises from the recognition that, faced with the collapse of the established narrative patterns on which meaning is founded, life is emptied of purpose, and identity dissolves. (Another player recognizes how the Parable, that is, a fiction, calls up identity: " 'We have no mothers [. . .] We are mere ideas, hatched whole and hapless.' " [UBA p. 230]; identity itself is a story we—or, indeed, others!—tell ourselves about ourselves.)

These extremities of feeling arise because the UBA is experienced by its members as a total order of meaning. It overarches their lives, determines the boundaries of their conceptual worlds. "He [Trench] wants to quit—but what does he mean ' "quit"? . . .' The game? Life? Could you separate them?" (UBA p. 238; cf. UBA p. 89). Whichever political party (be it Bogglers, Legalists, Guildsmen or, later, Caseyites and Damonites) is empowered to declare the meaning of the Association, that is, to disclose and define the patterns in its history, potentially controls a universal system of meaning. Thus Damonites and Caseyites compete to interpret the historic importance of the principal day in the Association's calendar, namely, "Damonsday" (which commemorates the deaths of the UBA legendary figures, Damon Rutherford and Jock Casey). The Damonites "hold that power itself is proof they are still in the right, that the continuing strength of this [i.e., *their*] story through time is evidence that it is somehow essentially true" (UBA p. 223). And for the Caseyites, " 'Casey must be made relevant to our times,' " Casey, extolled as the embodiment of "God active in man" (UBA p. 222). Thus, read from one standpoint, Coover's text is an inquiry into the political implications of meaning-systems whose truths are projected as "universal." But on what exactly does this process depend?

Henry's crucial insight is that it is the very act of recording history, simply writing it down, that validates and legitimizes what are, after all, only interpretations:

> "At 4:34 on a wet November afternoon, Lou Engel boarded a city bus and spilled water from his hat brim on a man's newspaper. Is that history?" "I . . . I dunno," stammered Lou [. . .]. "Who's writing it down?" Henry demanded. (UBA p. 50, cf. Coover 1973, p. 145)[5]

Of all the duties involved in his role as proprietor of the UBA, acting as its historian is "the job he enjoyed most" (UBA p. 55; cf. UBA pp. 19, 45). By year LVI of the Association, the archives run to "some forty volumes," in which are recorded everything conceivably relevant to the UBA: statistics, journalistic dispatches, seasonal analyses, and so on (UBA pp. 55–56). These records are accredited as "official," the title page of each volume bearing the words "Official Archives" (UBA p. 55). And it is the historian's power to institutionalize meaning that extends into the politics of the UBA itself where parties compete to write the history of the Association on their own terms.

The Game of the Name

Along with the politics of historical representation, another of the book's characteristically dissident postmodernist themes is what we might call the instrumentalization of meaning. To take an obvious example of this process, *The Universal Baseball Association* plays with two different orders of number. First, there are the numbers of the "real time" world (UBA p. 217), a world best exemplified by Horace Zifferblatt's accountancy firm, for which Henry works; there, number has meaning only in relation to capital assets and liabilities (e.g., UBA p. 135). Even in his baseball game, Henry cannot shirk "the dullest job——recording of fielding statistics," inert numbers "which didn't tell much of a story" (UBA p. 54). And under the Chancellorship of McCaffree, who was "forever yakking about distribution functions" (UBA p. 146), there is the danger that number, within the UBA, will be reduced to statistical data—in a word, instrumentalized. Then there are the numbers belonging to the world of "significant time" (UBA p. 217), those numbers in the Association which reveal astonishing symmetries (e.g., the "magic" number seven, UBA pp. 206, 219) and mythic patterns, like the 6–6–6 of the dice ("the number of the Beast" in Revelation) that determines the death of Casey by a line drive (UBA pp. 200–202). Here there is an order of number that resonates significance, that carries a mystical charge, in contrast to the purely functional figures Henry posts to his accounts ledgers. The fascination with numerology makes real baseball redundant. As Henry explains to his friend Lou,

"... I could spend unhappy hours at a ball park [...] Then, a couple days later, at home, I would pick up my scoreboard. Suddenly, what was dead had life, what was wearisome became stirring, beautiful, unbelievably real [...] I found out the scorecards were enough. I didn't need the games." (UBA p. 166)

Yet, when Henry feels depressed or ashamed of his solitary obsession, these numbers are suddenly drained of meaning; they only tell small stories, like the audits and trial balances of Zifferblatt's "real time" world. It is a comment on the fragility of discourses that open up orders of meaning alternative to those of instrumental or functionalist thought.

The process of instrumentalization, which threatens the semantic potential of number, is shown to threaten the entire culture, debasing all meaning to functional ends. This process is best illustrated through the novel's focus on the fate of meaning in a (so-called) Information Society. The issue is brought to the fore through the machinations of Fenn McCaffree. He is Chancellor of the UBA at a critical time in its history, when, partly in consequence of Rutherford's death, it is "undergoing a radical transformation" (UBA p. 145). And he is endeavoring to understand this transformation, to interpret this historic change. He responds to the problem by initiating an extensive and clandestine program of information-gathering. He uses an array of electronic devices, including secretly installed TV cameras and computers (UBA pp. 101, 145–50), to collect data on every aspect of the Association, from the performance of its players to the plans of its political parties. This state of affairs disturbs his predecessor, Woody Winthrop:

machinery, looking like big eyeless monsters conjured up from the depths, hummed and clicked, sucking up the information being fed to them [...] Special camera devices that McCaffree had invented to time runners, spy out jittery fielders [...] Woody suffered the intrusion of all this machinery, this detailed information gathering, the dossiers, the intense pattern studies and close-ups, the projections, the cumulative files. (UBA p. 149)

Moreover, Winthrop goes on to note that McCaffree's desire to understand the changes within the UBA cannot be divorced from his political ambition to maintain control of the Association—he is, after all, head of the incumbent Legalist Party. Hence "Fenn was even using the same methods to gauge and manipulate the political picture" (UBA p. 150); he has agents operating inside rival parties, secretly collating politically sensitive data (UBA p. 150). Data-gathering on this scale reduces meaning to the status of information. It reflects the tendency toward the rationalization of the Association, a tendency that limits the chances for the disclosure of those meanings or patterns that Henry found "stirring, beautiful." The situation is emblematic of the "Information Society" where those who control the communications technologies sacrifice potentially rich sources of meaning for those that are politically or economically exploitable. Indeed, the "blacksuited" McCaffree, ensconced in his secret office, is a parody of such a controller, sitting in his swivel chair, "hand gripping the chair-arm where his intercom buttons were rigged" (UBA p. 146).

The prominence, in the narrative, of terms drawn from game theory precisely conveys this tendency toward the instrumentalization of meaning within the UBA. Put simply, game theory is concerned with the question of the development of strategies that enable "players" (e.g., business competitors, military opponents, political parties), usually in conflict situations, to maximize "payoffs" without upsetting the equilibrium of the system in which they are "playing." This demands the study of the reasoning and dynamics of interdependent decision-making where one player's strategy depends on the likely strategy of another player and vice versa. The theory attempts to abstract the features common to a wide range of conflict situations and has most often found its application in the spheres of commercial, political, and military decision-making. In the case of the UBA, it is Chancellor McCaffree, head of the Legalist Party, who adopts a game theory approach to understanding the Association's crisis. Thus, in a statement where Coover parodies game theory, McCaffree observes:

"What if, Woody, we have passed, without knowing it, from a situation of sequential compounding into one of basic and finite yes-or-no survival, causing a shift of what you might call the equilibrium point, such that the old strategies, like winning ball games, sensible and proper within the old stochastic or recursive sets, are, under the new circumstances, *insane*! [. . .] The way things are going, we're apt to get a payoff *no*body wants." (UBA pp. 148–49)

Elsewhere McCaffree speaks of "compound decision problems" (UBA p. 146), "correlated strategies" (UBA p. 152), and so forth, which, together with the prominence, in the last chapter, of the game theorist, Raspberry Schultz (UBA pp. 234, 239), suggests the force of this current of thinking within the UBA. It is a way of conceptualizing the history of the Association in terms that strip it of mythological, re-ligious, and aesthetic significance—terms which, in Weber's famous expression, *disenchant* it. Within the conceptual framework of this dis-course, meaning is confined to contexts of "functionality," "utility" (UBA p. 146), and "payoffs" (UBA pp. 149, 150).

Woody Winthrop evidently feels estranged from McCaffree's func-tionalist talk. The linguistic divide between the two is often pointed up, for example: "the cumulative files which Fenn called CUMS——in Woody's day that was a dirty word" (UBA p. 149). "Cums," as Winthrop understands it, belongs to a language with which he is more familiar, namely, that of the locker room: the dirty jokes and bawdy songs which enliven the gatherings of the league players. The most poignant and sentimental episodes of the novel are those moments of male cama-raderie, as at the Rutherford wake, where a kind of communion is achieved through the medium of locker-room talk (e.g., UBA pp. 111–16). However, it is the game of baseball itself which is presented as an ideal model of communication,[6] that is to say, one which enables a profound experience of communality. Thus, in one passage, an all-too-solitary Henry suggests that the game may be valued insofar as it is felt to communicate a near-mystical sense of communion, of con-nectedness:

"I even had the funny idea that ball stadiums and not European churches were the real American holy places." Formulas for energy configurations where city boys came to see their country origins dramatized, some old lost fabric of unity. (UBA p. 166)

I have highlighted the difference between a worldly, functionalist order of meaning within the UBA and, at the other extreme, the experience of something like transcendent or mystical orders of mean-ing. But here, it must be stressed, there is no simple dualism at work in this novel; it is not just a matter of rich, complex, and vital patterns of meaning versus impoverished or utilitarian ones. Coover is conscious of a dialectic operating in the domain of culture whereby *any* animating or "efficacious" narrative eventually becomes exhausted and constric-tive (see note 4, Chap. 4). In time it will be challenged by new narratives whose authority and efficacy are themselves necessarily provisional, narratives which, in turn, are bound to be superseded. Hence Henry, recognizing the need for a new historical narrative which will reflect the profound changes that have occurred within the UBA, observes:

It was all there in the volumes of the Book and in the records, but now it needed a new ordering, perspective, personal vision, the disclosure of pattern because he'd discovered [. . .] that perfection wasn't a thing, a closed moment, a static fact, but *process*, yes, and the process was transformation. (UBA pp. 211–12)

In its metafictional capacity, the text projects Henry, the UBA's historian, as a surrogate writer, that is to say, as a producer/manipulator of narratives; for he is empowered—albeit within the limits or rules of his game—to construct meaning. (Henry may not be an omnipotent Yahweh-figure exercising total control over the UBA, but neither is he simply a creator enthralled by his creation. Rather, he plays a creative role as an historiographer, though always *within* culturally defined limits. Thus, " . . . the circuit wasn't closed [. . .]: there were patterns but they were shifting and ambiguous and you had a lot of room inside them" [UBA p. 143]). This capacity to construct meaning is made evident by way of Henry's insight into the power of naming and by way of his games with names:

Everywhere he looked he saw names. His head was full of them. Bus stop. Whistlestop. Whistlestop Busby, second base. Simple as that. Over a storefront across the street: Thornton's. He'd been looking for a name to go with Shadwell, and maybe that was it. Thornton Shadwell, Tim's boy. Pitcher like the old man? Probably [. . .] Henry was always careful about names, for they were what gave the league its sense of fulfilment and failure, its emotion [. . .] Names had to be chosen, therefore, that could bear the whole weight of perpetuity [. . .] Call Player A "Sycamore Flynn" or "Melbourne Trench" and something starts to happen. He shrinks or grows, stretches out or puts on muscle [. . .] Strange. But name a man and you make him what he is [. . .] The basic stuff is already there. In the name. Or rather: in the naming. (UBA pp. 46–48)

Here Coover affirms that the power to confer names is the power to assign meaning, to construct the significance of a person (or place or process). Of course, the creative act of naming is of little consequence unless it is institutionally underwritten; that is to say, if meanings are to gain currency and authority, they must be officially inscribed, committed to writing, ritualized—functions which Henry, as historian of the UBA, meticulously performs. However, while the operation of naming may be a means through which power is exercised, it is also a means through which power is challenged. For example, Witness Raspberry Schultz, the game theorist, has his authority progressively undermined by comical renaming: "the Witness, blushing Raspberry," "Witberry Yultz," and "witless Jerkberry" (UBA pp. 233–34).

When, in a sexual encounter with Hettie, a B-girl, Henry assumes the name of Damon, he acquires something of the force and charisma of his invented baseball hero:

"The greatest pitcher in the history of baseball," he whispered. "Call me . . .
Damon." "Damon," she whispered, unbuckling his pants [. . .] "Damon!" she
greeted, grabbing——and that girl, with one swing, he knew then, could bang
a pitch clean out of the park. "*Play ball!*" cried the umpire. And the catcher,
stripped of mask and guard, revealed as the pitcher Damon Rutherford,
whipped the uniform off the first lady ballplayer in Association history, and
then [. . .] they ran the bases, pounded into first, slid into second heels high,
somersaulted over third, shot home standing up, then into the box once more,
swing away, and run them all again, and "Damon!" she cried, and "Damon!"
(UBA p. 29)

And there will be situations in which names are divested of their power
and authority. For example, when Lou Engel pronounces the names of
the UBA ballplayers "they *did* sound like comic book names" (UBA
p. 189). But it is this very instability of meaning—owing to the fact
that the same word(s) may be cited in innumerable contexts, all words
having this general property of "iterability" (Derrida 1977)—which
saves language from ossification or univocality. Through Henry's
games with names, Coover illustrates how words may be freed from
their established significations and transferred into contexts which
animate them in fresh ways. It is this affirmation of the creative potential of language—the recognition that we can inhabit the world
through meaning-systems alternative to those that prevail—which is
the book's optimistic message.

Reading *The Public Burning*

The time frame of Coover's third novel, *The Public Burning*, is strictly
limited to the three days in 1953 leading up to the electrocution of the
Rosenbergs. Yet, by means of his critical engagement with the terms in
which the Rosenbergs were vilified and arraigned at the climax of
the McCarthy era, Coover interrogates and contests the master codes
through which postwar America's perceptions of politics and society
are mediated. However, many studies of the novel by Coover specialists
convey scarcely a hint of its adversarial force. Indeed, the theoretical
frameworks of commentaries tend all too often to foreclose on a political reading of the book.

One approach to *The Public Burning* privileges the book's *mythic*
frame of reference. Exponents of this approach (e.g., Hume 1979,
LeClair 1982, Ramage 1982) focus attention on the motifs of the sacri-
ficial victim, the Manichaean duel, the orgiastic rite—motifs which, to
be sure, figure prominently in this and other works by Coover, notably
The Origin of the Brunists, The Universal Baseball Association, and *A Politi-*

cal Fable. However, readings which thematize the novel's mythic perspectives tend to marginalize its sociohistorical perspectives. There is not a single reference to the Cold War in myth-centered readings by Kathryn Hume, Thomas LeClair, and John Ramage; this is not surprising when myth, in Coover's book, is understood to supplant history.[7] In contrast, my point of entry into the novel will be the thematic context of cold war history, with attention focused on the Cold War presented as a regime of discourse.

Another critical approach to *The Public Burning* yields what might be termed the "fabulationist" account of the novel. This account highlights Coover's model of man as a fiction-maker or fabulator through an examination of a central theme of the book: the fictional status of *all* "historical" (documentary, factual) narrative. Hence, in commentaries on *The Public Burning*, Robert Scholes speaks of "fabulative history" (Scholes 1979, p. 206), Larry McCaffery of "history-as-artifice" (McCaffery 1982, p. 87). To be sure, Coover illuminates history or, more precisely, historiography, as "fabulation" or "artifice." Indeed, in some important respects, Coover's views on writing history echo those of metahistorians like Hayden White. Speaking of "the extent to which 'invention' plays a part in the historian's operations," (White 1975, p. 7), White examines the "fictive" elements inherent in the types of explanation provided by historical narrative. For example, "explanation by emplotment" is "the way by which a sequence of events fashioned into a story is gradually revealed to be a story of a particular kind," that is, a history invested with the plot structure of, say, a "Tragedy" or "Comedy" (p. 7). White also explores what he sees as the unavoidable mediation of metaphor, metonymy and other tropes in the construction of historical accounts: "All historical narratives presuppose figurative characterizations of the events they purport to represent and explain," a view which prompts a conception of "the historical text as a literary artifact" (White 1978b, p. 56; see also White 1978a). Now critics like McCaffery and Scholes read *The Public Burning* as an exemplary work of metafiction precisely insofar as it "foregrounds" the artificiality of historiographical conventions; they recognize its epistemological challenge to our (Enlightenment/positivist) faith in the possibility of an objective grasp of history. Accordingly they privilege the following passage as the *locus classicus* of the novel (where Coover's Richard Nixon, endeavoring to sort out the ambiguities and contradictions in documents relating to the Rosenberg spy case, reflects on his confusion):

What was fact, what intent, what was framework, what was essence? Strange the impact of History, the grip it had on us, yet it was nothing but words. Accidental accretions for the most part, leaving most of the story out. We have not yet begun to explore the true power of the Word, I thought. What if we broke all the rules, played games with the evidence, manipulated language itself, made History a partisan ally? Of course, the Phantom [Coover's person-ification of communism] was already onto this, wasn't he? Ahead of us again. (Coover 1978, p. 172: Hereafter PB)

Yet this passage is not just about history-as-fiction, not just about the *primacy* of "art" and "fabulation" (Scholes) or the "fiction-making pro-cess" (McCaffery) in the writing of history; such remarks are in need of qualification. Insofar as this key passage explicitly connects historical discourse with power and political strategy (i.e., making a "partisan" use of history through the manipulation of language and evidence), it summarizes Coover's preoccupation with *political and ideological media-tions* in the "fictionalizing" of history. The problem with the "fabula-tionist" account of *The Public Burning* is that it is bound to a conception of metafiction as purely epistemological critique; a conception which does not embrace the adversarial potential of "metafictional" (or sign-reflective) writing. As we shall see, Coover's sign-reflective techniques work to undermine the authority of hegemonic historical narratives by exposing and contesting the ideology inscribed in them.[8]

The book's emphasis on the idea that history can only be appre-hended in narrative form necessarily threatens the validity of any political reading of history proposed by its author; for such a reading, within the novel's sign-reflective framework, becomes just one more narrative construct or fiction. As Raymond Mazurek observes in an essay on Coover's novel: ". . . the analysis of history as text displaces an analysis of history" (Mazurek 1982, p. 40).[9] This is a valid point, but perhaps Mazurek might moderate his criticism if he was to consider whether there are other reasons besides Coover's perception of history-as-text that inhibit or disable a political reading or critique of recent American history. Such a critique implies a faith in the tenability of a critical standpoint outside of the established order of meaning. How-ever, in our discussion of postmodernism (a concept absent from Ma-zurek's study), it was observed that the dissident postmodernist writer has little confidence in the possibility of a truly autonomous critical perspective. This attitude was seen to be derived from a view of post-modern consciousness as unable to transcend, or at least entirely free itself, from society's hegemonic codes. Accordingly, the narrative of *The Public Burning*, like the narratives of the Barthelme stories dis-cussed earlier, is almost exclusively mediated through the conscious-ness of minds (Nixon's, The Times Square crowds') enclosed within the prevailing ideologies. (Of course, in its sign-reflective dimension, the novel transcends the horizons of Nixon's or the cold war public's mind-set. But the sign-reflective frame of the narrative does not in itself constitute a standpoint from which Coover can offer a critical analysis or political reading of recent American history.)

Second, it is not purely at the abstract level of discourse theory that the problem of writing history is raised in the novel. Careful attention to the text will show that the problem is almost always raised in contexts which illuminate its *political* implications, particularly in the chronologically and socially specific context of American cold war politics.[10] The novel offers insights into the role of some of America's ideologically and politically dominant institutions—the press, the legal system, the Republican party, the FBI—in the propagation of cold war historical narratives and their promotion to hegemonic status. And while these insights probably fall short of Mazurek's idea (never specified) of an adequate political reading of cold war America, they nevertheless constitute a significant historical analysis of the role of privileged institutions in the production of "truth." In any event, the adversarial power of the book surely need not depend on a developed political analysis of recent American history. Rather, that power resides primarily in the novel's forceful deconstruction and de-mythification of the ruling historical narratives of cold war America—subversive operations which do not depend on some independent critical discourse but on the strength of formal, sign-reflective techniques.

The Limits of Political Discourse

Nixon continues his reflections on the Phantom's manipulation of language as follows:

What were his dialectical machinations if not the dissolution of the natural limits of language, the conscious invention of a space, a spooky artificial no-man's land, between logical alternatives? I loved to debate both sides of any issue, but thinking about that strange space in between made me sweat. Paradox was the one thing I hated more than psychiatrists and lady journalists. Fortunately, I knew, I'd forget most of this—these errant insights always fled and something more solid, more *legal*, sooner or later took over. (PB p. 172)

The thing to note about Nixon's thinking is that he believes that language has "natural limits" and that these are embodied in "logical alternatives" like either/or ("it's either/or as far as I'm concerned" [PB p. 64]) or true/false. And whatever concepts cannot be accommodated within this theory of language he experiences as "artificial" and "spooky," as not "solid," as "paradox." Later Nixon speaks of "mind-numbing paradox" (PB p. 292), and the Phantom is described as the "Creator of Ambiguities" (PB p. 414). What disturbs Coover's Nixon is that the "artificial no-man's land"—that is, the "undecidable," which according to the law of the excluded middle annuls the true/false distinction—threatens to invalidate the whole conceptual scheme which underpins his faith in "logical alternatives"; "that strange space in between" threatens to loosen his grip on reality. But Nixon quickly recovers his composure ("Fortunately, I knew, I'd forget most of this——these errant insights always fled.") and by the very next paragraph he has reverted to his black/white, either/or, true/false mode of thought. Contrasting himself with Julius Rosenberg he observes, "We were more like mirror images of each other, familiar opposites. Left-right, believer-nonbeliever, city-country, accused-accuser, maker-unmaker. I built bridges, he bombed them" (PB p. 173). But what Nixon cannot see is that the bi-polar concepts that structure his thinking are as artificial and as ideologically motivated as the language he accuses the Phantom of trying to invent.

Consider the novel's first "Intermezzo," "The War Between the Sons of Light and the Sons of Darkness." The title, with its Manichaean image of two fundamentally conflicting principles, gives an indication of what is to come: a sequence of the reified dualisms which limit popular political thinking in America. (What follows are documentary extracts from Eisenhower's addresses to the nation in 1953. In an interview, Coover has stated, "There's nothing of mine in any of those three Intermezzos. Every word spoken comes from some document or other" [Ziegler and Bigsby 1982, p. 90]):

The shadow of fear has darkly lengthened across the world.
We sense with all our faculties
that forces of Good and Evil are massed and armed and opposed
as rarely before in history. (PB p. 189)

Freedom is pitted against slavery;
lightness against the dark! (PB p. 190)

our civilization and our form of government
is deeply imbedded in a religious faith [. . .]
The enemies of this faith
know no god but force, no devotion but its use. (PB p. 191)

And so on. Coover juxtaposes extracts from Eisenhower's speeches in ways designed to highlight a kind of ideological/rhetorical process one might call "dichotomization," whereby political issues are simplified into emotionally charged pairs of opposing terms; superpower rivalry translated into a conflict between Good and Evil, Light and Darkness, God and Godlessness, Freedom and Slavery.

Cold war discourse drew on a lexicon of totemic words (e.g., freedom, loyalty, faith) and bogey words (e.g., communism, treason, conspiracy) which commandeered the terms of public debate and perverted the significance of the political issues in question. The invocation of these words could, and still can, be counted on to induce an instant and emotive response from an audience. The semiotician Charles Morris has suggested that certain forms of propaganda

seem to cut down the intervening sign-processes of which the individual is capable, and thus allow the interpretants of the signs with which the individual is confronted to take overt form more directly and quickly—laughing when something is signified as funny, crying when something is signified as unfortunate, responding to commands in an almost automatic fashion. (Quoted in Foulkes 1983, p. 24)

Morris is describing a kind of short-circuiting whereby "interpretants" have the power to bypass more complex cognitive processes like analysis and induce an immediate reaction. Coover parodies this reflex response in his portrayal of the crowd which has gathered in Times Square for the public execution of the Rosenbergs. Public figures, speaking from the Times Square stage, harangue a crowd whose feelings can be depressed or elevated at will by summoning the shibboleths of cold war rhetoric. (See, for example, Sister Emma Bennett Fowler's address [PB pp. 512–13].) In the warm-up to the executions, celebrities like Jack Benny and the Marx Brothers entertain the nation on the Times Square stage with comic turns that play on aspects of the Rosenberg spy case (the entertainment industry making its own contribution to the cold war propaganda campaign). And here again Coover parodies reflex reaction—the automatic laughter of people living under a political regime that thrives on the hyper-suggestibility of the public:

Out front, a hundred million mouths open wide, a hundred million sets of teeth spring apart like dental exhibits, a hundred million bellies quake, and a hundred million throats constrict and spasm [. . .] as America laughs. (PB p. 551)

This is a cruel caricature of the cold war public as a mindless, conformist mass (the sort of image which has provoked overpitched accusations that the novel is marred by "misanthropy," disfigured by a "protracted sneer").[11] It suggests clockwork behavior, responses triggered by, and thus under the control of, a repertoire of ideological signs. I want to read *The Public Burning* first and foremost as a text which combats the power of these signs. Taken together, these signs constitute a nationalist discourse—the discourse of "America."

The Discourse of "America"

> Every effort to speak of the world involves a kind of fiction-making
> process. There are always other plots, other settings, other inter-
> pretations. So if some stories start throwing their weight around, I
> like to undermine their authority a bit, work variations, call atten-
> tion to their fictional natures.
> Robert Coover in interview (McCaffery 1981, p. 50)

By discourse of "America," I mean that domain of language-use
which represents *the idea* of "America." In speaking of *the* discourse of
"America," I do not wish to imply that there is an absolute or definitive
discourse of "America"; depending on one's political perspective there
are several such discourses, and I have enclosed America in quotation
marks to suggest that that which is signified by the discourse may be
open to alternative representation or, indeed, may not be reliably
represented. I use the definite article to suggest the ruling version of
this discourse, that is, the discourse promoted and reproduced by
America's culturally dominant institutions; a *hegemonic* discourse insofar as it has articulated to itself populist sentiments, insofar as it creates
and "speaks" the consensus. It is for the most part an everyday discourse, relayed through popular forms of communication like the
press, television, and sermons. Even those elements of the discourse
which may strike non-Americans as exorbitant, like talk of Providence
or Armageddon, are familiar to millions of Americans through the
powerful mediation of the fundamentalist "electronic church." What
makes *The Public Burning* such a provocative and compelling text is
precisely that it critically engages a hegemonic discourse.

The discourse of "America" is a nationalist discourse. It is a definition
of America's historical situation vis-à-vis her enemies and allies and of
her assumed role as leading actor on the stage of history. It is an
acclamation of the American way of life, of its institutions, ideals, and
goals. It is an assertion of what is perceived as quintessentially American, of "Americanism," in tandem with what is perceived as un-
American or anti-American. It is, above all, an integrative discourse
appealing to, or "positioning," its subjects as *first and foremost* "Americans" whose patriotic duty is to preserve the established order.

The discourse of "America," like perhaps any nationalist discourse, is
a hybrid, conspicuously eclectic discourse, its elements drawn from
other, often mutually exclusive, discourses. Accordingly, its cardinal
concepts are not always compatible with one another; they do not
interlock to form a coherent system of thought.

The discourse of "America" that Coover opposes in *The Public Burning* is the one which flourished during the First Cold War. Yet, the paranoid and chauvinist feelings of that era, so vividly evoked in the novel, will be familiar to readers who lived through the Second Cold War. Indeed, the discourse that Coover interrogates, specifically the nationalist discourse of the 1940s and 1950s, has persisted in many respects throughout the 1980s and into the 1990s: the era of New Right ascendancy.[12]

In the following pages some of the key concepts of the discourse of "America" are individually discussed. The aim is to introduce the concepts and to examine Coover's deconstruction of the nationalist myths which permeate them.

Providence/Manifest Destiny/Novus Ordo Seclorum

The anonymous narrator of the "Prologue" quotes George Washington, Uncle Sam's "Primordial Incarnation" (PB p. 17):

" 'No people can be bound to acknowledge and adore the invisible hand which conducts the affairs of men more than the people of the United States. Every step by which they have advanced to the character of an independent nation, seems to have been distinguished by some token of providential agency!' " (PB p. 18)

And, meditating on America's "election" (PB p. 18) the narrator adds, "No, friends, America has not arisen: *it has been called forth*! It's like the Divine Hawthorne once said: 'There is a fatality, a feeling so irresistible and inevitable that it has the force of doom . . . !' " (PB p. 19). Nixon, like the narrator, believes in America's providential history. Playing golf with Uncle Sam, he reflects, "I had a feeling that everything in America was coming together for the first time: an emergence into Destiny" (PB p. 122). Yet later, when, symbolically, he is traveling *away* from the superpatriotic ambience of Times Square, Nixon has one of his "errant insights" (PB p. 172):

And then I'd realized what it was that had been bothering me: that sense that everything happening was somehow inevitable, as though it had all been scripted out in advance. But bullshit! There were no scripts, no necessary patterns, no final scenes, there was just *action,* and then *more action*! Maybe in Russia History had a plot because one was being laid on, but not here—*that was what freedom was all about!* (PB pp. 445–46)

This insight may be seen, among other things, to throw into question the nationalist myth of America's "inevitable" history: the theatrical language—"scripts," "final scenes"—suggests that the theory of a providential history is merely an elaborate fabrication. But, to be more precise, that theory is an *ideological* fabrication; this will be apparent in a moment when the theory is seen as a key component of two other nationalist myths: "Manifest Destiny" and the imperialist vision of a "New Order."

Some readers might be forgiven for thinking that in contending with the myth of America's providential history, Coover is contending with a dead issue. But, in fact, the myth remains credible for many. On the patriotic occasion of the Statue of Liberty's centennial (1986), Ronald Reagan delivered the following words:

I've always thought that a providential hand has something to do with the founding of this country. That God had his reasons for placing this land between two great oceans to be found by a certain kind of people. (Quoted in Brummer, 1986)

"God's reasons," it need hardly be said, implies a belief in a divinely ordained role for America.

Coover's Nixon says of Eisenhower that he "truly *believed* in Manifest Destiny" (PB p. 288), and the blackout in Times Square ends when Uncle Sam, the flying Superhero, is seen in the sky "bearing in his lean gnarled hands a new birth of freedom, a white-hot kernel of manifest destiny: a spark from the sacred flame!" (PB p. 603). In his essay, "Cuba, The Philippines, and Manifest Destiny," Richard Hofstadter discusses the ideological function of the concept of Manifest Destiny, noting how it has been invoked to justify expansion. For example, the annexation of the Philippines at the end of the Spanish-American War had to be justified. Hofstadter writes:

The doctrine that expansion was inevitable had of course long been familiar to Americans; we all knew how often Manifest Destiny was invoked throughout the nineteenth century [. . .] During the Nineties it came to mean that expansion "could not be resisted by Americans themselves, caught willing or unwilling," in the coils of fate [. . .]. Our aggression was implicitly defined as compulsory—the product not of our own wills but of objective necessity (or the will of God). (Hofstadter 1967, p. 177)

In short, we may say that Manifest Destiny had the ideological role either of consecrating imperialism, that is, imperialism as an expression of God's will, or of acquiescing in it, that is, imperialism as an expression of historical necessity. And, indeed, the first mention of Manifest Destiny, in the opening pages of the novel, links the concept with imperialism in precisely these terms (God's will and historical necessity). Uncle Sam says:

"It is our manifest dust-in-yer-eye to overspread the continent allotted by Providence for the free development of our yearly multiplyin' millions, so damn the torpedoes and full steam ahead, fellow ripstavers, we cannot escape history! [. . .] I tell you, we want *elbow-room*—the continent—the *whole* continent—and nothin' *but* the continent! And-by gum!—we will *have* it!" (PB p. 17)

The puns here deserve attention. "Manifest dust-in-yer-eye" for Manifest Destiny neatly reveals the ideological operation of the concept as an impairment of vision whereby people fail to "see" the mercenary nature of expansion and, instead, understand expansion as a providential or necessary process. "Elbow-room," as John Ramage points out, recalls *lebensraum:* Uncle Sam wants "the *whole* continent," the Nazis wanted all Europe. By representing the concept "manifest destiny" as "manifest dust-in-yer-eye" and linking it with an echo of *Lebensraum,* Coover undermines its lofty pretensions.

" 'The untransacted destiny of the American people is to establish a new order in human affairs' " (PB p. 608), says Uncle Sam on his majestic return to Times Square. Earlier, Nixon had read the motto *"Novus Ordo Seclorum"* over an entrance to the Senate Chamber and reflected: "Yes, this was what America was all about [. . .] this was the true revolution of our era. [. . .] It was our job now [. . .] to bring this new order of the ages to the whole world" (PB p. 78). But there is an awkward moment when he notes, "Of course, you had to be careful——revolution, new order, it was the kind of language people like the Rosenbergs used, too——but in ignorance, in darkness" (PB p. 79). It is a revealing observation; after all, it is the Communists who are accused of an ambition for world domination (PB p. 34). Yet when American global ambitions are conceptualized in such a grandiose formula as "Novus Ordo Seclorum," with its aura of enlightenment, civilization, a higher stage of history (and a concept further dignified by its Latin rendering), then those ambitions sound noble, magnanimous and are the more easily articulated in terms of destiny. Coover quotes *Time* magazine, which urged Americans to " 'accept the thrust of destiny,' to go out and take over the world, and 'create the first great American Century' " (PB p. 398).

Noam Chomsky, the bête noire of America's State Department, has researched American foreign policy in the era of cold war politics and unearthed a concept that, in the breadth of its imperialist vision, resembles that of the "new order":

They [the State Department planners] knew certainly by 1942 that the war was going to end with the US in a position of enormous global dominance, and the question then arose, "Well, how do we organize the world?" They developed the concept of Grand Area Planning where the Grand Area is understood as that which in their terms was "strategically necessary for world control." Their geo-political analysis attempted to determine which areas of the world would have to be "open"—open to investment, the repatriation of profits, access to resources and so on—and dominated by the United States. (Chomsky 1984, p. 25)

Similarly, the Marshall Plan, a major institution of the First Cold War, has been understood as an endeavor to establish an American new order, at least in Europe; a program for the reconstruction of Europe's war-devastated economies on a basis that would forestall the pursuit of "independent nationalistic policy" at the expense of U.S. interests. (See Armstrong, Glyn, and Harrison 1984, pp. 106–12.)

Material Progress

Coover's Richard Nixon has no doubts at all about what "America" means, about what defines "Americanness":

To think of the changes that this country had seen in the few years since I was a boy! Just look at that terrific layout Pat now had in her kitchen: who would want to change something that was working so well? These communists were crazy. Every time I flicked a switch, adjusted a thermostat, started a car, boarded a plane, walked through automatic doors, flushed a toilet, or watched a record drop on a turntable, I loved America more. And not just for her material progress. . . . (PB p. 230)

The passage reminds us of the ideological role played by the term "material progress." Communist states have, in terms of technological and economic performance, always lagged behind America. Hence "material progress" is used to connote the superiority of the American system of free enterprise. The ideological objective is to entwine the concepts of "America" and "material progress" so that America *qua* model capitalist economy becomes synonymous with "technological advance," "innovation," and "prosperity." Communism is then represented as the antithesis of progress: "The truth about the Phantom was that he was a *reactionary*, trying to derail the Train of Progress!" (PB p. 79).

It is significant that Coover represents Nixon's conception of material progress through examples of objects and practices *all* of which are plainly visible and/or tangible. It is through these empirical attributes that Nixon "reads" these objects and practices as a *natural* affirmation of American superiority and of what is quintessentially American. In *Mythologies*, Barthes investigated the ideological process whereby culturally determined meanings are naturalized. It is a process that ex-

ploits "what is immediately visible," that "organizes a world which is
without contradictions [. . .] and wallowing in the evident," such that
"things appear to mean something by themselves" (Barthes 1973,
p. 143). What Nixon cannot see is that his experience of everyday
technology as a self-evident indication of America's preeminence is at
bottom an ideological effect.

Freedom/Faith/Free Economy

> Upon all our peoples and nations
> there rests a responsibility to serve worthily
> the faith we hold and the freedom we cherish
> —which means essentially a free economy. (PB p. 193)
> —Dwight David Eisenhower

We find in the discourse of "America" a trinity of terms: freedom,
faith, and free economy. In the first "Intermezzo," Coover highlights
the ways these terms are ideologically entangled. After his editing (the
"Intermezzo" is an assemblage of extracts from Eisenhower's speeches
as recorded in "Public Papers of the Presidents" [PB p. 189]), the terms
recur with such frequency that they are revealed as the organizing
categories of Eisenhower's "vision" (PB p. 189). In his address to the
nation, Eisenhower repeatedly relates these terms to one another such
as to affirm that (a) there can be no freedom without faith; (b) there can
be no freedom without free economy; and (c) there can be no free
economy without faith. Coover illustrates the ideological effects of
linking terms which belong to essentially disparate discourses.

The principal theme of Eisenhower's address can be simply stated:
freedom, whose exemplary manifestation is to be found in the American way of life, must be defended against communism. In several
places, freedom is explicitly represented in religious terms: "We are
Christian nations, deeply conscious that the foundation of all liberty is
religious faith" (PB p. 190), "all free government is firmly founded in a
deeply felt religious faith" (PB p. 197), and so on. Yet, contrary to its
spiritual identification, the concept of freedom is identified elsewhere
at the level of the grossly material:

But to be free and stay free,
we must be strong—and we must stay strong! [. . .]
If we allow any section of the world that is vital to us,
because of what it provides us—say, manganese,
or uranium, or cobalt—anything that we need
—if we allow any of those areas to fall

to a form of government inimical to us,
that wants to see freedom abolished from the earth,
then we have trouble indeed! (PB pp. 194–95)

The issue raised here was a major cause of the Cold War. American capital, seeking a free-trade area nothing less than global, faced the prospect, after the war, of being denied access to the resources and markets of countries falling under the Soviet sphere of influence. Hence one of Uncle Sam's concerns is "securing the resources of poor nations from the Phantom's greed" (PB p. 19). Eisenhower evidently believes that freedom in part depends on access to other nations' resources, that is to say, it depends on a requisite of free enterprise. And he declares America's resolve to defend:

our traditional system of free enterprise.
Private investment has been the major stimulus
for economic development throughout this hemisphere;
this is the true way of the Americas—the free way—
by which people are bound together for the common good. (PB p. 194)

Once again, "the free way" is said to be the way of free enterprise.

In short, freedom is identified in *both* the terms of religion and free enterprise. In this way, Coover exposes a rhetorical ploy: a mercenary preoccupation with private investment and the acquisition of other peoples' raw materials can be ennobled by entwining it with a revered idea like freedom. It is easy to see how the appeal to freedom operates ideologically: if one wishes to maintain a way of life—in this case, the free economy of western capitalism—which is not universally approved, one represents it by a value—in this case, freedom—which is so approved. Coover quotes "Mother Luce," founder of the *Time-Life-Fortune* syndicate: "'Make money, be proud of it; make more money, be prouder of it! School yourself for the long battle of freedom in this country!'" (PB pp. 269–70).

To say that freedom is dependent on faith or free economy is not to define it. At this level of abstraction the meaning of the term is vague; it leaves unanswered such questions as: "freedom of what?", "freedom to what end?", "whose freedom?" However, freedom does *appear* to have an obvious meaning when contrasted with, say, "tyranny" or "slavery." Cold warriors have long exploited this illusion. Eisenhower's speeches, alerting the public to the communist "threat" to freedom, contain several such contrasts: "Freedom is pitted against slavery" (PB p. 190) or "to remain a free, independent, and powerful people [. . .] a soldier's pack is not so heavy a burden as a prisoner's chains" (PB

p. 195). It is the language we heard in the Cold War of the 1980s. In 1985, the strategically named "Committee for the Free World" met in London. There was fighting talk from, among others, Jeane Kirkpatrick, American representative at the U.N.; Star Wars luminary Richard Perle; and Norman Podhoretz, editor of the neoconservative weekly *Commentary* and, not by chance, hostile reviewer of *The Public Burning*. ("A cowardly lie" was the latter's shrill verdict on the novel [Podhoretz 1977].) In his message of support to the crusaders, Ronald Reagan suggested that the theme of the convention should be "how a decent political order might one day replace the terrible tyranny of Communism" (quoted in Schwartz 1985). And weeping televangelist Jerry Falwell, addressing America's Moral Majority on the Old Time Gospel Hour, declared: "Ask me if I'm willing to support the Contras: I'm willing to go there myself. I'm willing to do everything that's necessary to prevent my children growing up in slavery as in Afghanistan and Cuba and Nicaragua" (quoted in Schwartz 1987). As a consequence of the persistent linking of communism with tyranny and slavery, the notion of America as a "free nation" seems to express a concrete, verifiable condition.

Finally, a few words on the conjunction of the terms "free economy" and "faith." After expressing concern at the possible loss of access to raw materials, Eisenhower adds:

It is up to every American to realize
that he has a definite personal responsibility
in the protection of these resources—they belong
to the people who have been created in His image:
they must, at any cost, remain armed, strong,
and ready for the risk of War!
In that way only, can we permanently aspire
to remain a free, independent, and powerful people,
living humbly under our God. (PB p. 195)

Just as above, we saw free economy justified in terms of freedom, here we see it sanctified in terms of God. Elsewhere we learn that Eisenhower believes "Free economy was God's truth, that was all, plain as the nose on your face" (PB p. 288). Eisenhower's persistent invocation of God disposes the audience to interpret his speeches in religious terms. Again, Coover exposes a rhetorical ploy which, like the one discussed above, works on the basis of dissimulation: by appealing to God or religion, a profane concern (the "protection" of interests and resources) is cloaked in an aura of piety. The equation of free economy with Godliness continues to be upheld in America by a thriving Christian fundamentalism according to which: "If you're not rich, then God's not blessing you."[13]

The Center

> Out in the world, the frontiers are crumbling—but [. . .] the
> people draw back toward the center to restore their strength.
> (PB p. 264)

In an essay "Centre and Periphery" (1961), Edward Shils writes:

Society has a centre. There is a central zone in the structure of society [. . .]
Membership in the society, in more than the ecological sense of being located in
a bounded territory [. . .], is constituted by relationship to this central zone.
The central zone is not, *as such,* a spatially located phenomenon [. . .] The
centre, or the central zone, is a phenomenon of the realm of values and beliefs.
It is the centre of the order of symbols, of values and beliefs, which govern the
society. It is the centre because it is the ultimate and irreducible; and it is felt to
be such by many who cannot give explicit articulation to its irreducibility. The
central zone partakes of the nature of the sacred. In this sense, every society
has an "official" religion. (Shils 1970, p. 415)

The Public Burning suggests an American reverence for the idea of the
"center." The execution of the Rosenbergs will be staged in Times
Square because it is "the ritual center of the Western World" (PB
p. 209). Nixon, ambitious to host the incarnation of Uncle Sam, continually seeks the "center" of American life: "Being at the center was
everything" (PB p. 221); of Eisenhower, he says, "here, clearly, was a
man who had gone to the center and seen the sacred" (PB p. 231), and
he reflects:

[W]hile Julius Rosenberg at the age of fifteen was circulating a petition for
Tom Mooney, I nearly six years older was chairmanning the annual bonfire on
Fire Hill and establishing a new all-time record by topping it, not with the
traditional one-hole privy, but with a real four-hole collector's item [. . .] but
anyone with any understanding at all of the American mainstream will know
that in 1933 Tom Mooney was peripheral to it and that shithouse-crowned
bonfire was dead center. Now, twenty years later, Julius Rosenberg was still
outside, in fact he was colder than ever, while I was playing golf with Uncle
Sam. (PB p. 230)

The idea of the "center" of a nation has implications beyond the
expression of patriotic sentiment. Nixon's thinking illustrates how the
representation of attitudes or practices as either "central" or "mainstream" to a society may, in a political context, facilitate an ideological
interpellation, constituting dissidents like Rosenberg as "outsiders,"
deviants, or eccentrics. The aim is to marginalize or ostracize the
perceived adversary. In branding dissenting civil servants, labor activists, artists whose work exhibited a "communist" bias, and others as

communists and "hence" traitors, the inquisitorial HUAC (House Un-American Activities Committee) was, in effect, excluding them from the "center" or "mainstream" of American life. The process can, perhaps, be seen as a form of excommunication. The following definition of excommunication is one which, read from the perspective of *The Public Burning*, relates in many respects to the experience of the Rosenbergs:

> This is *excommunication*, the victim of which is excluded from further meaningful discourse as being insane, depraved, traitorous, alien, and so on. The excommunicated person is condemned, temporarily or forever, to ideological non-existence: he is not to be listened to; he is the target of ideological objectification; he is someone whose utterances are to be treated only as symptoms of something else, of insanity, depravity, and the like. Usually, ideological excommunication is connected with the material sanctions of expulsion, confinement, or death. (Therborn 1982, pp. 82–83)

In the light of these remarks, it is pertinent to recall that in the long narrative of *The Public Burning*, we only "hear" the Rosenbergs' political views (i.e., *their* version of their political views) in two brief "Intermezzos." One of them, "The Clemency Appeals," is subtitled "A Dramatic Dialogue by Ethel Rosenberg and Dwight Eisenhower," only there is no dialogue; as Coover's stage directions indicate, "At no time during the dialogue does the PRESIDENT address the PRISONER, or even acknowledge her presence on the same stage" (PB p. 307). Denounced as traitors, the fate of the Rosenbergs is ideological excommunication culminating in death.

Natives/Aliens

The American obsession with national identity is evidenced in numerous and well-known patriotic societies whose membership, in some instances, has at times run in the millions. Members take a pride in their being of "native stock"; they claim status by virtue of descent from, typically, Anglo-Saxon-Protestant-rural backgrounds. These societies vary in their political complexion from the genteel patriotism of the DAR (Daughters of the American Revolution) to the virulent racism of the Ku Klux Klan.

Large-scale immigration (approximately 24 million people emigrated to the United States between 1880 and 1920) was a powerful stimulus to the growth of chauvinist feeling. Those of old-American ancestry have cast doubt on the loyalty and patriotism of the immigrants and their descendants, questioned their "Americanism." (Coover's Nixon reflects: "Well, a Jew, a Catholic—maybe they lacked certain defenses, being spiritual outsiders, not quite true full-blooded Americans." [PB p. 42].) Immigrants have been seen as unassimilable Old Worlders, in general identified as alien. Such suspicion and hostility reflect a perceived loss, by those of "native stock," of cultural and political hegemony; they reflect a sense of dispossession on the part of those whose pioneering ancestors "settled" the country.

In Chapter 14, "High Noon," Fred Zinnemann's classic western (1952) is used to provide a parodic frame of reference for exploring this native/alien dimension of nationalist consciousness. Thus (native) Eisenhower, the "blue-eyed Westerner" (PB p. 298), is cast in Gary Cooper's role as the law-loving marshal, determined that justice be meted out to the "A-bomb rustlers" (PB p. 295). And the outlaws he must confront are the members of the (alien) Rosenberg Defense Committee, who are predominantly of Jewish-East European descent and who are identified with the "threat of . . . swarthiness" (PB p. 295). The Supreme Court has voted to vacate the stay of the Rosenbergs' execution, and the Defense Committee is petitioning the President for clemency. So now "It's all up to Ike" (PB p. 298). The crowds have gathered on the White House lawn, anxious lest the President cannot stand his ground at the final showdown. They seem to hear:

the clickety-clack of train wheels, galloping hooves—yes, it's as though the frontier is doubling back on the center, bringing wildness and danger, the threat and tumult of the wide open spaces [. . .] As they shuffle about under the White House balcony, they feel like they're [. . .] joining up with Roy Rogers's posse in *Bells of Rosarita,* [. . .] riding *The Big Trail* with John Wayne. (PB p. 297)

And as the clocks tick toward noon, when the President will announce his decision on the clemency appeal, "The crowd shifts about uneasily, like a movie audience deep in the third reel" (PB p. 300). That third reel is deep in the American psyche; the motifs of the western, the novel suggests, supply significant forms of intelligibility to the American consciousness. In particular, Coover reveals how the western has entered nationalist mythology as a discourse that signifies the ideal American and an authentic and natural American way of life. Thus we read of "Ike (Swede) Eisenhower" (PB p. 295):

The President [. . .] is a gunslinger, a tall, handsome, blue-eyed Westerner who looks a lot like Bill Boyd. Harry Carey. Randolph Scott in *The Frontier Marshall* [. . .] He is the Man Who Won the War, but he is also a man of the people, born and reared on the lonesome prairie, a man who knows what it's like to sleep out under the stars, listening to the howling of coyotes and the lowing of little dogies, a man who can ride and shoot and use his fists, a man who's walked through acres of dead men and kept his chin up to fight another day. (PB p. 298)

The pastoral vision of life in the Old West—open, spacious, whole-some—has its antithesis in the popular idea of the immigrant ghetto—urban, squalid, a breeding-ground for subversives:

the ghettos of the nation's cities [. . .] where the unassimilated live, speaking alien tongues, eating weird shit, their seed still frothy with unhomogenized Old World discontents; 90 per cent of all Commies in this country, as every G-man knows, are foreign-born or were dropped by foreign-born parents. (PB p. 28)

In short, Coover shows how the western, with its images of the out-doors, open country, plain living, self-reliance, and toughness, encodes the myth of a quintessentially American/"native" way of life.

Fifth Column

Nationalist discourses are not simply affirmative; they have a nega-tional side too. The discourse of "America" not only proclaims those ideals and practices which are held to be authentically American; it publicly negates those which are perceived as anti-American or, recall-ing the HUAC, as "un-American." The negational side of this dis-course is represented by key terms like "treason," "subversion," or "conspiracy," which embody myths of vulnerability—vulnerability to an "enemy within" (PB p. 25) or to attack from an external enemy (PB p. 34). It is in these terms, calculated to appeal to nationalist feeling, that the belligerent policies of an administration are legitimized; they are a means of securing the support of the public for repressive and unpopular measures. To be sure, the political expediency that gave rise to notions of vulnerability during the McCarthy era is, for reasons given later, scarcely examined in *The Public Burning*. Suffice to say here, most of the narrative has a willfully limited focus, that is, the para-noid/chauvinist mind-set of the American public of the 1950s, between one third and one half of which expressed approval of Senator McCar-thy's witch-hunt (Hofstadter 1967, p. 70n.).

Senator Joe McCarthy is introduced into the novel by extracts from his inflammatory speeches in which he spoke of " 'card-carrying Com-munists in the State Department' " and " 'A conspiracy so immense and an infamy so black as to dwarf any previous such venture in the history of man!' " (PB p. 27). Nixon, who continually vied with McCarthy for the prestige of being America's number one communist-hunter, also fueled public fears of communist subversion, insisting that " 'For the first time in American history, the security of the nation was directly and imminently threatened!' " (PB p. 587). In this climate of paranoia almost anyone was vulnerable to the charge of treachery, from New Dealers Henry Wallace (PB p. 26) and Alger Hiss to "Secretary of State

Dean Acheson [who] *might* be working for Stalin himself!" (PB p. 27). Yet, the majority of those under suspicion, like union activists or liberal intellectuals, were in fact patriotic. Most dissidents "lived" within the mythos of the discourse of "America." The Communist Party, which, by the early 1950s, had declined to around 30,000 members (Caute 1978, p. 185), could hardly be counted a threat. Nevertheless, the belief (sincere or feigned) in the existence of a deadly conspiracy against the nation worked to silence criticism of the social system and compelled dissidents, on pain of victimization (e.g., sacking, litigation, deportation), to demonstrate their patriotism.

In the late 1940s, early 1950s, it seemed to millions of Americans that a fifth column of spies, saboteurs, and subversives was operating in their midst, preparing "dangerous well-oiled schemes" for "socializing America" (PB p. 486) or smoothing the way for a Soviet invasion. Politicians (especially Republicans who were seeking a return to office on the anti-communist ticket), the FBI and CIA, churchmen, and the mass media (notably, the right-wing Hearst and Scripps-Howard press) whipped the public into a frenzy of panic and bred fear and suspicion with allegations of communist plots at home and abroad.[14] There may well have been a number of "Commiecrats" working in the State Department but, as David Caute has stressed in *The Great Fear,* his exhaustive study of the anti-Communist purge:

There is no documentation in the public record of a direct connection between the American Communist Party and espionage during the entire postwar period. Even during the Korean war, no evidence of Communist sabotage or attempted sabotage came to light. (Caute 1978, p. 54)

Nevertheless, popular fears of a vast clandestine network of traitors took root. The communist was typified as an insidious adversary, ubiquitous but always operating under cover, spreading a contagious ideology. Coover quotes J. Edgar Hoover: "'Whether you know it or not, your child is a target. His mind is the fertile plot in which the Communist hopes to implant his Red virus and to secure a deadly culture which will spread to others'" (PB pp. 134–35).

One of Coover's strategies for confronting the collective delusion of a colossal plot to destroy America is his use of the word "Phantom" as a generic term for the agents and ideology of communism.[15] It is a term which suggests both the flimsy basis for, and the mythical nature of, the belief in such a plot. First, "Phantom" may connote that which is shadowlike, without substance, and yet taken for real; phantoms, however illusory, have the power to haunt the mind. The term is synonymous with phantasm and figment. For these reasons, it is an appropriate appellation for the forces of a plot that has no basis in reality.

Significantly, the Phantom is referred to as that which is not solid: "The ungraspable Phantom. He was made of nothing solid, your hand would just slip right through " (PB p. 338). Second, just as Uncle Sam is personified as a comic-book "Superhero" with prodigious powers, so the personification of communism as "The Phantom" evokes the image of a comic-book arch-villain: the maniac or trickster that a Batman or Wonder Woman might have to deal with; the master of disguise (PB p. 24); the criminal mastermind who takes a sadistic pleasure in engineering disasters (PB pp. 412–13), in wanton terror (PB pp. 136–37). By figuring communism in comic-strip idiom, Coover exposes the lurid strain of fantasy in the American perception of communism as a baleful conspiracy. There is the further suggestion that comic books, avidly read by millions of Americans, have usurped their reality to the extent that political conflict can only be grasped in the simplified terms of the comic.

Armageddon/Millennium

> "The untransacted destiny of the American people is to establish a new order in human affairs, to confirm the destiny of the human race, and to pull that switch and shed a new and resplendent glory upon mankind!"
>
> (PB p. 608)

The switch to which Uncle Sam ostensibly refers is the one on the Times Square stage that will electrocute the Rosenbergs, but the visionary language evokes another frame of reference—Armageddon theory. "Pulling the switch" at a time when "Atomic Power [has] come of age" (PB p. 19) is shorthand for the gesture that will precipitate a holocaust. Yet, for believers in Armageddon, the fire/light of the holocaust ("resplendent glory") is also a sign of redemption for mankind. As the moment of the executions draws near, Armageddon theory is also on Nixon's mind:

Had Uncle Sam not announced, long ago, an uproarious tumult, a time of tribulation but a redemption which shall last forever? Was this more than a mere symbolic expiation? Were the Rosenbergs in fact the very trigger—living, high-explosive lenses, as it were—for the ultimate holocaust? (PB p. 415)

At the heart of Armageddon theory is a fundamentalist eschatology according to which salvation will be preceded by the devastation of the ultimate war. Coover cites a celebrated exponent of this doctrine:

The American Prophet S.D. Baldwin summed it up in a nutshell in the title of his 1854 classic: Armageddon: or the Overthrow of Romanism and Monarchy;

the Existence of the United States Foretold in the Bible, Its Future Greatness; Invasion by Allied Europe; Annihilation of Monarchy; Expansion into the Millennial Republic, and Its Dominion over the Whole World. (PB p. 18)

Today, Armageddon theory is proclaimed by America's Christian fundamentalists, with the difference that communism has replaced Romanism and monarchy as a principal agency of the Antichrist. Pat Robertson, the reverend who, in 1987, sought the Republican nomination for the presidency, prophesied Armageddon on his Christian Broadcasting Network. (His TV program, "700 Club," reaches an estimated 30 million households—White, M., 1987.) Apparently, it will come to pass, as the Books of Ezekiel and Revelation foretell, that Russia will invade Israel and be driven out by Ten Nations. A holocaust will then follow, and the Christian millennium will supersede the dominion of the Antichrist (Schwartz 1987). In a recent book of essays, *Armageddon?*, Gore Vidal cites a Yankelovich poll (1984) which found that 39 percent of Americans (Ronald Reagan among them) believe in Armageddon theory (Vidal 1987, p. 104).

Postwar America's obsession with the idea of Armageddon is probably best understood in the context of cold war ideology and propaganda. The American public believed stories concocted by the press, the CIA, and other agencies (cf. note 14, Chap. 4) that war with the Soviet Union was inevitable. A missile attack by the U.S.S.R. was thought to be imminent. Coover quotes extracts from the *New York Times* and *Time* magazine, published when the First Cold War seemed about to turn hot: "A *New York Times* headline announces: DANGER OF ATOM BOMB ATTACK IS GREATEST IN THE PERIOD UP TO THIS FALL!" (PB p. 34); *Time* magazine, "forecasting the imminent advent of the Third World War" (PB p. 399), had warned, " 'The Soviet Empire will continue to expand unless it is opposed with all our strength and that includes the steady, calm and constant acceptance of the risk of all-out War' " (PB p. 398). This was the era when school children were drilled in how to behave in the event of a sudden A-bomb attack, when "This Home is Prepared" stickers were displayed on front doors.

In the blackout which occurs in Times Square minutes before the Rosenbergs are due to be executed, and which coincides with Uncle Sam's sudden departure, the crowd is alarmed by a sense of impending apocalypse:

terror rips through the hooded Square like black wildfire, a seething conflagration of anti-light, enucleating the body politic [. . .]
"IT'S THE END OF THE WORLD!"
"UNCLE SAM IS DEAD!"
"WHO CAN SAVE US NOW?" (PB p. 595)

In the dark, panic spreads:

"OH LORD, THEY'RE ALL AROUND US!"
"COMANCHES!"
"I CAIN'T HOLD ON!"
"REDCOATS!"
"THEY'RE BURNING WASHINGTON!" [...]
"WE'LL ALL BE KILLT!"
"EEEEYAA-AA-AHH!" (PB pp. 598–99)

The picture of alarm and confusion parodies the panic scenes of the science-fiction horror film, a genre especially popular in the McCarthy era. Among the standard scenarios of this genre were A-bomb attacks on America, as in *Invasion USA* (1952), cities attacked by post-atomic mutants, as in *Them!* (1953), or Earth itself invaded by aliens from outer space, as in *The War of the Worlds* (1953). And when Uncle Sam returns with the illuminating "spark from the sacred flame" (PB p. 603) we read:

Yes! the sun hasn't set after all! Nothing has really happened, *they're still okay!* It's like coming out of a scary movie—nothing but camera tricks, the illusory marvels and disasters of Cinerama and 3-D, th-th-that's all, f-folks! Lights up and laugh! (PB p. 607)

The passage recalls an earlier episode in the novel where a man has just seen the 3-D movie *House of Wax* (1953). He leaves the Trans-Lux having forgotten to remove his 3-D glasses, thus "see[ing] everything through the eye-straining H-Polarizer haze of alcohol and iodine" (PB p. 351). He gets caught up in the crowd in Times Square and, through the distorting lenses of the glasses, experiences the confusion and excitement around him in the light of the film he has just seen. Crawling through the crowd, he recalls the catastrophic image of the blazing wax museum and:

it's all coming together—the stampeding masses, the creeping socialism and exploding waxworks, the tracks of history and time-lapse overviews—into the one image that has been pursuing him through all his sleepless nights, the billowing succubus he's been nurturing for nine months now, ever since the new hydrogen-bomb tests at Eniwetok: yes, the final spectacle, the one and only atomic holocaust, he's giving birth to it at last. (PB p. 354)

The chapter ends with the demented film-goer passing out under a tranquilizer thinking: "A misspent Friday, a curious episode on the way to Armageddon, nothing more" (PB p. 357).

Coover mocks the authority of Armageddon theory which, inflated by cold war propaganda, has assumed the generalized form of an apocalyptic sensibility. The distorted perceptions of a nation fed on images of impending doom are travestied in the figure of the film-goer wandering around Times Square in his 3-D glasses, the victim of illusions. Coover suggests that Armageddon theory has no more credibility than the plot of a "scary movie" and that, for many, the danger of superpower confrontation can only be grasped through the discourse of Hollywood films.

The Discourse of Social Cohesion

I have tried to identify the principal concepts in Coover's exposition of the discourse of "America." In particular, I have attended to how he reveals and unsettles the nationalist myths embedded in that discourse. An ingenious device for the presentation of those myths is the personification of the emblematic Uncle Sam. His speech radiates the nation's myths. Indeed, the distinctive feature by which we recognize him, and especially his authority, is his speech. He seems to have total command of the nation's idioms past and present: its regional dialects, its proverbs and colloquialisms. He is vox populi; he speaks the language of the nation's seers and sages, presidents and pioneers, heroes and Founding Fathers (or, put another way, their voices "leak through him" [PB p. 407]):

It seems like no one can hold back from celebrating the Poets and Prophets this morning, least of all the American Superhero, who speaks by custom with the grandeur of a nation of runesmiths, from Davy Crockett to Longfellow, the Carnegies and Cranes to Hank Williams and the Whittier Poets. (PB p. 214)

Uncle Sam is known as "The American Autolycus" whose "cunning powers of conjuration, transmutation and magical consumption" (PB p. 16) are not just confined to his tricks as a sharper but extend to his power over words. For example:

the electrical sign reading AMERICA THE JOKE OF THE WORLD begins once more to metamorphose, Uncle Sam accomplishing in three clean moves what it took the Phantom to do in sixteen dirty ones:
        AMERICA THE POKE OF THE WORLD
        AMERICA THE POPE OF THE WORLD
        AMERICA THE HOPE OF THE WORLD (PB p. 85)

In short, the Uncle Sam of *The Public Burning* is not just the Uncle Sam of the political cartoonist's imagination—the pugnacious, plug-hatted, striped-pantalooned figure who stands for America; on account of his prodigious powers of language, Coover's Uncle Sam is also the incarnation of the discourse of "America," specifically, the discourse of cold war America. He represents the way America understands herself, the way she understands her place and role in the world, her interests, her vulnerability. Such understanding is permeated by nationalist myths, and Coover's Uncle Sam functions conspicuously as the charismatic embodiment and tireless propagator of those myths. Hence his sudden flight from Times Square brings about not simply a blackout but "the nighttime of the people" (PB pp. 595, 596). With his departure, the nation is deprived, figuratively speaking, of its "vision." If we understand myth as an attempt to construct a coherent discourse about the world, the disappearance of myth, as symbolized by Uncle Sam's temporary absence, may be shown to result in a fragmentation of speech, an incoherence or babble (as exemplified by the confused exclamations of the crowd in Chapter 28) and, in consequence, a dissolution of the ideology which constitutes the nation's sense of reality, identity, and community:

People cry out to God, to Christ, Ike, Con Ed, the Pope, to anyone who might listen, who might help [. . .] In the nighttime of the people, everything is moving and there is nothing to grab hold of. The very pavements seem to dissolve into an undulating quagmire, vortical and treacherous. (PB pp. 595–96)

Panic ensues as the Times Square crowd loses what, elsewhere, Coover has referred to as the "mythic reinforcement of our tenuous grip on reality" (Coover 1970, p. 79).

At the end of the novel, Uncle Sam tells Nixon: " 'It ain't easy holdin' a community together, order ain't what comes natural [. . .] and a lotta people gotta get killt tryin' to pretend it is.' " (PB p. 649). The potent myths which animate the discourse of "America" play a crucial part in "holdin' [the] community together"; *qua* ideology, they function, to use Gramsci's term, as social "cement," as ratification of the "charter of the moral and social order" (PB pp. 117, 241). The projection of America as *the* nation of Freedom, Opportunity, Progress, and God promotes popular enthusiasm for and loyalty toward the social system. The discourse calls up nationalist identity, addressing all subjects first and foremost as "Americans" and thereby concealing class and ethnic divisions. It is a discourse of integration (though, needless to say, not all Americans are "recruited" by it). In America, where the mode of production is based on class division, the need to hold a community together is politically imperative. The apparatuses of the state often respond to this need by nurturing nationalist feeling with the aim of diminishing awareness of social divisions (Eisenhower accuses Communists of "seeking to promote [. . .] the deadliest divisions" [PB p. 193]) and fostering a spirit of patriotic solidarity, whereby subjects will give priority to national rather than factional interests.

Class division, expressed in the form of growing union activism and proliferating strikes, was at the root of domestic cold war politics.[16] "We have only two problems in America," said "Electric Charlie" Wilson in 1947, "labour at home and communism abroad" (Margolis 1986). To be sure, the issue of class division is not raised in *The Public Burning*. But this is not just because Coover's preoccupation with history-as-discourse displaces a reading of history (especially one as partisan as a class-based reading). Nor is it just because Coover writes as a liberal dissenter whose perception of politics excludes or, at least, marginalizes the class issue. Rather, it is primarily a question of the restricted viewpoint from which the events surrounding the execution of the Rosenbergs are narrated. Union activism was a feature of the late 1940s when the public could still distinguish between labor organizers, Communist Party members, and Soviet spies. But, by the early 1950s, as the McCarthyist paranoia reached fever pitch, the political issues had been simplified: now there were only loyal Americans and traitors. Class tensions were dampened by anticommunist hysteria and chauvinist fervor. Moreover, in the dangerous climate created by McCarthyism, the issue of class was not likely to be debated; communists, labor leaders, the Rosenbergs, and their supporters were inclined, for their own safety, to avoid raising such a "subversive" issue. Thus, for the time being, the reality of class struggle receded from public view. And the public view is the viewpoint of Coover's book; the text's narrative viewpoint is locked within the paranoid/chauvinist mind-set of the American public at the height of the First Cold War.

This restricted vision of the public is represented largely as an effect of the general structure of communications. There is simply no public sphere in Coover's cold war America, no forum for debating political issues. There are only vertical, one-way flows of information controlled by a virulently anticommunist press and the propaganda departments of the FBI and other state apparatuses. Mass-communication systems like the press are shown to amplify and repeat political messages to the point where meanings congeal into fixed, monolithic patterns. Furthermore, the restricted vision of the public is reflected in the narrow time span of the narrative—just three days in 1953, when the paranoia climaxed with the execution of the Rosenbergs. This strict temporal confinement suggests a popular consciousness devoid of historical perspective; for the crowds in the "Times Square" episodes, communism is the *eternal* enemy.

Coover also addresses the problem of "holdin' a community together," of maintaining social cohesion, by examining the practice of *contemporary* scapegoating.[17] Consider, first, this conclusion to a discussion of Sartre's views on scapegoating:

The doctrine of the scapegoat becomes necessary [. . .] in order to explain why the theoretically perfect society is not in fact perfect, and to avoid pressure for social change. Since the imperfections cannot be characteristic of the society, they must be due to elements which are in the society but essentially alien to it. Since these alien individuals are bad in their essential character, it is not necessary to establish their responsibility for any specific act. The elimination of these aliens will free the essentially perfect society of its only contamination. (Waterhouse 1974, p. 27)

The discourse of "America" proclaims a "perfect society," that is, for example, a society graced by God or a free society. Yet the "pressure for social change" from disadvantaged groups reveals the presence of imperfections. The Establishment, in an endeavor to contain or head off the pressure for change and to maintain the image of a perfect society, ascribes the imperfections to "alien individuals [who] are bad in their essential character." And it is precisely in these terms that the Rosenbergs are understood in Coover's book. Thus Uncle Sam tells Nixon: " 'No, guilt, real guilt, is like grace: some people got it, some don't. These people [the Rosenbergs] got it. Down deep [. . .] They are suffused with the stuff, it's in their bones, their very acids.' " (PB p. 112). Hence "it is not necessary to establish their responsibility." The "essentially perfect society" must then be purged of "its only contamination" by the "elimination of these aliens." This is the objective of "Uncle Sam's purification-by-fire spectacular" (PB p. 555), of the "public exorcism" (PB p. 12) in Times Square. The Rosenbergs had to be sacrificed to maintain the illusion projected by the myths of the discourse of "America," that is, the illusion of community, of order, in short, the illusion of a perfect society. (Ironically, twenty years after the execution of the Rosenbergs, the Watergate affair turned Nixon into a scapegoat. In order to save the honor of America's political institutions, evil had to be shown to reside in Nixon, not in the system. The result was a spectacular exorcism of the body politic: in the glare of the world's media, Nixon was ceremoniously banished from office as proof to everyone that the system had been purged of a contaminating influence and thus restored to its original state of purity.)

Finally, Coover exposes nationalism as a grotesque secular religion replete with rituals, incantations, iconographies (all especially evident in the "Sam Slick Show," [PB pp. 510–26]). It is a perceptive analysis of an important dimension of nationalism but an incomplete one. What remains to be said is that, in spite of its mystifications, nationalism also embodies an element of truth. That truth is to be found in its expression of human solidarity, albeit a displaced solidarity, a false substitute for the collective praxis that could transform society. And, accordingly, it becomes evident that nationalism can work as a discourse of social cohesion, as a medium of integration, precisely because it exploits the popular need for an *authentic* mode of cohesiveness.

Deconstructing Ruling Histories

Crucial elements of the discourse of "America" have been defined vis-à-vis narratives about America's historical situation. Broadly speaking, two interrelated narratives can be identified. There is the "paranoid" narrative—the perceived threat to the nation posed by communism at home and abroad. This provides the foundation for some of the concepts of the discourse ("Fifth Column," "Natives/Aliens," and "Armageddon"). And there is the "chauvinist" narrative—America's emergence as a superpower seen as confirmation of her destiny to play the leading role on the stage of world history. Hence the relevance of other concepts of the discourse ("Providence," "Manifest Destiny," "Novus Ordo Seclorum," "Material Progress," and "Millennium"). If we take a broad clinical view of paranoia, perhaps the narratives may be seen as different sides of the same coin: delusions of persecution (Communist malevolence toward America) alternating with delusions of grandeur (America as the millennial Republic).

Coover highlights the role of some of America's dominant institutions—for example, the press, the legal system, the FBI, the Republican Party—in the elaboration and propagation of these historical narratives. Aware of the power of some institutions to fabricate histories, Coover's deconstructive technique is to present institutional histories in terms which exaggerate their factitiousness. First, there is the American press. Chapters 10 and 18 are extended reflections on the narrative powers of the *New York Times* and *Time* magazine, respectively. *Time,* personified as "The National Poet Laureate" (PB p. 395), is characterized by his bold constructions of history, for example, "his dream of 'The American Century'" premised on his "accept[ing] the thrust of destiny," and "his vision of perpetual war" premised on his belief that "The Soviet Empire will continue to expand" (PB pp. 397–98). But note Coover's terminology: "dream," "vision"—*Time* is, after all, a "poet." Thus Coover suggests the fabulative status of *Time's* pronouncements. In respect of the *New York Times* we read:

In the old days, before *The New York Times,* if you wished to destroy a man, you inscribed his name on a pot and smashed it [. . .] Now you attach his name to a sin and print it. Such an act is beyond mere insult or information, *it is a magical disturbance of History* [. . .] Is Alger Hiss a Communist? Is Joe McCarthy a Fascist? Is Justice Douglas a Traitor? [. . .] *What matters is: where are such questions being asked?* (PB p. 245. My emphases)

The authority or truth of a statement, we are reminded, is but a function of the apparatus which enunciates it.[18]

The FBI is revealed as another institution with the power to manufacture history. In extensive sections of Chapters 7 and 21, Nixon describes the fraudulent operations of the FBI ("hell, the FBI has a special section which does nothing but produce fake documents" [PB p. 156]), particularly its role in forging evidence against the Rosenbergs. There are suggestions that its chief, J. Edgar Hoover, *invented* the idea of a spy ring: "Hoover was in many ways a complete loony, arbitrary in his power and pampered like a Caesar, and if he dreamed up a spy ring one day, then by God it *existed*" (PB p. 456). Hoover's famous statement on the Rosenbergs' alleged espionage is quoted so as to sound like a trite piece of detective fiction: "The Crime of the Century, by J. Edgar Hoover" (PB p. 166). Yet, at the same time, the FBI is depicted as a publicly revered and admired institution, its pronouncements received as the literal truth:

Saypol hinted that there was a lot of FBI material he wasn't free to use because of these continuing investigations [. . . But if he] held up a handful of FBI documents and told them [the jury] to imagine Julius Rosenberg "reaching out like the tentacles of an octopus," then an octopus is what everyone willingly saw, surprised only that it had a moustache and wore double-breasted suits. (PB p. 454)

The legal system is a third institution whose power to construct history is explored by the novel. The courts played an active role in propagating and "proving" the theory that Communists at home had plotted against the United States. For example, Coover quotes Irving Kaufman, the judge presiding over the trial of the Rosenbergs, who in passing sentence spoke of a " 'diabolical conspiracy to destroy a God-fearing nation [. . .] By your betrayal *you undoubtedly have altered the course of history* to the disadvantage of our country!' " (PB p. 37). But the trial of the Rosenbergs, as Coover gives ex-lawyer Nixon to understand and emphasize, was pure theater. Observing how Kaufman persistently biased his judgments in favor of the prosecution (PB pp. 150–51), Nixon comments:

He was like the director of a play who knows how to boost his actors' egos and give them a sense of participation in the staging and interpretation, while in fact pulling all the strings—a fantastically smooth performance, Bloch [the Rosenbergs' defense counsel] himself had to applaud it at the end.
    Applause, director, actors, script: yes, it was like—and this thought hit me now like a revelation—*it was like a little morality play for our generation!* [. . .] in order that my generation might witness in dramatic form the fundamental controversy of our time! (PB pp. 151–52)

Then Nixon turns his thoughts to Irving Saypol, the Prosecuting Attorney who had once remarked, " 'A well-turned case is just like a stage play really' " (PB p. 153): "Saypol [could] make what might later seem like nothing more than a series of overlapping fictions cohere into a convincing semblance of historical continuity and logical truth" (PB p. 154).

In addition to the press, the FBI, and the legal system, other institutions shown to be implicated in the construction of paranoid and chauvinist accounts of American history are the Republican Party and the entertainment industry. And in most instances, Coover employs literary and theatrical metaphors to suggest the fabricated character of the histories which are produced/reproduced by these institutions.

To speak of a "fabricated" history is not to imply that the functionaries of the above institutions cynically disbelieved in the histories they retailed; on the contrary, most judges and G-men, politicians, journalists, and others were probably sincere in their beliefs in a communist conspiracy and/or "The American Century." There is a revealing passage where, in the face of contradictory evidence, Nixon's belief in the Red Plot remains firm:

I could perceive a lot of backstage scene-rigging and testimony-shaping by the prosecuting team that deprived the courtroom performances of some of their authenticity and power, but there was no shaking off the basic conviction: the Rosenbergs were guilty as hell. (PB p. 105)

Nixon's acute ex-lawyer's perception of "scene-rigging" and "testimony-shaping" is overruled by a gut reaction—"guilty as hell"; evidence of framing cannot dislodge a "basic conviction" that has the force of instinct. The novel shows that such reactions or convictions are founded on factitious narratives, histories promulgated to the point where they are experienced as common sense, as obvious, as natural. Thus Nixon *qua* historian, trying to sort through the "facts" of the Rosenberg case, can be seen to inhabit a world already interpreted by a regime of nationalist discourses.

Coover's Nixon places a high premium on his skills as an orator and debater (PB p. 365): "I'm a rhetorician, not a general, and for me that's power" (PB p. 279). And he defines power in rhetorical-textual terms: "The essence of power is paradox and ambiguity" (PB p. 287). It is Nixon who grasps the possibilities of "explor[ing] the true power of the Word" (PB p. 172). The exploration of the power of the Word is what preoccupies Coover in *The Public Burning*. The book simultaneously shows off and interrogates the discourse which seized the public imagination, which fostered a demonology of international communism and elaborated fantasies of America's grandeur. Though written in the late 1960s–early 1970s (LeClair and McCaffery 1983, pp. 75–76), the novel that deconstructs the discourse of a superpower has an even greater claim to political relevance today, that is, at a time marked by the strident nationalism of a hegemonic New Right.

Linguistic Bondage

Spanking the Maid may be read as continuing a theme elaborated in *Pricksongs and Descants:* the need to transcend the exhausted genres in which the imagination is trapped. Jackson Cope proposes one such reading, where the literature of pornography serves as a model for the enervated genre. He finds in the narrative's high incidence of repetition—repeated phrases, recurring dreams, habitual beatings—a suggestion that the old formulas have been tried and tried again, an "allegory" about writing within the limits of genres. And, in conclusion, he says of the book:

> It is about the stunning simplicity with which one can, with the manual of generic prescription, proscription, with "method and habit," write oneself out of "communication" with an audience, with one's own text, with one's own self. (Cope 1986, pp. 57–58)

He points out the numerous references to "blank sheets" and "communication" and then offers a lively reading of this text as an (apolitical) commentary on the problems of writing fiction itself. In other words, Cope reads *Spanking the Maid* as an introverted postmodernist text; the kind of reading which, typically, does not address the way in which the book confronts the political dynamics of language. Yet this is a remarkable omission when one considers that a parody or critique of pornographic discourse in its specifically sadomasochistic form is surely evidence of a strategic choice, one calculated to raise the issue of power relations. But exactly what kind of power relations?

The punishment rituals in *Spanking the Maid* signify more than just eroticized power play. Rather, the rituals are made intelligible, first and foremost, in the context of an ideology that constructs subjects in a relation of domination. The acts of domination and submission encode and dramatize an ideology appropriate to a stratified and exploitative social order; an ideology whose key terms include "station," "deference," "obedience," "duty." This ideology forms the content of the sadomasochistic discourse—perhaps Coover's paradigm for other discourses founded on notions of superiority and obedience. And it is this content which Coover seeks to expose and contest. The ideology in question constructs the subjectivities of maid and master such that they find their identities (and gratification?) in obedience and submissiveness or in authority and domination.

"Every state and condition of life has its particular duties," he has taught her. "The duty of a servant is to be obedient, diligent, [. . .] submissive and respectful toward her master. She must be contented in her station, because it is necessary that some should be above others in this world, and it was the will of the Almighty to place you in a state of servitude." (Coover 1988, p. 34: Hereafter SM)

Parodied here are precisely the identities needed to integrate subjects into a system founded on social stratification and exploitation.

"Duty" and "service" are probably the most recurrent words in the text. Again and again, the lesson given by the master and recited by the maid is that an inward state of grace is achieved by "devotion to duty" and "service." Hard work is given a religious justification: the maid sets about her tasks as if she was "doing the will of God" (SM pp. 56, 91). This explains the archaic tone of much of the text that parodically uses the diction and syntax of those closely identified with the promotion of a pious and stringent work ethic—the Victorians and Puritans. Accordingly, verses by the Victorian hymnodist John Keble and the devotional poet George Herbert are frequently cited. The text quotes almost verbatim a stanza from Keble's "Morning": "The trivial round, the common task, [. . .] will furnish all she needs to ask, room to deny herself, a road [. . .] to bring her daily nearer God." (SM pp. 13, 46). And the maid repeatedly sings lines from Herbert's "The Elixir" (SM p. 100):

"Oh, teach me, my God and king, in all things thee to see, and what I do in anything, to do it as for thee [. . .] A servant with this clause makes drudgery divine: who sweeps a room as for thy laws, makes that and th'action fine!" (SM pp. 14, 24, 41, 55, etc.)

More than just a disciplinarian, the master functions principally as an ideologue, an instructor in the code of compliance and service. It is remarkable that on nearly every page of the text there is reference to learning, teaching, or instruction; to teachers, lessons, or lectures. Moreover, every beating is preceded or accompanied by a lecture on obedience or a recital of the master's teachings:

"When you are ordered to do anything, do not grumble or let your countenance betray any dislike thereunto, but do it cheerfully and generously!" "Yes, sir, but—" "What? WHAT—?!" Whish-*CRACK!* "OW!" SLASH! [. . .] "Be respectful—?" "Be respectful and obedient, sir, to those—" swish-*THWOCK!* "—placed—OW!—placed OVER you—AARGH!" (SM pp. 73–74, see also pp. 26, 68)

Clearly, the beatings are not coercive; the maid does not have to be forced to work. She works, we are told, because "she is driven by a sense of duty" (SM p. 21), because she *believes* that "true service (*he doesn't have to tell her!*) is perfect freedom" (SM pp. 18–19, 47, 83, my emphasis). That freedom is to be found in service is *obvious* to her and to the master. Moreover, to say that neither can recall the origins of their arrangement—"When, she wants to know [. . .] did all this really begin?" (SM p. 22); " . . . he wonders [. . .] when it all began" (SM pp. 30, 42)—is to suggest that their positions as subjects have always-already been produced by ideology as, respectively, subordinate and superordinate. In respect of the maid, it is not a question of complicity in this arrangement but rather a question of the "merciless invention of souls" (SM pp. 48, 34, 67), that is, of her subjectivity as an ideological construct. She recognizes herself in her master's service, in submission to his authority.[19] As for the master, far from being a free, self-determining agent, he "lives out" his relation to the maid and understands their situation always "according to the manuals" (SM p. 70) and "in terms of the manuals" (SM p. 51)—the manuals being the source of ideology. Here I would add that Coover's highly repetitive prose—clusters of sentences recited again and again—creates a tight verbal structure that suggests confinement within the narrow limits of the ideology which positions maid and master.

However, as the story progresses, there are hints that the subjectivity of master and maid is not entirely fixed by, cannot be wholly accounted for in terms of, ideology; it is as if the ideology of duty, obedience, and faithful service is (like an exhausted narrative) beginning to lose its hold, its efficacy:

He goes to gaze out into the garden, vaguely dissatisfied. The room is clean [. . .], the maid whipped, why isn't that enough? Is there something missing in the manuals? No, more likely, he has failed somehow to read them rightly. (SM p. 71)

The master would sooner admit his own fallibility than that of the manuals; acknowledgment of the latter would undermine his and the maid's rigidly ordered existence. Accordingly, as the gaps and ambiguities in the manuals become more evident, master and maid cleave more desperately to the stern disciplinary system sanctioned by the manuals. The maid seeks "the comforting whirr and smack of his rod" (SM p. 98), and feels "dread" at the prospect of dismissal (SM pp. 90–91). The master contrasts their ritualized, rule-governed world with the world of Nature:

Outside in the sleepy afternoon heat of the garden, the bees are humming, insects chattering, sounds [. . .] strangely alien to him, sounds of *natural confusion and disorder from a world without precept or invention.* (SM p. 71. My emphasis: See also SM p. 63)

Nature, then, is feared as an anarchic force, a chaos for want of the ordering power of man-made laws.[20] Yet, as the text repeatedly suggests, Nature is a figure for something else, namely, the disorderly impulses of the unconscious or psyche ("inner nature") and, in particular, of repressed sexuality. Hence the sexual undertones in matters relating to the garden: the garden teems with "birds and bees" (SM pp. 35, 55, 71, 83, etc.); "She screams. The garden groans, quivers, starts, its groves radiant and throbbing" (SM p. 101); and "She asked him [. . .] if he was afraid of the garden, whereupon he ripped her drawers down [. . .] and flogged her [. . .] mercilessly" (SM p. 89). The perceived danger, in other words, is repressed, unacknowledged "intentions" (SM p. 71), proscribed energies, which threaten at all times to erupt into consciousness. And, indeed, the ideology that binds the master and maid in a power relation that validates the beatings is punctured and subverted by an unconscious play of energies, which are, for the most part, expressed in the puns of dreams. The master—a caricature that fuses Victorian pedantry with Puritan piety to create an oppressive superego—reports dreams in which the key words of his discourse mutate into words that mock or negate the preceding meanings. Thus, "lectures" becomes "lechers" (SM p. 29), "order" becomes "odor" (SM p. 39), "utility" becomes "futility" (SM p. 11), "humility" becomes "humor" (SM p. 16), and so on. Elsewhere, the master's professed spiritual commitment to "some high purpose" (SM p. 24) is ironically undermined by what must be taken as an unconscious expression of desire: "Has he devoted himself to a higher end, he wonders [. . .] flexing a cane" (SM p. 78), where "higher end" suggests the maid's raised buttocks, bared for a beating.

These involuntary expressions, generated by the dynamics of the unconscious, and which seem to challenge or negate the accredited order of meaning, occur only sporadically, as it were in the margins of the text. For the most part, it is only the master's voice, speaking the ideology of the manuals, that we hear. The maid is bound to silence: "'You may speak when spoken to [. . .] unless it be to deliver a message or ask a necessary question'" (SM pp. 35–36, 52, 57). Then, in the closing section of the text (SM pp. 99–102), the language in which the ideology is inscribed, the language we recognize from the master's citations of the manuals, breaks up. The contradictions of a split subjectivity seem to erupt into language. Signifiers from the master's dreams and from earlier images of the garden collide with or displace signifiers from the (oft-repeated) maxims and precepts of the manuals, that is, the signifiers of the master-discourse:

for what she really wants is to [. . .] give him a lecture (she says "elixir") on method and fairies, two dew-bejeweled habits you can roast chestnuts over [. . .] Is she testing him, perched there on his stout engine of duty like a cooked bird with the lingering bucket of night in her beak (see how it opens, closes, opens), or is it only a dimpled fever of the mind? [. . .] "Something about a higher end," he explains hoarsely, taking rueful refuge, "or hired end perhaps. [. . .]" (SM pp. 100–101)

Accordingly, as the master-discourse disintegrates—its words re-inflected by the countervailing force of repressed or marginal signifiers—master and maid are displaced from the positions its ideology had assigned to them. It is a terrifying experience in which they feel abandoned to "that natural confusion and disorder" of a world devoid of the familiar ideological patterning, a condition thought of by the master as a "bottomless hole" (SM pp. 40, 66, 102). Yet, at the same time, it is a liberating experience, the dissolution of old identities. The closing words—"*Perhaps today then . . . at last!*'" (SM p. 102, Coover's italics)—may express hope. For a new space for subjectivity is opened up as the bonds of a repressive discourse come unraveled, as words are released from the meanings to which ideology had enthralled them.

Chapter 5
Thomas Pynchon

Temporal Communication

Bellow's *Herzog* inveighs against contemporary representations of humankind suffering "down in the mire of post-Renaissance, post-humanistic, post-Cartesian dissolution, next door to the void" (Bellow 1965, p. 99). And, later, he observes, "We must get it out of our heads that this is a doomed time, that we are waiting for the end [. . .] We love apocalypses too much, and florid extremism with its thrilling language. I've had all the monstrosity I want" (p. 324). Behind Herzog's words we hear Bellow's impatience with a body of fiction designated by some as "post-humanist" or "apocalyptic" (see Fiedler 1968, 1975; Hassan 1971; Sontag 1983). Pynchon's *V* (1963), published a year before *Herzog*, would, no doubt from Bellow's standpoint, be a target for Herzog's condemnation (although the principal bête noire here is probably Burroughs; cf. Tanner 1971, p. 298). However, Bellow's rejection of the post-humanistic strain in contemporary fiction appears to rest, in large part, on his faith in some essential humanity which, after Pascal, he calls the "heart" (hence *Herzog*).[1] But if, for Bellow, humanity is essential to Homo sapiens, for Pynchon it is a precarious cultural construct that, under certain historical conditions, may disappear. And *V* is, in the first instance, an examination of how a history of colonialism, consumerism, and reifying technologies impacts on the humanity of individuals precipitating (what Pynchon fears may be) a decline into an "inanimate" existence, "a falling-away from what is human" (Pynchon 1975, pp. 405, 321; hereafter *V*). Here I want to discuss how problems of language and communication are raised in the context of *V*'s pervasive theme, namely, the drift into a post-humanistic condition.

In "Mondaugen's Story" (Chapter 9), it is recounted how in German South-West Africa, in 1922, one Herr Foppl sets up a model community with the aim of recreating the adventurist, colonial spirit of '04—the days of the genocidal General von Trotha. The community, shut in a plantation house, is sealed off from time; it inhabits a past where historical details as minute as the "04" fashions in lipstick and mascara are followed. There is riotous partying day and night which, in the spirit of the von Trotha era, includes the torture and murder of native Hereros. This hermetic community, living in its own artificial time, may be seen as the analogue of a closed system of meaning. This is implied by the experience of Kurt Mondaugen, principal of the novel's voyeurs (*V* pp. 236, 256). By virtue of his radio equipment, he is the only member of Foppl's household with a link to the outside world (*V* 275). Shut away in a turret (another form of enclosure), he obsessively seeks meaning in the random sounds of atmospheric radio disturbances (*V* pp. 230, 246). Eventually, the "spherics" are decoded as "The world is all that the case is" (*V* p. 278). This is the famous first line of Wittgenstein's *Tractatus* where, loosely speaking, "the case" is the world as given by the logical limits of language.[2] And the irony of this "message" is that, far from amounting to contact with the outside world, it suggests the enclosure of Foppl's community in its own "case," that is, within the claustral limits of a nostalgic-romantic conception of colonial history. Moreover, the *Tractatus,* insofar as it identifies metaphysical and ethical statements as nonsensical (on the grounds that their truth or falsity is not empirically testable), is an eminently temporal philosophy, that is to say, one which rules out the legitimacy of any transcendent perspective. Thus, Pynchon's allusion to this text points up the silence surrounding a *Fasching* of colonial murder; a moral language cannot be spoken because the realm of the intelligible is limited to a voyeuristic, empirical world of the visible—of skin, surfaces, and historical spectacle (e.g., '04 period costume and cosmetics). Note, for instance, the extreme conditionality of this description of Mondaugen's moral response to a massacre of innocent Hereros: " . . . he was starting to feel those first tentative glandular pressures that one day develop into moral outrage" (*V* p. 277).

The book's poet, Fausto Maijstral, observes: "To have humanism we must first be convinced of our humanity. As we move further into decadence this becomes more difficult" (*V* p. 322). It is difficult to be convinced of our humanity in the face of prestigious discourses that explain human beings without reference to humanity. For example, Benny Profane, drifter and schlemiel, finds work in a laboratory that uses "synthetic human objects" on which to test the effects of radiation. What disturbs Profane is that these "objects" precisely reflect how the prevailing sciences understand human beings:

In the nineteenth century, with Newtonian physics pretty well assimilated and a lot of work in thermodynamics going on, man was looked on more as a heat-engine, about 40 per cent efficient. Now in the twentieth century, with nuclear and subatomic physics a going thing, man had become something which absorbs x-rays, gamma rays and neutrons. (*V* p. 284)

Written during the consumer boom of the Kennedy years, *V* reveals a society where the space of personal meaning has been largely occupied by the signifying power of commodities. Marcuse, also writing at this time, famously observed: "The people recognize themselves in their commodities; they find their soul in their automobile, hi-fi set, split-level home, kitchen equipment" (Marcuse 1966, p. 9). *V* has many characters who understand themselves first and foremost in relation to their commodities. It is a relationship that disturbs Benny Profane: "Love for an object, this was new to him" (*V* p. 23). And in a passage which parodies such love he overhears his girlfriend talking to her MG: "'You beautiful stud [. . .], I love to touch you [. . .] Do you know what I feel when we're out on the road? Alone, just us? [. . .] Your funny responses, darling, that I know so well . . .'" (*V* p. 28). Furthermore, there is the reifying logic of the commodity which may, *inter alia,* be expressed through the extension of its aesthetics of styling and packaging from the product to the consumer. Thus, one woman— adorned with the accoutrements of high fashion, "expressionless, poised like one of her own mannequins"—invites the observation: "Who knew her 'soul' [. . .] It was her clothes, her accessories, which determined her" (*V* pp. 400, 401). The fetishistic sexuality which this chapter explores (*V* pp. 401–4) seems particularly appropriate to an era of hyperconsumption when an obsessive pursuit of, and attachment to, commodities has become the principal source of meaning. It is a state of affairs that prompts one character to say, "'we foist off the humanity we have lost on inanimate objects '" (*V* p. 405). This fetishism is a mark of "decadence" (*V* pp. 321, 405), of the drift into a cultural void whose landscape in *V* is "the Street": "The street of the 20th Century, at whose far end or turning—we hope—is some sense of home or safety" (*V* pp. 323–24). The street is the temporal world of consumer traffic through which Benny Profane and other *déracinés* wander seeking an exit: "Streets had taught him nothing [. . .] He walked; walked, he thought sometimes, the aisles of a bright, gigantic supermarket, his only function to want" (*V* pp. 36–37). Even Profane feels the pressure of consumerism's claim on his identity.

Benny's surname—"Profane"—implies the condition of being mired in the temporal world, the world which he has come to think of as "a single abstracted Street" (*V* p. 10). A crucial sign of this temporality is the condition of language, the prevalence of a profane mode of communication. Thus we read of Profane "who knew that one wrong word would put him closer than he cared to be to street level, and whose vocabulary it seemed was made up of nothing but wrong words" (*V* p. 137). The "wrong words" are those which limit mental horizons to street level, which cut the mind off from any transcendent or spiritual understanding. Therefore, Profane and others yearn for the "gift of tongues" (*V* pp. 122, 461, 472, 92); it is a wish for communication that transcends the temporal order. For example, as Profane points a gun at an alligator trapped in the New York sewers—an alligator which he is under orders to kill, we read: "He waited. He was waiting for something to happen. Something otherworldly, of course. He was sentimental and superstitious. Surely the alligator would receive the gift of tongues" (*V* p. 122). The experience of glossolalia or speaking with tongues is described in Acts of the Apostles 2:2–13. On Pentecost, when the disciples had gathered in a house "a sound came from heaven like the rush of a mighty wind [. . .] And they were all filled with the Holy Spirit and began to speak in other tongues, as the Spirit gave them utterance." Moreover, although all those speaking are Galileans, a cosmopolitan mix of onlookers are amazed "because each one heard them [the disciples] speaking in his [the onlooker's] own native language."[3] This, then, is an account of an ecstatic and, it seems, telepathic mode of communication in which those who speak are possessed by an inexpressible, numinous power. The gift of tongues may, indeed, be an "otherworldly" phenomenon, the longing for it "sentimental and superstitious." Nevertheless, as an ideal, this mode of communication serves Pynchon as a standard against which to critique the debased language forms of this world.

A distinctive feature of Profane's motley circle of friends—sailors, dropouts, failed artists and others—is their run-down "temporal" mode of communication. Rachel Owlglass, whose most intimate relationship is with her MG (*V* pp. 28–29), talks to Profane in "nothing but MG-words, inanimate-words he couldn't really talk back at" (*V* p. 27). This idea of a language whose reified ("inanimate") condition precludes response is also conveyed in a comic description of an artist called Slab who "refer[s] to himself as a Catatonic Expressionist and his work as 'the ultimate in non-communication'" (*V* p. 56). Slab, moreover, is a member of a rollicking set of artists known as "The Whole Sick Crew" whose "Conversations [. . .] had become little more than proper nouns, literary allusions, critical or philosophical terms linked in certain ways" (*V* p. 297). These terms, we are told, may be combined and recombined in many novel ways but, without fresh and spirited inputs of meaning, the Crew's discourse, like any closed system, will become subject to the law of entropy. And the exhaustion of all meaning-systems amounts to the expiration of human culture.

The "paranoid," patterning intelligence that organizes discrete and randomly occurring phenomena into global narratives may be valued as a negentropic force, as the generator of meaning in a culture suffering from a deficit of meaning. From his accidental encounters with V-signs in the context of political crises and disasters—for example, a tourist called Victoria in the proximity of Fashoda; Valletta as a center of riots in Malta—Herbert Stencil postulates the existence of a figure called "V," the agent, he believes, of a worldwide conspiracy of dehumanization—"the ultimate Plot Which Has No Name" (*V* p. 226). Hence, Stencil projects a "V-structure" onto history, a construct that lends his existence purpose and identity as "He Who Looks for V" (*V* p. 226), and without which he would simply lapse into a state of "half-consciousness" or "sleep" (*V* pp. 55, 346). (We might say the V-sign serves as a metonym for signs and languages in general which may be experienced as either pregnant with meaning or devoid of it.) However, although Stencil's paranoid projection may work to compensate for the near-exhaustion of meaning in a decaying culture, it is no substitute for the gift of tongues, for the desired epiphanies. For Pynchon reveals Stencil's patterning as an essentially fictionalizing activity, presenting him as a surrogate novelist who weaves dispersed incidents into a Big Story: "Stencil caught up in a compulsive yarning. [. . . He left] pieces of himself—and V—all over the western world. V by this time was a remarkably scattered concept" (*V* pp. 388–89). Moreover, it may be that the paranoid *grands récits* which informed McCarthyism and Stalinism in the years immediately preceding the writing of *V* inspired not only the scale of Stencil's fantasy—"the century's master cabal" or "the ultimate Plot" (*V* p. 226)—but also the desire to deconstruct it, presumably on the grounds that totalitarian politics often find their legitimation in totalizing narratives.

In one of the book's most remarkable passages, Pynchon vividly illustrates how language in a temporal, entropic condition necessarily issues in an impoverished, superficial image of the world. The narrator comments on:

a world if not created then at least described to its fullest by Karl Baedeker of Leipzig. This is a curious country, populated only by a breed called "tourists." Its landscape is one of inanimate monuments and buildings; near-inanimate barmen, taxi-drivers, bellhops, guides [. . .] More than this it is two-dimensional, as is the Street, as are the pages and maps of those little red handbooks [. . .] War never becomes more serious than a scuffle with a pickpocket [. . .]; depression and prosperity are reflected only in the rate of exchange; politics are of course never discussed with the native population. Tourism thus is supranational, like the Catholic Church, and perhaps the most absolute communion we know on earth: for be its members American, German, Italian, whatever, the Tour Eiffel, Pyramids, and Campanile all evoke identical responses from them; their Bible is clearly written and does not admit of private interpretation [. . .] They are the Street's own. (*V* pp. 408–9)

The Baedeker guide projects a two-dimensional image of the world. Landscapes are just the space around monuments, the native population just local color. Baedeker discourse positions the tourist as nothing more than a spectator of the (ahistorical) "picturesque." "Politics" is only what inconveniences the tourist or else is generally understood without reference to the viewpoint and interests of the natives. Baedeker discourse, then, is distinctively temporal: it shuts out the transcendent or critical perspectives which could enlighten the traveler. It is a discourse invested with the authority of a church—maintaining a churchlike monopoly of interpretation—but one which presides over "profane" subjects: a communion of the unilluminated.

Finally, in an era of temporal discourse, the quest theme in fiction becomes susceptible to parody; at least, that is, the type of quest whose goal is knowledge or illumination, as in the detective story or *Bildungsroman*. Such a narrative, often figured in the form of a journey, is essentially a search for philosophical insight, knowledge of a situation, or self-understanding and, typically, the protagonist will find an answer or arrive at some truth (even if only in the form of a disillusionment.) In *V*, however, in a characteristically self-reflexive gesture, we are informed that "There are no epiphanies, no 'moments of truth' " (*V* p. 330, repeated on p. 337). Accordingly, the last words of Benny Profane are, " 'offhand I'd say I haven't learned a goddamn thing' " (*V* p. 454). And the last we hear of Stencil is that his search for V goes on, as he heads for Stockholm following "the frayed end of another clue" (*V* pp. 451–52). In short, Pynchon's anti-quest formally signifies the impossibility of enlightenment or intellectual growth in a culture characterized by a deficit of meaning.

Communication and Community

The possibility of an alternative cultural order supplanting America's late-capitalist system is a question which haunts *The Crying of Lot 49* (1966). This cultural order is represented by the "Tristero System" which is, or is imagined to be, an underground communications network used by those alienated from the official culture. The latter are thought of by Oedipa Maas, the novel's mediating consciousness, as a community of internal exiles—marginals, drifters, deviants, visionaries—who may be "truly communicating" (Pynchon 1976, p. 128, hereafter CL) in terms of an order of meaning which is *radically discontinuous* from the hegemonic one. The Tristero System is understood not simply as an oppositional or confrontational force; it is, for Oedipa, among other possibilities, an *alternative* mode of communication whose emergence into mainstream life is conditional upon the dissolution of America's capitalist order. It is idealized by her as a promise of "revelation," another universe of meaning waiting to supersede America's ruling ideologies. She hopes for the time, though she also fears it may be a time of reckoning, when a mode of communication will restore meaning to a society perceived to be in the grip of cultural entropy. The acronym "D.E.A.T.H." (CL p. 90), which Oedipa interprets as a sign of the Tristero, suggests that some form of apocalypse or annihilation may be the price to pay for the institution of a redemptive order of meaning. "There is nothing to do/For our liberation, except *wait* in the horror of it," wrote John Ashbery in 1962 ("They Dream Only of America," Ashbery 1971, p. 23). That ominous mood of waiting pervades *Lot 49:* "Tristero [. . .], if it existed, in its twilight, its aloofness, its waiting. The waiting above all" (CL p. 136). Oedipa imagines the disenfranchised Tristero communicants, those condemned to communicate in secret, *in silence,* waiting for Another America in which they can find a voice. (Another acronym, "W.A.S.T.E." signifies "We Await Silent Tristero's Empire" [CL p. 127].) One character remarks to Oedipa: "'You know what a miracle is [. . .] another world's intrusion into this one'" (CL p. 88).[4] In *Lot 49,* "this world" is a culturally debased late-capitalist society from which a mass of its people are alienated. Yet, in their alienation resides the subversive potential to reverse society's entropic course by transforming the latent or fantasized existence of Tristero's dominion into actuality. That dominion is the intrusive "other world," a new world struggling to be born.

Pynchon's interest in the question of those alienated from and excluded by the social system has as its likely source the countercultural milieu that developed during the Kennedy/Johnson years, when New Left dissident movements rallied under the banner of "Participatory Democracy." The hope was to transform the reputedly "representative" institutions of a bureaucratic, mass society through the development of direct, decentralized, and democratic forms of decision-making. (In 1964, for example, the Students for a Democratic Society, working through the Economic Research and Action Project, set up a series of community-based projects with the aim of organizing inner-city poor around local, single issues. However, the results of these political initiatives were meager and inconsequential. See Buhle 1987, pp. 230–32 and Wohlforth 1989, pp. 111–13.) Yet millions of Americans in effect continued, and still continue, to live outside the system. A notable symptom of this situation is the much-observed phenomenon of the high level of voter abstentionism. H.J. Ehrlich noted that "In the [presidential] election of 1968 [. . .] 7 million registered voters did not vote because they thought the election was meaningless" (Ehrlich 1971, p. 296). And even by the 1970s, Afro-American and Hispanic voter registration barely exceeded fifty percent of its potential (Davis 1986, p. 224). The idea of the Tristeros surely owes a great deal to the submerged presence of this "silent," that is, politically unrepresented, mass of the socially alienated and poor. What, Oedipa asks, if it ever mobilized?

When Pynchon wrote *Lot 49*, something of a schism occurred within the sphere of public discourse in America. Dissenting views on the Vietnam War and other divisive issues were, in general, excluded from the established channels of communication like the big newspaper chains and TV networks, which proved servile in their support of the administration. Dissidents responded by establishing their own alternative channels. Paul Buhle, a founding editor of *Radical America*, recalls the importance of the "underground" media at the height of the campus insurgency:

We gave ourselves to the same tasks that any previous radical intelligentsia would have tackled in our place: popularization and communication. The local underground newspaper (produced in dozens of locations by 1968–69), a more significant communications medium than all the national publications put together and the most important grassroots information network since the heyday of the Socialist Party, became at once a means for practical and theoretical expression. (Buhle 1987, p. 239)

While the term "Tristero" denotes groups which cannot simply be identified with the New Left or countercultural radicals, one can see how, for a politically conscious author of the mid-1960s, the alternative communications network might also serve as a symbol of mass alienation from the official culture, as an expression of a profound rift within a community. Hence the following passages where Oedipa reflects on the withdrawal of the Tristeros from the established communications channels (the latter metonymically represented by the U.S. mail/government delivery system):

For here were God knew how many citizens, deliberately choosing not to communicate by US Mail. It was not an act of treason, nor possibly even of defiance. But it was a calculated withdrawal, from the life of the Republic, from its machinery. (CL p. 92)

a network by which x number of Americans are truly communicating whilst reserving their lies, recitations of routine, and betrayals of spiritual poverty for the official government delivery system. (CL p. 128)

One issue adumbrated in the preceding remarks is a characteristic concern of dissident postmodernism, namely, the politics of communication (see Chapter 2). Suffice to note here that the exponential increase, in the postmodern period, of channels of mass communication has prompted questions such as: Who controls the means of communication? Who are empowered to speak? Who are voiceless? I want to discuss Pynchon's meditations on the politics of communication in the context of two questions in particular: (1) What are the conditions (ideological, institutional) that impede the development of an alternative mode of communication which could serve as a foundation for a new cultural order? (2) What forms ("channels") and orders of meaning might this mode of communication take? Within the sphere of inquiry opened up by this second question, Pynchon includes fiction itself. I shall argue that he fashions a discourse which shadows the subversive effects imputed to the Tristero System. The result, one might say, is a Tristero novel.

Oedipa suspects that the machinations of a deceased lover, Pierce Inverarity, may lie behind the arcane symbols she reads as clues to the existence of the Tristero System. Those "clues" may have been planted by hired agents of Inverarity, in which case she is the victim of a hoax or conspiracy (CL p. 128): "Every access route to the Tristero could be traced also back to the Inverarity estate" (CL p. 127). But beyond his role as the possible agent of a "pure conspiracy" (CL p. 134) against Oedipa, Inverarity's principal role in the novel is to personify a dynamic, aggrandizing capitalism. Oedipa recalls that this "California real estate mogul" (CL p. 1) slept beneath a bust of Jay Gould, "the only ikon in the house" (CL p. 2). Gould (1836–92), a railway baron, gold speculator, and money dealer, was the archetypal American capitalist—which is precisely how the anarchist Jesús Arrabal sees Inverarity: "'He is too exactly and without flaw the thing we fight'" (CL p. 89). And Oedipa reflects on Inverarity's "need to possess, to alter the land, to bring new skylines, personal antagonisms, growth rates into being" (CL p. 134). As executor of Inverarity's will, Oedipa travels to "San Narciso" which had been his "domicile and headquarters." As she sorts through the tangled assets of the estate, they appear, like the "Gould System" of railways, to ramify indefinitely, accounting, possibly, for all investments in San Narciso. The thought disturbs her and culminates in a kind of epiphany when the natural barriers between San Narciso and the rest of the continent seem to dissolve. Whence:

There was the true continuity, San Narciso had no boundaries. No one knew yet how to draw them. She had dedicated herself, weeks ago, to making sense of what Inverarity had left behind, never suspecting that the legacy was America. (CL p. 134)

It is an intuition of the pervasive power of capital in America, a point reinforced by a reference to arch-capitalist Inverarity as a "founding father" (CL p. 14).

The America of *Lot 49* is an America under the dominion of capital, a social order which is understood to isolate individuals and create self-centered forms of subjectivity which militate against genuine communication and, by extension, against authentic community. The society of *Lot 49* is populated by self-enclosed egos. Images of enclosure abound in the novel; there are repeated references to closed systems, towers, furrows and cul-de-sacs. A further instance of enclosure is in the form of the narrative itself whereby events are exclusively mediated through, or enframed by, Oedipa's "paranoid" consciousness (a departure from the multiple focalization used in *V* and *Gravity's Rainbow*). These elements of the narrative serve primarily to reflect the entrapment of the subject in his/her ego (a condition of the egocentrism fostered by the capitalist order), precisely the form of entrapment which is at the heart of Oedipa's crisis. She experiences her consciousness as a state of confinement, a consciousness given its objective correlative in the insulated world of Kinneret-Among-the-Pines, a bourgeois milieu of Tupperware parties, psychotherapy, and herbal diets, where Oedipa lives the "Rapunzel-like role of a pensive girl somehow, magically, prisoner among the pines and salt fogs of Kinneret" (CL p. 10). It is this sense of entrapment which largely explains her identification with the girls in the Remedios Varo painting:

prisoners in the top room of a circular tower, embroidering a kind of tapestry which spilled out the slit windows and into a void, seeking hopelessly to fill the void: for all the other buildings and creatures, all the waves, ships and forests of the earth were contained in this tapestry, and the tapestry was the world. (CL p. 10)

Oedipa sees the painting as a potent symbol of her predicament: it suggests there is "no escape" from the tower of one's ego (CL p. 11), that the "tower is everywhere" (CL p. 11); it serves as an image of solipsism, exposing the limits of bourgeois egocentricity. Accordingly, Oedipa fears that she may only be fantasizing (or "embroidering") the existence of the Tristero, that it may be no more than an alienated bourgeoise's dream of escape. For the Tristero, if it exists, with its promise of a system of communication that will connect people in an authentic community, may bring to an end her isolation; it may be "a real alternative to the exitlessness, to the absence of surprise to life, that harrows the head of everybody American you know" (CL p. 128).

The insular subjectivity of bourgeois egocentrism is also implied in Pynchon's allusions to the Narcissus myth. (Recall that Oedipa's business as executor of Inverarity's will lands her in "San Narciso," a town which, insofar as it "had no boundaries" [CL p. 134] may be seen as a microcosm of America.) Pynchon's use of the myth is more than simply a statement about the narcissism of American culture; the myth also relates intimately to the book's metaphors of enclosure and entrapment. Narcissus, enthralled by his reflection, "had adapted to his extension of himself and had become a closed system" (McLuhan 1967, p. 51). Hence his world became no more than a *projection* of his own image. Similarly, Oedipa, shut inside the tower of her own ego, worries that the "Tristero System" (which, she hopes, may "bring to an end her encapsulation in her tower" [CL p. 28]) may be no more than the projection of a paranoid's fantasy, the "paranoid" being defined in conspicuously egocentric terms: "The true paranoid for whom all is organized in spheres joyful or threatening about the central pulse of himself" (CL p. 95). Oedipa's entrapment in a monadic ego is highlighted to contrast with a diametrically opposed condition—a communion of minds, an *intersubjectivity.* Consider the following passage where Oedipa is drawn into a deaf-mute's ball:

Each couple on the floor danced whatever was in the fellow's head: tango, two-step, bossa nova, slop. But how long, Oedipa thought, could it go on before collisions became a serious hindrance? There would have to be collisions. The only alternative was some unthinkable order of music, many rhythms, all keys at once, a choreography in which each couple meshed easy, predestined. Something they all heard with an extra sense atrophied in herself. She followed her partner's lead [. . .] waiting for the collisions to begin. But none came. She was danced for half an hour before, *by mysterious consensus,* everybody took a break. (CL p. 97. My emphasis)

Now, on one level, this absurd scene has the appearance of having been carefully contrived to illustrate, in a parodistic manner, the reliance on the imagination as a source of explanation: Oedipa, who cannot possibly *know* what is in the heads of the deaf-mutes, can only account for their harmonious and synchronized behavior in the fanciful terms of "an extra sense atrophied in herself" and a "mysterious consensus." Yet, within the larger framework of the narrative as a whole, these very terms find their validation in Oedipa's hope for, in the novel's utopian image of, an interference-free (telepathic?) mode of communication, that is, an intersubjectivity. There are, moreover, passages in *Gravity's Rainbow* which, without a hint of parody, express the same quasi-mystical ideas, in similar words, as those in the passage quoted above.[5] And I have emphasized the use of the word "consensus" because it serves as an expression of Pynchon's ideal of intersubjectivity—the word being used earlier in the novel with precisely the same connotation (CL pp. 88–89).

I have discussed how the egocentric, atomistic consciousness is understood to obstruct the operation of the Tristero as an (intersubjective) medium or "channel" of communication. Next, I want to discuss how a prescribed mode of cognition is understood to leave the subject unattuned to (what Oedipa can only imagine *may* be) the Tristero's "messages" or order of meaning.

Positivist Closure

Popular talk of the "Californianization" of America implies, among other things, an acknowledgment of the impact on the national economy and life-style of the pioneering center of computer technology. In his choice of San Francisco and Berkeley as principal sites of Oedipa's quest, Pynchon provides the appropriate ambience in which to raise questions about culture in the age of the computer. One remarkable feature of this culture is the widespread automation of clerical labor; in particular, the substitution of the computer for human brain power. One character, believed to be a Tristero communicant, is an executive who, at the behest of an "efficiency expert" was "automated out of a job by an IBM computer" (CL pp. 83–84). The elegant binary logic of the computer, which enhances managerial and industrial performance by producing knowledge of a functional, exploitable kind, has inevitably acquired prestige as an *exemplary* model for human thinking. It is with this last point in mind that I want to consider the following passage:

Perhaps she'd be hounded someday as far as joining Tristero itself, if it existed, in its twilight, its aloofness, its waiting. The waiting above all; if not for another set of possibilities to replace those that had conditioned the land to accept any San Narciso [. . .], then at least, at the very least, waiting for a *symmetry of choices* to break down, to go skew. *She had heard all about excluded middles; they were bad shit, to be avoided;* and how had it ever happened here, with the chances once so good for diversity? For it was now *like walking among matrices of a great digital computer, the zeroes and ones twinned above,* hanging like balanced mobiles right and left, ahead, thick, *maybe endless.* Behind the hieroglyphic streets there would *either* be a transcendent meaning, *or* only the earth [. . .] Tremaine the Swastika Salesman's reprieve from holocaust was *either* an injustice, *or* the absence of a wind [. . .] *Ones and zeroes.* So did the couples arrange themselves [. . .] *Either* Oedipa in the orbiting ecstasy of a true paranoia, *or* a real Tristero. (CL pp. 136–37. My emphases)

Here, Pynchon gives us an insight into the positivist mentality. According to the principle of the excluded middle, anything must be included either under a given term or its negative: a proposition may be either true or false; it may signify either x or not-x. Therefore, a third value which postulates a class of undecidable propositions that are *both* true *and* false, that signify *both* x and not-x, cannot be admitted. The binary oppositions ("ones and zeroes") on which computers operate have reinforced this iron either/or logic. In *The Postmodern Condition,* Lyotard has observed that in advanced societies statements which cannot be translated into quantities of information (i.e., the binary digits or "bits," the "ones and zeroes," of computer language) no longer count as knowledge: "Along with the hegemony of computers comes a certain logic, and therefore a certain set of prescriptions determining which statements are accepted as 'knowledge' statements" (Lyotard 1984a, p. 4).

Pynchon relates the principle of the excluded middle to the difficult business of interpretation. Oedipa's "mind's plowshare" has become "unfurrowed" (CL p. 95); her thoughts are no longer, so to speak, in the groove of a system of meaning which can conclusively define reality for her. Having drifted beyond the "buffering," "protective" space of inflated metaphors (CL p. 95), she must learn to live in an unstructured void ("For this, oh God, was the void" [CL p. 128]) where signs have no determinate meaning. Thus the numerous signs which she encounters may be read as: (a) "clues" to, or empirical proof of, the objective reality of the Tristero System; (b) random occurrences which, however, she has patterned into a constellation of meaning relevant to her hopes or fears (in which case, the Tristero is no more than a "paranoid" construct); (c) forgeries "planted" for her attention as part of a plot against her (in which case, the Tristero *is* a conspiratorial fabrication); (d) forgeries when, however, no plot is intended (in which case, the conspiracy is another paranoid construct). The evidence for each alternative is of equal measure so that there is no compelling reason for putting one interpretive option before another (CL p. 128). Indeed, her predicament demands that she entertain all four simultaneously, that she recognize the *coexistence of contradictory possibilities.* This, precisely, is the space of the excluded middle, of the undecidable, and it is a space in which Oedipa feels lost; for under the binary (either/or) logic sanctioned by positivism, she cannot admit the existence of this space.

Thus positivism, defined by its intransigent either/or logic, is seen to effect a form of closure; it abolishes the conceptual space of indeterminacy, diversity, and paradox.[6] Recall these crucial lines: "[Tristero's] waiting. The waiting above all, if not for another set of possibilities [. . .], then at least, at the very least, waiting for a symmetry of choices to break down, to go skew." Evidently "symmetry of choices" refers to the either/or mode of cognition in which the positivist mind is furrowed. And until the ideology of positivism is dethroned, the Tristero must remain silent, its post horn muted.[7]

The principle of the excluded middle is invoked not only to raise questions about the ontological status of the Tristero (for example, "Either Trystero did exist in its own right, or it was being presumed, perhaps fantasied by Oedipa" [CL p. 80]), but also to intimate something of the semantic range of messages that *might* be relayed through it.[8] Until the "symmetry of choices" dictated by positivism "breaks down," the conformist consciousness will not be *attuned* to the Tristero's messages. (However, for a partially "sensitized" Oedipa [CL pp. 29, 66], it is "As if, *on some other frequency* [. . .] words were being spoken" [CL p. 13].) As for the computer it is "ones and zeroes," so for the positivist mentality it is either x or not-x, either true or false. On the other hand, the Tristero System is anticipated (or, if unreal, imagined) as the negation of this polarizing logic; its communications, when activated, speaking in the terms of the excluded middle, an order of meaning that privileges indeterminacy and "ambiguity," "diversity" and paradox. I now want to discuss how Pynchon's writing itself aims to reproduce the subversive effects ascribed to messages relayed (or that might be relayed) through the Tristero; for, as I said earlier, *Lot 49* may be read as a Tristero novel.

Speaking the Excluded Middle

A good deal has been written about Pynchon's skillful appropriation of the concept of entropy. (See, for example, Abernethy 1972; Mangel 1976; Plater 1978.) Here, I want to say no more about the place of entropy in *Lot 49* than is necessary to introduce the theory underpinning Pynchon's adversarial mode of writing. In *Lot 49,* Pynchon exploits the difference between "two distinct kinds of entropy" (CL p. 77), which, following the narrative, we may refer to as "thermodynamic" and "informational" entropy (CL p. 80). Thermodynamic entropy, suffice to say here, refers to the heat loss or dissipation of energy which impels a closed system toward a terminally static condition. (The system, "closed" to fresh inputs of energy, loses its dynamism and "runs down.") The idea of thermodynamic entropy may be used metaphorically to suggest, as Henry Adams put it, a "heat-death of culture." Thus, in Pynchon's early short story, "Entropy," we learn of one Callisto that:

he found in entropy or the measure of disorganization for a closed system an adequate metaphor to apply to certain phenomena in his own world [. . . for example] in American consumerism [he] discovered a similar *tendency from the least to the most probable, from differentiation to sameness* [. . .] and envisioned a heat-death for his culture in which ideas, like heat-energy, would no longer be transferred [. . .] and intellectual motion would accordingly cease. (Pynchon 1985, pp. 84–85. My emphasis)

It is that entropic tendency towards the "most probable" and "sameness" that explains Oedipa's experience of "days which seemed (wouldn't she be first to admit it?) more or less identical" (CL p. 2); of "the absence of surprise to life, that harrows the head of everybody American you know" (CL p. 128); of her entrapment between binary alternatives, prompting the question: "How had it ever happened here, with the chances once so good for *diversity*?" (CL p. 136). In short, translated into social terms, thermodynamic entropy may suggest the loss of differentiation, a state of cultural uniformity. It is an appropriate metaphor for a late-capitalist society where the monopolistic practices of big corporations have standardized patterns of consumption. Indeed, the culture of Oedipa's America is largely characterized by the consumption of mass-produced commodities like Tupperware and Muzak (CL pp. 1, 2). Above all, under the condition of a generalized uniformity, where differentiation, "diversity," and "surprise" are absent, communication is impoverished; the order of meaning is routine, conformist, and predictable; *"messages" convey the "most probable" or certain meanings.*

Informational entropy denotes the measure of disorganization for a closed system. Here, however, "disorganization" refers to the *uncertainty* of a message, and the closed system is a communication circuit. The crucial difference is that whereas entropy in a thermodynamic system denotes a decrease in complexity (a "running down" from a dynamic disequilibrium to a terminal stasis), entropy in a communication system denotes an increase in complexity—*semantic* complexity. There is no information in a message that is a priori certain (a state of degree-zero entropy; "Information [being] that which removes prior uncertainty" [Brown 1966, p. 119]). But as the measure of uncertainty increases, the meaning of a message becomes less probable and more *ambiguous*. In excess, informational entropy may be regarded as undesirable, a state of communication marked by irrelevance, redundancy (repetition), and leakage; a matter of "noise" drowning "signal." But, within limits, this entropy may be positively valued as enriching a message, making its significance less predictable and investing it with a diversity of meaning through ambiguity or indeterminacy.

While some critics recognize that it is Pynchon's practice to exploit informational entropy in the very form of his writing, they tend to disregard the *adversarial* value of this practice and discuss only its aesthetic or philosophical significance in apolitical terms (e.g., see Abernethy 1972; Mangel 1976; Plater 1978). Pynchon's objective is to fashion a discourse which maximizes the effects of ambiguity, indeterminacy, and paradox *with a view to occupying the domain of the excluded middle*. It is a strategy designed to fracture the positivist logic which orders meaning into uniform, standardized patterns (binary oppositions, prefabricated alternatives), a logic, that is, which represses diversity of meaning. This strategy may, perhaps, be clarified in the terms of post-structuralist literary theory: in opposition to the closure effected by the principle of the excluded middle that restricts the free play of signifiers (binding signifiers to signifieds; the meaning of Oedipa's "clues" limited to a "symmetry of choices"), Pynchon cultivates a mode of writing which, insofar as it privileges ambiguity or uncertainty, "liberates" the signifier and guarantees its productivity.

In summary, we may say that in *Lot 49* the two concepts of entropy operate in the following way: Pynchon uses the idea of thermodynamic entropy as a metaphor to illustrate the tendency toward cultural uniformity, where communication is degraded by the certainty or probability of the message. However, his use of informational entropy is quite literal; in the text itself, messages are encoded so as to maximize their uncertainty or improbability in a defiant reversal of the prevailing tendency. Now, I want to identify the presence of uncertainty at different levels of Pynchon's text and illustrate its adversarial function.

Insofar as the protagonist of *Lot 49* behaves like a sleuth or "private eye" (CL p. 91), the novel invites comparisons with the detective story (cf. Tanner 1982, p. 56). Typically, the narrative of the latter progresses from a state of enigma (uncertainty) to one of knowledge; one by one hypotheses are eliminated by clues which (obligingly) cohere into a master explanation that resolves the enigma in its entirety. However, in *Lot 49*, no such explanation emerges; instead, the hypotheses multiply as clues and "revelations [. . .] come crowding in exponentially" (CL p. 58), leaving Oedipa (and the reader) suspended between a *range* of explanations (see above, under "Positivist Closure"). In short, in what reads like a parodic inversion of the classic detective tale, the degree of uncertainty in *Lot 49 increases;* the enigma (of the Tristero System) ramifies, complexifies, and its resolution is postponed beyond the timespan of the story. I would suggest that we recognize this postponement as, in the first instance, a negation of the habits of thought sanctioned by positivist ideology. In the conventional detective story, the resolution of the enigma is located in the positivist's domain of empirical facts (the sleuth's world of circumstantial evidence), where it is assumed that, on the basis of induction, there comes a point when facts speak for themselves, "disclosing" their meanings as if the latter were univocal and determinate. But, in *Lot 49*, this is precisely the domain whose laws

disallow the order of meaning identified with the excluded middle—
the ambiguous, the undecidable, and the paradoxical. Thus when
Pynchon presents an enigma which cannot be resolved within the
positivist's preestablished limits of meaning, this must be seen not so
much as the expression of an epistemological impasse (although to his
bourgeois "Young Republican" butt, Oedipa, it may appear this way),
as a *strategic refusal* of a scheme of thought which, in the name of truth
and certainty, represses "diversity" of meaning. This, then, is one
respect in which we may think of *Lot 49* as speaking the language of the
excluded middle, that is, the language of the Tristero (insofar as the latter is imagined or idealized as an alternative mode of communication).

The strategy of the postponed resolution may be discussed in the
more general context of what, following Barthes, we may call the
"hermeneutic code." In *S/Z*, a structural analysis of a short story by
Balzac, Barthes introduced this literary code as one among others
whose systems of rules serve to make narratives intelligible to the
reader. He writes: "Under the hermeneutic code, we list the various
(formal) terms by which an enigma can be distinguished, suggested,
formulated, held in suspense, and finally disclosed" (Barthes 1974,
p. 19). Later, under the rubric "Voice of Truth," Barthes indicates the
final unit of this code: "disclosure, decipherment, which is, in the pure
enigma (whose model is always the Sphinx's question to Oedipus), a
final nomination, the discovery and uttering of the irreversible word"
(pp. 209–10). (In view of the preceding points, it should be evident that
the genre which preeminently exploits the hermeneutic code is the
detective novel in which an enigma is, after tantalizing deferrals, resolved.) But Pynchon's text, in resisting any such resolution, trans-
gresses this code. Thus he frustrates the expectation of, or desire for, a
narrative closure that will enthrall the text to a definitive representation of reality. He eschews the "Voice of Truth," the final disclosure
which will pattern Oedipa's clues into a "pulsing stelliferous Meaning"
(CL p. 58). To speak the Voice of Truth, that is, to conclude *Lot 49* by
authorizing one reading of Oedipa's clues and rejecting the others,
would be to establish a *closed system* of meaning. Therefore, instead of "a
final nomination, the discovery and uttering of the irreversible word,"
it is the case in *Lot 49* that "the direct, epileptic Word, the cry that might
abolish the night" (CL p. 87) and hence reveal the mysterious Tristero,
is never uttered. The narrative is held in suspense with Oedipa/the
reader left in an acute state of uncertainty. This condition constitutes
the text as an open system of meaning where diverse possible explanations coexist without the chance of any one becoming the Voice of
Truth.

"Had a plot finally been devised too elaborate for the dark Angel to hold at once, in his [. . .] head, all the possibilities of?" (CL p. 134), Oedipa asks herself, wondering if the Tristero is a conspiracy engineered by Inverarity in an effort to "survive death as a paranoia." But, surely, Oedipa's question encodes a pun which draws our attention to an elaborate "plot" of another kind—that of *Lot 49* itself, a labyrinth of clues, symbols, and allusions whose supernumerary possibilities for meaning cannot be sorted *in the reader's head* into a final explanation of the enigma of the Tristero. (The reader's perspective is necessarily that of Oedipa's, the novel's mediating consciousness.) The effect is one of maximum uncertainty which, for Pynchon, avoids the "closed system" of meaning that (to extend the entropy metaphor) culminates in mental inertia.[9]

Uncertainty is a conspicuous feature at another level of the text—the proper noun. There are many names in the novel—for example, "Pierce Inverarity," "Maas," "Tristero"—that have been deliberately contrived to suggest a variety of meanings. Consider the implications of the name "Tristero" (sometimes spelled "Trystero": e.g., CL pp. 52, 65). One might read it as "triste" + "terror" thereby inferring that the "wretched" or "sad," that is, those disinherited by the official culture, will be the agents of some terrible nemesis against society. (Hence the apocalyptic mood of the novel.) Alternatively, one might read it as "tryst" + "error" thereby inferring that it is erroneous to believe in some kind of "appointment" with (or teleological conception of) history. The disaffected Oedipa would like to think of the Tristero System as the agency of a redemptive historical process, the antithetical stage of a dialectic through which the disinherited will be delivered from their wretched condition. Later, when Oedipa combs obscure texts for information about the origins of the Tristero rebels (at times she resembles a Foucauldean historian disinterring an insurrectionary history) further meanings accrue to the word.

The effect of uncertainty is also sustained by the technique of investing names or their predicates with contradictory (and hence ambiguous) meanings. This technique has strategic value not only insofar as it opens up the semantic space of the excluded middle but also in the context of Pynchon's doubts about standard oppositional practices. He subscribes to the characteristically postmodern view that, in the late-capitalist era, oppositional movements may work to the advantage of the system against which they are directed. Lyotard exemplifies this thinking when, in *The Postmodern Condition,* he comments, "struggles and their instruments have been transformed into regulators of the system" (Lyotard 1984a, p. 13). In *Gravity's Rainbow,* opposition to the "They-system" discovers itself to be a "We-system [. . .] playing Their game" (Pynchon 1978, p. 638). Pynchon denies the subversive value of opposition based on binary alternatives such as Left/Right or religious/secular. He suggests that a truly revolutionary movement would not be a reversal or inversion of the prevailing order of things because such options remain within the orbit of established oppositions; rather, the revolutionary movement must be radically discontinuous from the prevailing order (a relationship which can only be conceptualized in quasi-religious terms as the "miracle [. . .] of another world's intrusion into this one" [CL p. 88], as the revelation of some "magical Other" [CL p. 136] or sublime "unnamable act" [CL p. 136].) Accordingly, Pynchon indicates that the Tristero System is not a mirror image of that which it opposes by representing its communicants (real or imagined) in ways which *conflate* contradictory alternatives. For example, one Mike Fallopian, thought to be a Tristero communicant, while dressed in a "modified Cuban ensemble" cheerfully implies he has been, or will be, a customer at "Tremaine's Swastika Shoppe" (CL p. 126). And, in a similarly paradoxical vein, another figure who appears to be communicating through the Tristero network is a church-hating anarchist called Jesús (CL p. 88).

Finally, I want to note the implications of the contradictory meanings condensed in one of the novel's key terms—"waste." A dying sailor gives Oedipa a letter and directs her to a mailbox which resembles a trash can. "On the swinging part were hand-painted the initials W.A.S.T.E. She had to look closely to see the periods between the letters" (CL p. 96). Those "periods" could make all the difference between constituting a message as either mere *refuse* or (to compound the punning) a *refusal* of the official culture as represented by the government delivery system. For, as Oedipa learns from a motto on a stamp, WASTE is the acronym for "WE AWAIT SILENT TRISTERO'S EMPIRE" (CL p. 127) and it serves as the sign under which society's rejects communicate through an underground, alternative channel. Since the narrative offers no basis for privileging one interpretation over another, the reader must entertain both simultaneously in their contradictory relation: "waste" signifies the Tristeros as both those *refused* (rejected) by society and those actively *refusing* society. The contradiction is an affront to positivist either/or logic, an instance of an adversarial mode of writing that contests the binary coding which, in a technological-rationalist age, structures meaning for functional ends and which, says Pynchon, leads to cultural entropy.

A Total System of Meaning

In *Gravity's Rainbow*, a V-2 technician tells his interrogators: "'I couldn't go with von Braun . . . not to the Americans, it would only just keep on the same way . . . I want it really to be over, that's all. . . .'" (Pynchon 1978, p. 456, hereafter GR). "It"—that is, war or intensive preparations for it—*has* kept on in the same way; today, we are all citizens of the Rocket State (NATO, Warsaw Pact) of which von Braun may be thought of as a founding father.[10] Pynchon suggests that behind the nation-state fighting of World War II, some larger process was invisibly unfolding, a new order emerging: "Oh, a State begins to take form in the stateless German night, a state that spans oceans and surface politics, sovereign as the International or the Church of Rome, and the Rocket is its soul" (GR p. 566). Pynchon urges us to think of the war not as a conflict that was terminated in 1945 but as a key point of transition to, and perhaps the agency of, a new global order that superseded "a European and bourgeois order [. . .] destroyed forever" (cf. GR pp. 644–65). The rocket is the totem of this new order, this transnational "war-State."

In the age of the Rocket State, advanced societies, locked into supranational alliances or "Rocket-cartels" (GR p. 566) have rationalized their economies to support colossal military machines. (Pynchon, like William Burroughs, presents a war-model of society.)[11] *Gravity's Rainbow* is a dramatic illustration of how unceasing mobilization for missile-centered warfare gives rise to a hypertrophied bureaucracy, a "cartelized state" which can regulate the economy, administer resources, and supervise research and development. "The real War is always there" (GR p. 645), says Pynchon. Hence people's lives are shown to be ordered by a historically unprecedented level of state control: men and women subjected to a "rationalized power-ritual" (GR p. 177), obeying directives which issue unceasingly from "the State's oversize paper brain" (GR p. 421), working on projects where "organization charts [are] plan-views of prison cells" (GR p. 402).

The foregoing points indicate some of the integrative tendencies of a society conceived on the model of a *total system.* To be sure, the concept of a total system is both contentious and, given the variety of ways in which it has been theorized, always in need of specification (cf. Jameson 1981, pp. 90–93). Suffice to say here, Pynchon's total system incorporates elements of Weber's "iron cage" model of capitalist society, as seen in his preoccupation with "rationalization" (GR pp. 81, 177, 230, 588), "routinization" (GR pp. 325, 464), and other (usually noncoercive) forms of control.[12] Furthermore, it appears to be endowed with, precisely, a *systemic* logic; that is to say, it is believed to function as a self-regulating whole, *all* of whose parts are interrelated as compatible subsystems. We can understand, therefore, how "paranoia"—"the onset, the leading edge, of the discovery that *everything is connected*" (GR p. 703)—is an appropriate response to living in a total system in which (it is feared) every part is, or will be, adapted to the needs of the whole. Thus, not by chance, does one Father Rapier's account of such a system echo the above definition of paranoia: "Once the technical means of control have reached a certain size, a certain degree of *being connected* one to another, the chances for freedom are over for good" (GR p. 539).

One narrator reflects: "Only the demands of the Operation. Each of us has his place, and the tenants come and go, but the places remain" (GR p. 616). In Pynchon's model of the total system, each of us has an assigned place, a perception which surely prompted his use of the Calvinist categories "Elect" and "Preterite," which denote predestination of the subject. Moreover, the Elect/Preterite division, unlike class division, is seen as immutable. Indeed, in *Gravity's Rainbow,* there is little faith that "some dialectic is still operating in History" (GR p. 540; see also p. 678). Opposition and conflict are (as in Parsonian systems theory) perceived to exert a regulatory, stabilizing effect on the system as a whole. It is no surprise, then, that the hope placed in "Malfunction" (GR pp. 586, 738) or "Murphy's Law" (GR pp. 275, 471) sounds hollow—a desperate, last-ditch stand in the face of a virtually omnipotent, omnipresent System (albeit a system which is shown to be heading, ultimately, for self-destruction [GR p. 412]).

Pynchon may be criticized for offering a functionalist, reified model of society, but then we need to take account of the historical and intellectual context in which he was writing. This was the moment— 1960s, early 1970s—of late capitalism when the crises and contradictions of the market economy *appeared* to have been successfully managed, contained, or averted by the regulative function of the state. It was the moment when the ideologues of "organized capitalism" acclaimed the benefits of global planning and the technical-bureaucratic organization of production and consumption. It was the moment when synchronic models of society, culture, and communications—especially structuralism and cybernetics—were at the height of their prestige. It was the moment of Parsonian systems theory which, at least in America, was the paradigm guiding most research into questions of social order and stratification.[13] In Marcuse's influential essay, *One-Dimensional Man* (1964), everything affirmed the status quo, and contradictions had been "flattened out." The incorporation of the working class into the capitalist order was understood to have been successfully accomplished. Marcuse perceived a total system, "an omnipresent system which swallows up or repulses all alternatives" (Marcuse 1966, p. xvi).

In the total system of *Gravity's Rainbow,* opposition and dissent are also incorporated. Roger Mexico, a rebel, anticipating the collapse of the "Counterforce," reflects: "They will use us. We will help legitimize Them. . . ." (GR p. 713). The Counterforce rebels suspect that their political identity has been defined by Them: that they are just a "we-system" that is "playing Their game" in the terms dictated by Their "delusional systems" (GR p. 638). In Pynchon's Rocket State, rebellion is "lived" within a frame of reference established by the official "delu-sions" (ideology) of the System and is perceived to work to the advan-tage of the latter. The freaks and rebels of the Counterforce, South American anarchists, pre-capitalist communities, heretics, and dissi-dents—all, in time, are absorbed by the System. Slothrop fears, "They [have] busted the sod prairies of his brain, tilled and sown there, and subsidized him not to grow anything of his own" (GR p. 210). And in the subsection entitled "Weissmann's Tarot," we read:

The King of Cups [. . .] is the fair intellectual-king. If you're wondering where he's gone, look among the successful academics, the Presidential advisers, the token intellectuals who sit on boards of directors. He is almost surely there. Look high, not low. (GR p. 749)

The intellectual, once idealized as a social critic or society's conscience, has been professionalized, allocated a prestigious position within the System and hence co-opted into serving it.

Inevitably, given Pynchon's obsessive concern with incorporation, the very process of narrating is questioned. This concern accounts, in part, for a work which reflects on the possibility of its own autonomy. At one point, Pynchon interjects an anguished confession into the narrative: "[Yes. A cute way of putting it. I am betraying them all . . . the worst of it is that I know what your editors want, *exactly* what they want. I am a traitor. I carry it with me. Your virus.]" (GR p. 739). It is a slick or "cute" joke (GR pp. 738–39)—symptomatic, perhaps, of the kind of humor a publisher might welcome as a book's selling point—which occasions Pynchon's intervention. He is, like William Burroughs, acutely conscious of having to communicate on others' terms, terms which he sees as complicitous with a system defined by its betrayal of human hopes and needs. Pynchon's judgment of himself as a traitor may be unduly severe. Nevertheless, this self-criticism *qua* practicing artist together with his remarks on the co-optation of today's intellectuals and the predefinition of political identities reveal an anx-iety about the power of the late-capitalist social order, that is, the "System," to control meaning.

In short, we can observe the link, in *Gravity's Rainbow*, between society conceived as a total system and the emergence of a *total system of meaning*. What largely defines Pynchon's novel as a dissident postmodernist work is its critique of the System's control over the processes of signification.

No Public Sphere

In *Gravity's Rainbow*, a total system of meaning implies, among other things, the absence of critical space. Pynchon highlights changes in the forms and channels of discourse which have abolished that space, that is, changes which deny us a vantage point from which we can adequately interpret the social order and hence articulate, in coherent and rational terms, our opposition to it. This theme can, to a large extent, be discussed in the name of a postmodern phenomenon: the erosion of the public sphere. The sphere in which socially significant information is freely and openly exchanged, in which political issues are rationally debated and critically examined, has been substantially eroded in the late-capitalist period. Institutionalized regulation and manipulation of public opinion impedes the growth of political understanding based on information and analysis. (See Chapter 2, under "Erosion of the Public Sphere.") This is a condition of the social order described in *Gravity's Rainbow* where people live without a critical discourse which can supply adequate and appropriate terms for interrogating and contesting the exercise of power.

In the age of the Rocket State—the hypertrophied war-State of which we are all citizens—developments in the field of propaganda are one important factor in the loss of critical space. The production of propaganda by large state (or civil) apparatuses is, of course, not exclusive to the period in question, but what is new is the exponential increase, dating from World War II and the First Cold War, in the quantity of propaganda systematically produced and in the number of channels available for its transmission. A healthy public sphere depends on the free circulation of reliable information. However, the incessant stream of state-managed propaganda is a good example of the vertical and one-way flow of information which, via the mass media, has imbued the public sphere with perverted accounts of political events. Propaganda agencies abound in *Gravity's Rainbow*:

P.W.E. [Political Warfare Executive] laps over onto the Ministry of Information, the BBC European Service, the Special Operations Executive, the Ministry of Economic Warfare, and the F.O. Political Intelligence Department at Fitzmaurice House. Among others. When the Americans came in, their OSS [Office of Strategic Services], OWI [Office of War Information], and Army Psychological Warfare Department had also to be coordinated with. Presently there arose the joint SHAEF Psychological Warfare Division (PWD), reporting direct to Eisenhower, and to hold it all together, a London Propaganda Coordinating Council, which has no real power at all. (GR p. 76)

With so many agencies at work, public consciousness is besieged by fabricated accounts of the war: "But 'Roger,' she'd smile, 'it's *spring*. We're at peace.' No, we're not. It's another bit of propaganda. Something the P.W.E. planted" (GR p. 628). Or: "The German-and-Japs story was only one, rather surrealistic version of the real War" (GR p. 645). *Gravity's Rainbow* presents a society permeated by false reports and fraudulent histories (e.g., GR pp. 164, 326), a public entrapped in "a cooperative structure of lies" (GR p. 728). The late-capitalist state is portrayed as seeking not merely to mobilize public opinion in support of its aims but, through an extensive restructuring of the institutions of mass communication, to constitute public consciousness. What chance is there for free independent discourse in a social order which, as one character puts it, "bring[s] the State to live in the muscles of your tongue" (GR p. 384)?

Another factor in the dissolution of the public sphere is the drive, historically unprecedented, for the systematic regulation of political debate. This is a broad issue which, of course, includes policies of censorship and misinformation (whose effectivity depends on the co-option of the major public channels of communication by the state or hegemonic interests). Habermas has discussed another aspect of the matter. In *Toward a Rational Society,* he notes the tendency, greatly intensified in the postwar era, toward the "rationalization" of political debate. Formerly, it was public opinion which defined the arena of political debate in terms which were "rooted in social interests and in the value-orientations of a given social life-world" (Habermas 1971, p. 68). However, evidencing structural changes in the public sphere, public discussion of political issues is now bypassed by government "experts" who have redefined the arena of political debate in terms that pay regard to the stability of the social order. Social administrators define the horizons of political consciousness by setting an agenda of what should and should not be discussed by "fixing" the terms in which discussions are to be conducted. Pynchon is conscious of these practices:

"How high does it go?" is not even the right kind of question to be asking, because the organization charts have all been set up by Them, the titles and names filled in by Them, because
Proverbs for Paranoids, 3: If they can get you asking the wrong questions, they don't have to worry about answers. (GR p. 251)

We may cite as a third factor in the dissolution of the public sphere the phenomenal expansion of mass culture to the point where its principal discourses have colonized the greater part of our public (not to say private) cultural space. Their stereotyping of people and their reduction of social processes to formulaic narratives tend, in general, to impede critical reflection. Habermas's concern about the "increasing substitution of images for words" (see Chapter 2, under "Erosion of the Public Sphere") reminds us of the predominantly visual character of the mass media. Our late-capitalist environment is suffused with reproduced visual images whose primary function is to enchant the spectator, a process which depends on the suspension of his/her critical powers. Accordingly, for some, the film-goer is the quintessential model of the late twentieth-century public man or woman, his/her sense of reality derived from hypnotic screen images. The scene on the last page of *Gravity's Rainbow* is a cinema where "we" are the audience, "old fans who've always been at the movies (haven't we?)" (GR p. 760). "We" are in the "Orpheus Theatre" of which Richard M. Zhlubb is "night manager" (GR p. 754). Richard M. *Zhlubb* (*oaf* in Yiddish) "who is fiftyish and jowled" is evidently Nixon (president at the time Pynchon was writing) and the film theater he "manages" is America. The book's closing scene of the audience inside the theater shouting for the show to start, while outside, immediately above the theater, a rocket is falling in silence, is a poignant metaphor for a public made oblivious to the politics of the real world. This is, after all, the *Orpheus* Theatre, whose program is to entrance the public, to lull it to sleep. And these are *Hollywood* films (the theater is situated in "Los Angeles"), purveying "wretched Hollywood lies" (GR p. 641); Hollywood seen as the foremost instance of a deceitful and mesmerizing mass culture; Hollywood which has taught us to see in romantic clichés so that a bright point in the sky is perceived as a wishing-star, not an approaching rocket (GR p. 760).

Finally, as remarked earlier, the Enlightenment ideal of the public sphere assumed conditions for the free circulation of reliable and truthful information whereupon political issues would be subjected to open debate and critical judgment. However, in the age of the Rocket State, the unceasing flow of propaganda, the institutional regulation of political debate and the ritualized and reductive modes of thought fostered by mass-cultural discourses, make it virtually impossible for citizens to comprehend or "read" their political reality. Reliable information is sought, but in vain. Hence Pynchon draws the radical conclusion that, at the present time, it is altered states of consciousness which offer the best chance, however remote, of yielding insights into the true nature of the social order:

Bland [a business magnate] or his successors and assigns, could've bought programmers by the truckload to come in and make sure all the information fed out was harmless. Those like Slothrop, with the greatest interest in discovering the truth, were thrown back on dreams, psychic flashes, omens, cryptographies, drug-epistemologies, all dancing on a ground of terror, contradiction, absurdity. (GR p. 582)

Accordingly, the dreams and drug-induced visions of Slothrop, Tchitcherine, Enzian, and others are to be understood as substitutes for empirical methods of inquiry which, in Pynchon's view, are inadequate as a means of "reading" the present political conjuncture. The Enlightenment faith in Reason as a critical force and the sovereign mode of understanding is undermined by a social order whose political reality is beyond the *rational* grasp of its citizens. Therefore, in contrast to an "Elect" graced with knowledge (i.e., "Those Who Know" [GR p. 665]), "The rest of us, not chosen for enlightenment [. . .] must go on blundering inside our front-brain faith in Kute Korrespondences," this ignorance being one of the conditions of "our preterition" (GR p. 590). The narrative often seems poised on the "leading edge" of revelation (GR pp. 257, 566, 703) but revelation does not occur because the power structure, the precise configuration of controlling forces, cannot be grasped or represented.[14]

Technological Rationality

The years Pynchon worked on *Gravity's Rainbow*, 1966–1971 (GR p. 739), belong to a period when the social orders of America and western Europe found their legitimation in the appeal to productivity, performance, and efficiency; that is to say, a period when technological rationality was the ruling ideology. This ideology was a reflection of the long wave of capitalist expansion, which began around 1940 and ended in the early 1970s. (In the 1980s, a period marked by economic crisis and the new Cold War, the social orders of western capitalism were primarily legitimated in the name of "democracy" and "freedom.") Thus Ernest Mandel, writing in 1972, remarks that:

Belief in the omnipotence of technology is the specific form of bourgeois ideology in late capitalism. This ideology proclaims the ability of the existing social order gradually to eliminate all chance of crises, to find a "technical" solution to all its contradictions, to integrate rebellious social classes and to avoid political explosions. (Mandel 1978, p. 501)

He refers to these beliefs collectively as "the ideology of 'technological rationalism'" (p. 503). And in an essay published in 1968, Habermas writes: "For the leading productive force—controlled scientific-technical progress itself—has now become the basis of legitimation." He sees this as a new type of ideology, a substitute for the ideology of "just exchange" that can no longer legitimate political power: "technocratic consciousness . . . today's dominant, rather glassy background ideology, which makes a fetish of science, is more irresistible and farther-reaching than ideologies of the old type" (Habermas 1971, p. 111).

Technological rationality does not only serve as a basis for legitimation; it is also the practical consciousness of late-capitalist society. Both Mandel and Habermas explain late capitalism as a new stage of social development, a predominantly technical-bureaucratic order where production and consumption are no longer under the "steering medium" of the market but are, to an unprecedented degree, regulated by the state. The goal is a rationalized economy, a total system, as Habermas sees it, each of whose parts is adapted to the needs of capitalist production in order to ensure its smooth functioning. Hence "The model according to which the planned reconstruction of society is to proceed is taken from systems analysis" (Habermas 1971, p. 106). (All this is not to say that late-capitalist society *is* a stable, rational system—indeed, Mandel and Habermas, among others, are conscious of the paradox that our putatively rational society is essentially irrational—only that much administrative effort is directed toward achieving that end.) In a system which seeks not only to guarantee the conditions of commodity production but to optimize them through global planning and technical expertise, technological rationality becomes the most pervasive ideology. Our evaluations and calculations, our ideals and goals, are predominantly defined by the criteria of functionality, efficiency, and organization.

One influential proponent of the primacy of technological rationality with whose views Pynchon was very likely acquainted was Herbert Marcuse. In *One-Dimensional Man* (1964), an essay widely circulated among American dissidents of the 1960s, Marcuse discussed this ideology not only as a source of legitimation and not only as the primary form of practical consciousness but, above all, as a "logic of domination." He developed the thesis advanced by Adorno and Horkheimer in *Dialectic of Enlightenment* that science and "technological consciousness" have become the principal instruments of domination. Marcuse writes:

In the medium of technology, culture, politics, and the economy merge into an omnipresent system which swallows up or repulses all alternatives. The productivity and growth potential of this system stabilize the society and contain technical progress within the framework of domination. Technological rationality has become political rationality.

And:

In this universe, technology also provides the great rationalization of the unfreedom of man and demonstrates the "technical" impossibility of being autonomous, of determining one's own life. For this unfreedom appears neither as irrational nor as political, but rather as submission to the technical apparatus which enlarges the comforts of life and increases the productivity of labour. Technological rationality protects rather than cancels the legitimacy of domination, and the instrumentalist horizon of reason opens on a rationally totalitarian society. (Marcuse 1966, pp. xvi, 158–59)

Gravity's Rainbow was produced at a time when the ascendancy of the ideology of technological rationality was the focus of an influential debate. Pynchon investigates the operation of this ideology across a spectrum of cultural and social practices. However, the aim here is to concentrate on his presentation of it as a force which subjugates discourse to its instrumental criteria.

The dominant institutions of the late-capitalist order—industrial, bureaucratic, educational—have elevated technological rationality to the status of sovereign meaning-system. Accordingly, it is institutionally empowered to constitute the "truth." Its prescribed forms of thinking—positivist, causal, pragmatic—have become the basis for determining what qualifies as knowledge or science. It dictates the mode of comprehension. Consider the following exchange between Leni Pökler and her husband, Franz, a rocket engineer:

He was the cause-and-effect man: he kept at her astrology without mercy, telling her what she was supposed to believe, then denying it. "Tides, radio interference, damned little else. There is no way for changes out there to produce changes here."
"Not produce," she tried, "not cause. It all goes along together. Parallel, not series. Metaphor. Signs and symptoms. Mapping on to different coordinate systems. I don't know. . . ." She didn't know, all she was trying to do was reach.
But he said: "Try to design anything that way and have it work." (GR p. 159)

Here we see the logic sanctioned by technological rationality used to disqualify the truth-claims of an alternative meaning-system. And it is not only a matter of Leni refusing to think in terms of cause and effect. In his concluding objection to her beliefs, Pökler argues from the essentially functional or instrumental criteria of technological rationality. Under a "System" which "demand[s] that 'productivity' and 'earnings' keep on increasing with time" (GR p. 412), discourses with a technological orientation (e.g., sciences which issue in techniques of production or control) prevail over other types of discourse and, indeed, become a force in the constitution of truth.

Another example of the power of this ideology to control meaning is the account of Kekulé von Stradonitz's famous dream in which, according to the chemist, the molecular structure of benzene was revealed to him (GR pp. 412–13). (The dream had far-reaching consequences, serving as a kind of blueprint that led to the development of polymer chemistry, that is, the industrial synthesis of molecules.) The dream-image of the snake with its tale in its mouth might have been read in the terms of an older mythic discourse, that is, as a symbol of a "cyclical, eternally-returning" world (GR p. 412), as a promise of renewal. In the event, it was subjected to the reading of an instrumental rationalist discourse, one which interpreted the sign of the coiled serpent as the symbolic form of benzene's structure. The rationalist discourse, insofar as it is explicitly linked with the needs of an exploitative and rapacious "System" ("Taking and not giving back . . . ," etc. [GR p. 412]), is empowered by it to usurp the terms of signification (to the extent that it even recodes the signifiers of a dream).

A distinctive feature of *Gravity's Rainbow* is the substantial space allocated to the discourse of prestigious sciences, notably polymer chemistry, ballistics, behaviorism, and pharmacology. (Numerous passages are composed almost exclusively of the specialized language of these disciplines: GR pp. 90, 250, 345, 517–18.) Pynchon's strategy is to enframe these discourses in contexts which highlight what he perceives to be their immanent logic—precisely, the logic of regulation and control that defines technological rationality. We can see how this strategy works in the case of behaviorism. Pynchon's mobilization of the behaviorist lexicon works to suggest something of the cogency and force of this discourse, its scientific pretensions and intellectual assertiveness (and, certainly, behaviorism has a reputation for being an overweening science). There are lengthy passages written in an uncompromising Pavlovianese, with strings of recondite terms like "reciprocal induction," "ultraparadoxical phases," "irradiation," "summation" (GR pp. 55, 90). This discourse, moreover, pretends to objectivity—as instanced in the precise, technical terms that describe an experiment by Pynchon's behaviorist, Pointsman, which replicates Pavlov's famous laboratory test of 1905 (see GR p. 78). But, for Pynchon, this objectivity is only a veil to be stripped away: "And how much of the pretty victim straining against her bonds does Ned Pointsman see in each dog that visits his test stands . . . and aren't scalpel and probe as decorative, as fine extensions as whip and cane?" (GR p. 88). Here, as elsewhere, Pynchon suggests an underlying orientation of behaviorism toward domination and control of *human* subjects. Roger Mexico fears that Pointsman "wants *him*. As one wants a fine specimen of dog" (GR p. 46). And Pointsman thinks of the war as a "laboratory" (GR p. 49) providing the opportunity for experiments in the conditioning of deranged survivors of the Blitz. In the "war-neurosis ward" of a hospital, his hopes are revealed:

Out of each catharsis rise new children, painless, egoless for one pulse of the Between . . . tablet erased, new writing about to begin, hand and chalk poised in winter gloom over these poor human palimpsests shivering under their government blankets [. . .] How Pointsman lusts after them, pretty children [. . .] to use their innocence, to write on them new words of himself, his own brown Realpolitik dreams. (GR p. 50)

Here Pynchon suggests that for the science of conditioned behavior the ultimate goal is to "re-write" identity—a secret, "Realpolitik dream" of totalitarian control over the human subject.[15]

In the 1960s, when Pynchon was writing, the claims of many established sciences to objectivity came under critical scrutiny. There arose a number of counter-discourses that investigated such matters as the "politics of psychiatry" and "politics of medicine." This was the moment of the adversarial, interrogatory studies of, among others, Thomas Szasz, R.D. Laing, Ivan Illich, and Michel Foucault.[16] Further, it will be recalled that the Enlightenment's faith in the critical and emancipatory potential of science had, in the postwar period, been radically questioned, notably by theorists of the Frankfurt School. Adorno and Horkheimer perceived a logic of domination embedded in the Enlightenment program of systematically promoting the "scientific attitude": "What men want to learn from nature is how to use it in order wholly to dominate it and other men" (Adorno and Horkheimer 1979, p. 4). In *One-Dimensional Man*, Marcuse expressed a similar view: ". . . science, by virtue of its own method and concepts, has projected and promoted a universe in which the domination of nature has remained linked to the domination of man" (Marcuse 1966, p. 166). *Gravity's Rainbow*, insofar as it vividly illustrates the ways in which scientific knowledge, under the sovereignty of technological rationality, operates to augment control, is very much in the mold of the Critical Theorists' polemic.

Critical Perspectives

Nearly everything that is experimental, excessive, and extravagant about *Gravity's Rainbow* acquires significance in relation to the colossal task that Pynchon sets himself: a radical critique of Western meaning-systems. These are identified as "white" or Eurocentric (GR pp. 264, 285, 325, etc.), patriarchal (GR pp. 674–81, 712, 64), and, above all, technological-rationalist. Strictly speaking, the *oppositional* meaning-systems which serve as a basis for Pynchon's critique should not be read as counter-hegemonic. Hegemony implies a notion of culture as an arena of struggle where social groups compete to define common sense in terms of their own intellectual and moral vision. However, since Pynchon sees postwar society as a total system—an administered whole into which the formerly autonomous cultural sphere has been incorporated—counter-hegemonic resistance is virtually ruled out as a possibility; the conditions for contesting cultural and ideological supremacy have been eroded: "The Man has a branch office in each of our brains" (GR p. 712). Alternative and oppositional tendencies are not only effortlessly absorbed by the System, they are understood to sustain it. While in *Lot 49* Pynchon at least keeps alive the possibility of a viable opposition, in *Gravity's Rainbow* he does not identify any progressive or emergent countermovements which may pose a serious challenge to the status quo. (Hence the repeated question: Is there a way back? [GR pp. 693, 556]. Pynchon does not point a way forward and can only suggest that eventually the law of entropy will undermine the System.) The novel's critical perspectives are quite consciously derived from cultural practices which are either archaic or marginal; in other words, they cannot affirm any course of action which, under the prevailing conditions, could deliver humanity from the System. Therefore, we should think of them not as rallying points but as vantage points from which to mount a critique of the West's dominant codes. There are four major critical perspectives in *Gravity's Rainbow* and I shall represent them as follows:

Anti-Eurocentrism

Non-western cultures occupy a prominent place in the novel: those of the Kirghiz tribesmen of Central Asia, the Gaucho anarchists of the Argentine Pampas, and the Hereros of South-West Africa. And in each case a European/Europeanized metropolis seeks to incorporate the non-western culture into its own social order. Hence Moscow's "Russification" (GR p. 354) of Central Asia; hence "Buenos Aires sought hegemony over the provinces" (GR p. 264); hence Berlin's administration of "Sudwest" (GR p. 315). "'In Africa, Asia, Amerindia, Oceania, Europe came and established its order of Analysis and Death'" (GR p. 722). I shall illustrate the process of Europeanization as it is critically reflected upon by the Herero Enzian, beginning with his perception of the Rocket.

The Rocket haunts the novel not just as a material power threatening global destruction but as an oppressive meaning-system—a potent symbol of the primacy of technological rationality in western culture, a charismatic, cultural force. This is most apparent to a non-westerner like Enzian:

It began when Weissmann [i.e., *white* man] brought him [Enzian] to Europe: a discovery that love among these men [Europeans], once past the simple feel and orgasming of it, had to do with masculine technologies, with contracts, with winning and losing. Demanded, in his own case, that he enter the service of the Rocket. . . . Beyond simple steel erection, the Rocket was an entire system *won*, away from the feminine darkness, held against the entropies of lovable but scatterbrained Mother Nature: that was the first thing he was obliged by Weissmann to learn, his first step toward citizenship in the Zone. He was led to believe that by understanding the Rocket, he would come to understand truly his manhood. (GR p. 324)

The African Hereros seek to perpetuate a vision of "an era of inno-cence," of "Pre-Christian Oneness" (GR p. 321), before European col-onization. And this vision is partly embodied in the Herero words Pynchon employs (GR pp. 314–25 passim); taken collectively as a lexicon, they constitute a counter-discourse, a *weltanschauung* sum-moned in opposition to "the closed white version of reality" (GR p. 264). "Njambi Karunga," for example, signifies "God is creator and destroyer, sun and darkness, all sets of opposites brought together, including black and white, male and female" (GR p. 100). This stress on synthesis or union (see also GR p. 563) sets up a forceful contrast with the western analytical approach to understanding ("It wasn't Eu-rope's Original Sin—the latest name for that is Modern Analysis" [GR p. 722]). However, the Hereros, "Europeanized in language and thought [are] split off from the old tribal unity" (GR p. 318). Enzian's dream of a return to the "Eternal Center" (GR p. 319) has become obsolete in the epoch of European/Western supremacy: "But it is *their* time, *their* space, and [Enzian] still expects, naively, outcomes the white continuum grew past hoping for centuries ago" (GR p. 326).

Anarchism

Pynchon's critique of capitalism is, in many respects, Weberian (see above, under "A Total System of Meaning"). Capitalism is assailed not in the name of class exploitation but in that of "the grim rationalizing of the World" (GR p. 588). As in Weber's classic study *The Protestant Ethic and the Spirit of Capitalism* (1904), capitalism is traced back to the systematic profit-seeking of the Puritans (GR p. 278), and its inherent need for a "rationalized" (or administered) society is perceived to have culminated in "the System." Pynchon's hostility to rationalization suf-fers, I think, from overgeneralization. He comes to reject not just its excesses, notably bureaucracy and cultural programming, but any practice which may be conceived of as "rational" (organizing, planning, scientific inquiry) and, indeed, the whole cognitive dimension of con-sciousness (GR p. 720). This partly explains why Pynchon does not consider Marxism a redemptive creed: a self-proclaimed science, often associated with bureaucratic regimes and industrial planning, it would appear to Pynchon not so much as an obvious alternative to the (capitalist) System as akin to it.[17] One alternative, however, to which Pynchon seems attracted is anarchism, albeit an anarchism of a mystical cast wherein freedom is envisaged as an "anarchic oneness" (GR p. 264). (Certainly Pynchon's anarchism is not to be identified with the politico-economic philosophies of Kropotkin, Proudhon, and other libertarian thinkers.) This conception of anarchism requires a few words of explanation.

Slothrop meets one Squalidozzi who recalls the "openness" of Argentina before Buenos Aires fenced off the pampas:

"In the days of the gauchos, my country was a blank piece of paper [. . . But, later] Fences went up, and the gaucho became less free [. . .] We [European Argentinians] are obsessed with building labyrinths, where before there was open plain and sky. To draw ever more complex patterns on the blank sheet. We cannot abide that *openness:* it is terror to us. Look at Borges. Look at the suburbs of Buenos Aires [. . .] The Argentine heart [. . .] longs for a return to that first unscribbled serenity . . . that anarchic oneness of pampas and sky. . . ." (GR p. 264)

The allusions to Borges and "labyrinths," to "patterns" on blank sheets of paper, suggest that the "openness" to which this idea of anarchism aspires is not only that of an unfenced/decentralized space but also an open, unpatterned state of consciousness, a mind not enclosed by systems of meaning or the constructs of language.

Squalidozzi's nostalgia for the days of the gauchos explains his interest in the "Zone," the "decentralized" (GR p. 265) space created by the war: " 'In the openness of the German Zone, our hope is limitless' " (GR p. 265). There he hopes to set up an anarchist commune where the gaucho way of life can be revived. But he fears that the Zone cannot indefinitely remain an open space. Indeed, centralization proceeds as sectors of Allied occupation and numerous closed communities are established (e.g., GR pp. 519, 613–64). Nevertheless, a commune is founded, but the project fails when its members agree to collaborate with the arch-profiteer von Göll in making a film of the legendary gaucho hero, Martín Fierro (GR pp. 386–88). As a result of the collaboration, the commune is eventually reduced to a film set (GR p. 613); a comment perhaps on the power of capitalism to turn alternative cultures into spectacles. From the outset the reader is prepared for the failure of this project. Slothrop observes that Squalidozzi's paper "La Revolución" is fifteen years old (GR p. 263). (Similarly, Oedipa Maas observes that Arrabal's anarcho-syndicalist paper "Regeneración" is dated "1904." See Pynchon [1966] 1976, p. 89.) Pynchon's point seems to be that anarchist ideals are archaic, an outmoded response to the colonizing powers (centralization, commodification) of a total system.

Naturism

Gravity's Rainbow identifies two antithetical temporalities: a natural process which is cyclical and an historical process which is linear. The System's ruthless exploitation of nature "violates" the eco-cycle (GR pp. 412–13) and inserts humanity into History; it "demand[s] that 'productivity' and 'earnings' keep on increasing with time," and thus induces a perception of time as a "resource [which is] of no value to anyone or anything but the System" (GR p. 412), the "hopeless [. . .] one-way flow of European time" (GR p. 724). This history, moreover, is seen as terminal insofar as it is ultimately identified with the evolution of the Rocket (GR p. 209).

Several binary oppositions are founded on this central antithesis between Nature's eco-cycle and the System's terminal history, notably the Rainbow/Rocket (GR p. 209) and Green/White (e.g., "the living green against the dead white" [GR p. 268]) oppositions. They involve issues that may appear to situate Pynchon in the ecologists' camp except that in the last third of the novel they acquire a quasi-mystical cast which is extrinsic to conventional green politics. For example, Pynchon exhorts us to adopt an animistic view of nature. Animism bound the primitive subject to the natural world in a sacrosanct relationship: "Animism spiritualized the object."[18] However, living under a system whose attitude to nature is purely instrumental and dominative, the subject has become alienated from the natural world. Pynchon's response is to project as an ideal (though not as a viable means of redemption) humankind's reconciliation with nature, a goal expressed in terms of an animistic reverence toward natural objects: "Slothrop [. . .] understand[s] that each tree is a creature, carrying on its individual life, aware of what's happening around it, not just some hunk of wood to be cut down" (GR pp. 552–53); "There are harpmen and dulcimer players in all the rivers, wherever water moves" (GR p. 622); and in the last lines of the novel "we" sing of "a face on ev'ry mountainside / And a Soul in ev'ry stone" (GR p. 760, see also p. 590).

Ultimately, reconciliation with nature is understood to depend on a retreat from those "higher" mental processes cultivated by the System: specifically, the rational or cognitive processes of reflection, ratiocination, and analysis. The dissolution of Slothrop's mind is seen as the precondition of his resurrection as a natural being (*from this "naturist" perspective*, this is a redemptive state, signified by the appearance, as in *Genesis*, of a rainbow):

and now, in the Zone, later in the day he became a crossroad, after a heavy rain he doesn't recall, Slothrop sees a very thick rainbow here, a stout rainbow cock driven down out of pubic clouds into Earth, green wet valleyed Earth, and his chest fills and he stands crying, *not a thing in his head,* just feeling natural. . . . (GR p. 626. My emphasis)

This return to nature inevitably involves a reversion to a *pre-linguistic* consciousness insofar as the "higher" mental processes are necessarily embodied in language. And, indeed, after his transfiguration, Slothrop's command of language declines until he can no longer communicate (GR pp. 682, 740–41). Furthermore, it might be argued that the loss of language guarantees the reconciliation with nature insofar as it is understood that "name-giving, dividing the Creation finer and finer, analyzing, *set[s] namer more hopelessly apart from named*" (GR p. 391, my emphasis). The compulsion to name, which separates human beings from the natural world, has culminated in the taxonomies of science whereby "disqualified nature becomes the chaotic matter of mere classification" (Adorno and Horkheimer 1979, p. 10). Finally, Slothrop's road to, an albeit ambiguous, redemption is surely not intended to serve as a viable option for the rest of us. Rather, we should understand this episode as instantiating the (Edenic?) myth of primal oneness whose function in the novel is to highlight humanity's present estrangement from the natural world.

Clown-Freak Mentality

This critical perspective is embodied in the mind-set and behavior of a loose grouping of rebels known as "The Counterforce." Their revolt is, in part, expressed in performances of gross buffoonery calculated to upset the norms of propriety and rational behavior sanctioned by the official culture. Thus, in one instance, Counterforce partisans scandalize a functionary of the System by staging a surprise combat between clowns wielding giant foam rubber penises (GR p. 708). Their tactics also include the use of obscene language for subversive ends. Pig Bodine, dressed like a clown (GR p. 710), and Roger Mexico disrupt a formal dinner party for big-corporation executives with a mock-menu of nauseating dishes: "fart fondue," "bowel burgers," "Diarrhea Dee-lite," and so on (GR pp. 716–17).[19] Some critics have perceptively noted the relevance of Mikhail Bakhtin's concept of "dialogic interaction" to this and other scenes like it (see White, A., 1984, pp. 135–36; Mendelson, E., 1976, pp. 173–74). Suffice to say here that Bakhtin has remarked on the subversive and animating power of "low" (e.g., scatological) discourse in contexts which demand solemn and decorous language in deference to authority.

A later offshoot of the Counterforce is active in Nixon's America. Doped, wacky types drive recklessly along the Santa Monica Freeway, "a freeway for freaks [. . .] They come gibbering in at you from all sides, swarming in, rolling their eyes through the side windows, playing harmonicas and even *kazoos* in full disrespect of the Prohibitions" (GR pp. 755–56). They are described as being in an "unauthorized state of mind" (GR p. 755). And perhaps we should think of the Counterforce as primarily a state of mind: zany, anarchic, spontaneous, in short, from the viewpoint of the technological-rationalist System, *irrational*. Thus one partisan remarks: " '*They're* the rational ones. We piss on Their rational arrangements' " (GR p. 639) (after Mexico has climbed onto a boardroom table and urinated over a gathering of oil magnates [GR p. 636]).

For reasons discussed earlier, the Counterforce fails (GR p. 713). However, its descendants remain active in America (GR pp. 754–57). And while their extempore antics are not seriously presented as capable of defeating the System (but, then, given Pynchon's premise of the virtually omnipotent total system, resistance is reduced to impotent gestures), at least their "unauthorized state of mind" may be a way, albeit a temporary one, of seceding from the System's totalitarian order of meaning. The idea that redemption may be achieved in the form of some radically transformed state of consciousness is perhaps a product of that conjuncture in American history (1960s, early 1970s) when an affluent society had *apparently* contained its contradictions. Indeed, the term "System," commonly used at the time, connoted a static, functionalist model of society rather than an unstable, dialectical one. Under these circumstances, many "countercultural" dissidents were inclined to the view that liberation lay not in the class dynamics of productive activity but in a "revolutionary consciousness" or "new sensibility." (Theodore Roszak's *The Making of a Counter Culture* (1970) is symptomatic of this viewpoint.) In short, *Gravity's Rainbow* bears the marks of a moment when, for many, an assumed social stasis shifted the prospect of emancipation from a collective praxis to the individual's subjective transcendence of "technocratic" (Roszak) or technological-rationalist consciousness.

Pynchon, it must be said, is all too aware of the limitations of the Counterforce, those "doomed pet freaks" (GR p. 713) with "brains ravaged by antisocial and mindless pleasures" (GR p. 681). However, since the novel does not affirm any viable course of action which may deliver humankind from the late-capitalist order, it is the Counterforce's clown-freak mentality which remains as the best hope of emancipation. It is this irrationalist, anarchic frame of mind which Pynchon most often evokes in opposition to the routinized cognition demanded by the System.[20]

"Situations, Journeys, Comedy"

Many of the Counterforce are "dopers" as well as buffoons. Chu Piang is both: an opium addict and a factotum who *enjoys* tripping over his mop (GR pp. 346, 347). These qualities make him a "sub rosa enemy of order" (GR p. 346), someone living in an "unauthorized state of mind." The Chu Piang episode may serve as an example of how the clown-freak mentality of the Counterforce is embodied in Pynchon's narrative techniques. (The passage, quoted in full—the ellipses are Pynchon's—has been divided into numbered sections as a means of ready reference for the commentary which follows.)

[i] Chu Piang being a monument to all this [i.e., to Victorian Britain's trade policy of forcing opium onto the Chinese market], nowadays whole tourist caravans come through to look at him, usually while he's Under The Influence [of opium] . . . "Here ladies and gentlemen, as you may have observed, the characteristic sooty-gray complexion. . . ." They all stand peering into his dreamstruck faces, attentive men with mutton-chop sideburns, holding pearl-gray morning hats in their hands, the women lifting their skirts away from where horrid Asian critters are seething microscopically across the old floor-boards, while their tour leader indicates items of interest with his metal pointer, an instrument remarkably thin, thinner than a rapier in fact, often flashing along much faster than eyes can really follow——"His Need, you will notice, retains its shape under all manner of stresses. No bodily illness, no scarcity of supply seems to affect it a whit . . ." all their mild, their shallow eyes following gently as piano chords from a suburban parlor . . . [ii] the inelastic Need turns luminous this stagnant air: it is an ingot beyond price, from which sovereigns yet may be struck, and faces of great administrators engraved and run off to signify. [iii] It was worth the trip, just to see this shining, worth the long passage by sleigh, over the frozen steppe in an enormous closed sleigh, big as a ferryboat, bedizened all over with Victorian gingerbread——inside are decks and levels for each class of passenger, velvet saloons, well-stocked galleys, a young Dr. Maledetto whom the ladies love, an elegant menu including every-thing from Mille-Feuilles à la Fondue de la Cervelle to La Surprise du Vésuve, lounges amply fitted out with stereopticons and a library of slides, oak toilets rubbed to a deep red and hand-carved into mermaid faces, acanthus leaves, afternoon and garden shapes to remind the sitter of home when he needs it most, hot insides poised here so terribly above the breakneck passage of crystalline ice and snow, which may be seen also from the observation deck, the passing vistas of horizontal pallor, the wheeling snowfields of Asia, beneath skies of metal baser by far than this we have come to watch. . . . [iv] Chu Piang is also watching them, as they come, and stare, and go. They are figures in dreams. They amuse him. They belong to the opium: they never come if it's anything else. He tries not to smoke the hashish out here, actually, any more

than courtesy demands. That chunky, resinous Turkestan phantasmagoric is fine for Russian, Kirghiz and other barbaric tastes, but give Chu the tears of the poppy any time. The dreams are better, not so geometrical, so apt to turn everything——the air, the sky——to Persian rugs. Chu prefers situations, journeys, comedy. Finding the same appetite in Tchitcherine, this stocky, Latin-eyed emissary from Moscow, this Soviet remittance man, is enough to make anybody trip over his mop, suds hissing along the floor and the bucket gong-crashing in astonishment. In delight! (GR 346–47)

In [i], the tourists who come to gaze at Chu Piang are evidently Victorians—"men with mutton-chop sideburns, holding pearl-gray morning hats." The tour leader, using his metal pointer in a demon-strative, almost authoritarian, fashion is a caricature of the Victorian pedagogue. His approach to the object of study (Chu Piang under the influence of opium) is positivistic, strictly empirical; a matter of what can be "observed" or "noticed." And he endeavors, with the aid of the pointer, to dictate his positivist terms of understanding to the tourists. But by [ii] these terms have given way to the capricious logic of a sustained conceit rendered in a courtly Elizabethan diction, a marked deviation from the tour leader's punctual, expository mode of address. In [iii], "the long passage by sleigh" is justified in the name of the conceit itself (i.e., Chu Piang's "Need" *compared* to a luminous "ingot beyond price") and *not* in the name of its subject (i.e., Chu Piang's "Need"). Hence "It was worth the trip, just to see this *shining*," and the account of the journey by sleigh ends "beneath skies of metal baser by far than this we have come to watch." In other words, the figurative dimension of the conceit takes over from its subject and constitutes the controlling viewpoint of the passage. This is a technique which one might refer to as "vehicle autonomization." As a rule, the "vehicle" or figurative meaning of a metaphor serves to express or enhance the "tenor" or literal meaning. However, one component of Pynchon's adversarial discourse involves the vehicle displacing the tenor, break-ing away from it to become a reality in its own right.[21] The strategic function of this technique can be explained in the light of a remark, quoted earlier, by Leni Pökler: contesting the linear logic of her hus-band's "cause-and-effect" thinking, she spoke of "'Metaphor. Signs and symptoms. Mapping on to different coordinate systems'" (GR p. 159). A discourse whose rules permit the figurative dimension of a metaphor to supplant the literal dimension "map[s] on to [a] different coordinate system," in this case, one which is not governed by the continuity or linearity of causal thinking. Of course, such a discourse is not inherently subversive but, in the context of *Gravity's Rainbow*, where technological rationality privileges the logic of cause-and-effect, it ac-quires subversive value. (Pynchon emphasizes how the thinking of, for example, rocket engineers and behaviorists is grounded in causal logic. See, for example, GR pp. 89, 159, and 752.)

There is another sense in which section [iii] may be read as an instance of "mapping on to different coordinate systems." The amazing description of the sleigh is plausible only if it is understood as one of Chu Piang's opium dreams (a view which section [iv] appears to confirm). And it is not just the surreal images but also the movement of the narrative itself that suggest an opium-induced experience. (Here, perhaps, there is a pun on "trip.") The narrative progresses by abrupt switches of perspective and scale, imitating the viewpoint of an erratic camera, at one moment zooming in on the minutest details of the sleigh (e.g., focusing on the impossibly intricate features of the oak toilet), at another, panning across the steppe, opening a view onto the "snow-fields of Asia." This disjunctive mode of perception is a characteristic feature of experience under opium and other hallucinogens. Suffice to say here, Chu Piang's opium dreams, like the use of metaphor in [ii] and [iii], are governed by the logic of an alternative "coordinate system"; alternative, that is, to the causal, functionalist logic of technological rationality.

The deictics of [iii] are notably volatile. Deictics are the reference points in a narrative which orient the reader, enabling him/her to identify character, time, and place; they indicate *who* spoke or acted, *when* or *where* something was said or done. Section [iii] begins: "It *was* worth the trip, just to see this shining . . . ," the verb tense denoting that the journey has been completed. But in the subsequent description of the sleigh ride, the tense switches to the present thereby suggesting that the journey is in process: "a young Dr. Maledetto whom the ladies *love*," "to remind the sitter of home when he *needs* it most." And in the phrase "hot insides poised *here*," the adverb suggests *in this place now* rather than *there and then*. Furthermore, while the subjects of [iii], the Victorian tourists, are indicated in the third person ("passenger," "he"), in the closing line it is "we" who have traveled to gaze at Chu Piang. In short, the shifting deictic coordinates also reproduce the disjunctive logic of the opium dream.

I have drawn attention to elements of Pynchon's writing that resist the ruling ideology of technological rationality. The digressive and capricious course of his narrative appears to imitate drug-induced mental states where cognition is unconstrained by the principle of causation. Pynchon's writing eschews the "narrative continuity [of] the average *Reader's Digest* article" (GR p. 703). Continuity, or the linear logic of cause-and-effect thinking, is seen in the novel as the form of cognition prescribed by the System and preferred by those of "us" who live within the System's domain of meaning: "You will want cause and effect. All right" (GR p. 663). (The System cannot tolerate the experience of that which is outside of its control: "surprises," "indeterminacy," "statistical oddity," "psychological quirks.") Pynchon's adversarial discourse is premised on the assumption that narrative continuity has ideological implications, that it embodies and extends an oppressive logic. Hence his cultivation of a mode of writing which, employing such devices as those discussed above, persistently strays from the syntagmatic axis.[22]

In [iv] we learn that Chu smokes opium rather than hashish because "The dreams are better, not so geometrical [. . .] Chu prefers situations, journeys, comedy." And Chu's preference is also Pynchon's. "Situations, journeys, comedy" is a phrase whose meaning resonates beyond the lines just quoted, suggesting those escapades and deviations of the narrative which express the clown-freak mentality. Briefly, there are the farcical, semi-staged "situations," like Chu's addiction turned into a tourist attraction or Slothrop's ritual tasting of mouth-burning sweets at Mrs. Quoad's (GR pp. 115–19); "journeys" denotes not simply travel but the labyrinthine digressions of the imagination, as in the fantastic account of the journey by sleigh or Lord Osmo's Adenoid fantasy (GR pp. 14–16); "comedy" is slapstick or buffoonery, as in Chu tripping over his mop or "A Moment of Fun with the Komikal Kamikazes" (GR pp. 690–92). "Situations, journeys, comedy" comprise those elements of the text which mock the rationalist and functionalist norms prescribed by technological rationality in the interests of a planned society and economic performance.

Preterite Signs

The ideal of a realm of meaning whose truth is assured is expressed in terms of the Puritan conception of a pure, prelapsarian language. "Slothrop's own Puritan hopes for the Word" (GR p. 571) recalls the notion of a divine language, that is, the perfect adequation of name to thing in God's originary nomenclature. God's speech is the "single root" from which the ramifying languages of man have become disconnected:

Is there a single root, deeper than anyone has probed from which Slothrop's Blackwords only appear to flower separately? Or has he by way of the language caught the German mania for name-giving, dividing the Creation finer and finer, analyzing, setting namer more hopelessly apart from named, even to bringing in the mathematics of combination, tacking together established nouns to get new ones, the insanely, endlessly diddling play of a chemist whose molecules are words. . . . (GR p. 391)

The single root is lost, the unified, pristine language of the Creation has fragmented into idioms whose inferiority is suggested in terms of fabrication and fraudulence—the "tacking together" and "diddling play" of words. Divine speech is Pynchon's metaphor for a language of revelationary power, an imaginary criterion that illuminates the base condition of language in the age of the System. Postlapsarian language is seen to have been distorted by propaganda, attenuated by the reductive stereotypes of pop-cultural discourses and, above all, to have been instrumentalized by the logic of technological rationality.

Accordingly, strategic importance is attached to a whole domain of *nonverbal* signs, specifically those marginal ones that have been "passed over" by the System. They are idealized as sources of revelation, enclaves of meaning uncontaminated by the System's codes:

Crosses, swastikas, Zone-mandalas, how can they not speak to Slothrop? He's sat in Säure Bummer's kitchen, the air streaming with kif moirés, reading soup recipes and finding in every bone and cabbage leaf paraphrases of himself . . . news flashes, names of wheelhorses that will pay him off enough for a certain getaway . . . He used to pick and shovel at the spring roads of Berkshire, April afternoons he's lost [. . .] picking up rusted beer cans, rubbers yellow with preterite seed, Kleenex wadded to brain shapes hiding preterite snot, preterite tears, newspapers, broken glass, pieces of automobile, days when in superstition and fright he could *make it all fit,* seeing clearly in each an entry in a record, a history: his own, his winter's, his country's . . . instructing him, dunce and drifter, in ways deeper than he can explain, have been faces of children out the train windows, two bars of dance music somewhere, in some other street at night, needles and branches of a pine tree shaken clear and luminous against night clouds, one circuit diagram out of hundreds in a smudged yellowing sheaf, laughter out of a cornfield in the early morning as he was walking to school, the idling of a motorcycle at one dusk-heavy hour of the summer. . . . (GR pp. 625–26)

"Crosses, swastikas [. . .], how can *they* not speak to Slothrop?"; "*Instructing him* [. . .] in ways deeper than he can explain. . . ." (i.e., ways which elude verbal formulation). This passage evokes the *ideal* of the revelationary nonverbal sign, that is, the sign which, apprehended at an intuitive level of consciousness, yields meanings radically alternative or opposed to those encoded in the System's closed and repressive order of discourse. Such an ideal serves as an indictment of language in its prevailing forms, distrusted as an instrument of mass deception, limiting consciousness to modes of intelligibility which conform to the functional demands of the System.

Pynchon, like Barthelme and Burroughs, seeks a domain of meaning outside of society's ruling codes. Hence the innumerable artifacts and natural phenomena in *Gravity's Rainbow* which are read and valued as alternative sources of meaning; for example, faeces (GR pp. 65–67), beach pebbles (GR p. 106), used toothpaste tubes (GR p. 130), shivers (GR p. 641), and hair (GR p. 643), in addition to those listed in the above extract. Moreover, a significant proportion of the novel's nonverbal signs are conspicuous as forms of refuse: the used Kleenex and prophylactics, the rusted beer cans and sewage. And insofar as these comprise precisely those things excluded by and from the System as "waste" (i.e., that which cannot enhance the System's functioning or performance), they are valued by the novel's dissident characters as signs untainted by the System's mendacity and ideology, as sources of illumination. (Pynchon reinforces the point that these signs lie outside the System by explicitly associating the rejectamenta with the "preterite" [GR p. 626], that is, those with no place in the Providential scheme which, by the terms of the narrative, means those "passed over" by the System.)

In the quoted extract, Pynchon is describing occurrences and *objets trouvés* which are read as signs. These signs may be connected into personal or ephemeral patterns of meaning in the way that Slothrop could "make it all fit," but given their evidently fortuitous existence they cannot be controlled or exploited by the System. And, for Pynchon, it is precisely their resistance to rational systematization which saves these signs from becoming total systems of meaning that entrap the subject. Recall that what largely defines the late-capitalist order as presented in *Gravity's Rainbow* is that it has enlarged and developed apparatuses for managing the processes of signification and globalizing its meaning-systems: "'These are our letters, our words: they too can be modulated, broken, recoupled, redefined, co-polymerized one to the other in worldwide chains'" (GR p. 355). Accordingly, when language is manipulated for the purpose of building totalitarian master-narratives, fortuitous, transient, nonverbal signs acquire value as an alternative source of meaning. They may yield insights suppressed by the master-narrative, insights which, as remarked earlier, can only be apprehended at a preverbal, intuitive level of consciousness.[23]

In the "Kirghiz Light" episode, Pynchon also opposes the revelationary nonverbal sign to the "chain-link fields of the Word" (GR p. 705), that is, language understood as restricting the bounds of consciousness. In the early days of Stalin, one Vaslav Tchitcherine, an official of the NTA (New Turkic Alphabet) mission, is posted in Central Asia to impose an alphabet on a preliterate community of Kirghiz tribesmen: "it was purely speech, gesture, touch among them, not even an Arabic script to replace" (GR p. 338). There, he learns from an aqyn ("a wandering Kazakh singer") of the "Kirghiz Light" and goes in search of it. It is a mystical illumination promising spiritual rebirth which is possible only:

In a place where words are unknown [. . .]
If words were known and spoken,
Then the God might be a gold ikon,
Or a page in a paper book.
But It comes as the Kirghiz Light—
There is no other way to know It.

(GR p. 358)

Subsequently we are told that "Tchitcherine will reach the Kirghiz Light, but not his birth. He is no aqyn, and his heart was never ready" (GR p. 359). As a literate European his mind-set is closed to the vision. Literacy, understood as the *prioritizing* of language as the medium of cognition, is seen as limiting the range of consciousness. Like his NTA colleague, Galina, he is "shut in by words" (GR p. 339).

Tchitcherine is an agent of Moscow's program of "Russification" (GR p. 354), a form of colonization whose principal instrument is language—the imposition of a Europeanized "New Turkic Alphabet" on a preliterate Asian folk culture. The campaign of enforced literacy also bears the marks of the System insofar as it depends on, and is parodied as, an overgrown bureaucracy. (The NTA project operates through a vast network of committees like the "glottal K Committee" and "G Committee.") Tchitcherine recognizes that literacy will destroy the folk culture (GR p. 357), that it will function as a vehicle of rationalization, eliminating the magic of the shamans (GR p. 355). Thus, once again, language is perceived as a medium of incorporation, a means of drawing the subject into the cultural orbit of an alien and oppressive order.

In the Zone, at the limit of his "anti-paranoia" ("where nothing is connected to anything" (GR p. 434), Slothrop exits from the symbolic order, "not a thing in his head, just feeling natural" (GR p. 626). This reversion to a prelinguistic consciousness seems to guarantee his release from the System, a System which is chiefly defined by its near-monopolistic control of meaning. And while Slothrop's condition is not offered as unequivocally desirable (thenceforth, others see him as little more than a living ghost [GR pp. 740–42]), less still as a viable option for the rest of us, this episode serves to illustrate what Pynchon sees as the polarized alternatives of the present conjuncture: silence or participation in a total/totalitarian system of meaning. Perhaps Pynchon's attitude can be summed up by a line in that episode which recounts the "Conversion of the Dodoes": "No language meant no chance of co-opting them in to what their [. . .] invaders were calling Salvation" (GR p. 110).

Colonizations

In one of the last episodes of *Gravity's Rainbow*—"The Occupation of Mingeborough," Slothrop witnesses the military occupation of his home town. Barricades block the way to his house, but his response suggests a situation with deeper implications; he feels like the victim of a dispossession that reaches beyond the loss of one's house: "But there is the occupation. They may have already interdicted the kids' short cuts along with the grown-up routes. It may be too late to get home" (GR p. 744). Zoyd Wheeler, leading figure in *Vineland*, suffers the same fate as Slothrop; his house is seized by the military when armed convoys occupy Vineland (a fictitious county in northern California). And, like Slothrop, Zoyd experiences the loss as more than just the dispossession of property:

> attempting to get back his own small piece of Vineland [. . .] But every other night lately he was visited by the dream of the burning house. Each time it became clearer to him that his house [. . .] was asking him to torch it, as the only way left to release it from its captivity. Having glided out to visit [. . .], Zoyd would soundlessly enter and haunt, finding nothing inside anymore of himself [. . .], only stripped and vacuumed spaces, public or hired security shift after shift. (Pynchon 1990, p. 374: Hereafter VL)

Those stripped, vacuumed and patrolled spaces of the house suggest the occupation of another kind of interior, namely, the psyche. But, before I expand on this theme, I want to focus attention on the high profile of the military given in the book.

The military occupation of Vineland, headed by one Brock Vond, a federal prosecutor, is legitimized in the name of the "War on Drugs" (VL p. 348). There are "Brock's troops [. . .] running up and down the dirt lanes in formation chanting 'War-on-drugs! War-on-drugs!' strip-searching folks in public [. . .] and acting indeed [. . .] *as if they had invaded some helpless land far away,* instead of a short plane ride from San Fransisco" (VL p. 357, my emphasis). This and other passages like it have their historical basis in the tactics used by the Los Angeles Police Department in its "war on drugs." Mike Davis has described the military style operations launched by the LAPD against black youths suspected of drug trafficking. In his account of the militarization of federal drug enforcement, he compares the LAPD's "Operation Hammer" (Los Angeles, April 1988) to a "Vietnam-era search-and-destroy mission." He remarks on elite tactical squads "'jacking up' thousands of local teenagers at random like surprised peasants." He quotes the head of the operation, Chief Daryl Gates: "'This is war [. . .] This is Vietnam here'" (Davis 1988, pp. 37–38; see also p. 59). The military occupation of Vineland is presented as an instance of "Vietnam here." The air controllers at Vineland airport "sounded like they used to in Vietnam" (VL p. 355). And Brock Vond reconnoiters the wooded hillsides of Vineland from a Huey slick, dressed in "flak jacket and Vietnam boots" (VL p. 375). Pynchon is suggesting that the kind of force which the U.S. government unleashed on Vietnam (and other parts of the Third World—[see VL pp. 49, 103, 334]) is being *turned inward* on the U.S. population itself.

In a discussion with Sylvere Lotringer on the overdevelopment of the military sector in late-capitalist societies, Paul Virilio has observed: "The military class is turning into an internal super-police. [. . .] It's no longer exo-colonization (the age of extending world conquest), but the age of intensiveness and endo-colonization. One now colonizes only one's own population" (Virilio and Lotringer 1983, pp. 94–95). Endo-colonization, I would suggest, is a process that may be readily applied to events in Vineland, Pynchon's model of late-capitalist America. (In passing, one might add that in *V*, Pynchon, among other things, examines the opposite phenomenon of exo-colonization, focusing on inter-imperialist rivalries in East Africa in the 1890s and the German occupation of South-West Africa in the 1920s. The change of perspective in *Vineland* may, in part, be explained with reference to another observation by Virilio: "If you decolonize without, you'll colonize all the more intensely within" [p. 157]. The American retreat from Southeast Asia is replaced by an intensified colonization at home.) Pynchon conveys the fact of military overdevelopment by representing Vineland as a militarized space. It is perceived as a "garrison state" (VL p. 314); a place of mass-detention camps and blockhouses (VL pp. 249–55, 264); a space of military maneuvers (like "national-emergency" exercises) and military freeways (VL pp. 339–40, 355, 249). The militarization of space (which, of course, also includes the proliferation of silos, bunkers, and bases) is the consequence of a burgeoning military budget. In another study—a remarkable examination of the recent history of American political economy—Mike Davis has pointed to military overdevelopment as a crucial component of the "boom" manufactured by the Reagan administrations. He explains the role of an exorbitant military budget—one trillion dollars for 1985–87—in the recovery of key industrial sectors like aerospace and metals and in stimulating the massive growth of electronic technologies (Davis 1986, pp. 242–43). "Military Keynesianism," he observes, "has been reborn as Reaganomics" (p. 202).

The principal time frame of the narrative, we learn from the opening line, is 1984 (VL p. 3)—the year of Reagan's reelection. Indeed, the Reagan era is quite explicitly the sociohistorical context of the novel.

Pynchon considers how Reaganomics impacts on the lives of Americans. There are "the Reaganomic ax blades [. . .] swinging everywhere" (VL p. 90), the "Reaganomics [. . .] cutbacks" which, among other things, deprive Zoyd's ex-wife, Frenesi—anarchist-turned-informer—of "Witness Protection" (VL pp. 26–27, 354). And, while in *V*, we must get along with the anonymity of "the ultimate Plot Which Has No Name" (*V* p. 226), in *Vineland*, the plot has a specific identity: " ' . . . the whole Reagan program [to] dismantle the New Deal, reverse the effects of World War II, restore fascism at home and around the world' " (VL p. 265). The reelection of Reagan, therefore, prompts one dissident to observe: " 'we all have to be extra paranoid' " (VL p. 262). For, within the book's frame of reference, Reagan's program is, principally, to advance the process of endo-colonization.[24]

Brock Vond's military operation—which has "some connection with Reagan's so-called readiness exercise, code-named REX 84" (VL p. 353)—must be read as a sign of the massive expansion of state power necessary for endo-colonization; it is a reflection of "the State law-enforcement apparatus which was calling itself 'America' " (VL p. 354). And there is the "federal-state Campaign Against Marijuana Production" whose helicopters, on crop-destruction missions, fly over north California which "like other U.S. pot-growing areas [. . . joined], operationally speaking, the third world" (VL p. 49). As CAMP forces move into "unincorporated country" (VL p. 222), "neutralizing" towns friendly to pot growers, "taking [them] back under government control" (VL p. 220), we are offered this arresting image of internal colonization:

Sooner or later Holytail was due for the full treatment, from which it would emerge, like most of the old Emerald Triangle, pacified territory—reclaimed by the enemy for a timeless, defectively imagined future of zero-tolerance drug-free Americans all pulling their weight and all locked in to the official economy, inoffensive music, endless family specials on the Tube. (VL pp. 221–22)

Endo-colonization—the "pacification" and total administration of one's own population by means of intensive military-policing—cannot alone guarantee social control. It is also necessary to structure the consciousness of the population, to colonize the universe of discourse by imposing the terms in which people understand themselves and their social reality, by fixing the coordinates of thought. The practice of agenda-setting is crucial to this process. Proceeding from an order of priorities constructed out of political expedience rather than social need, state administrators seek to define (a) which social problems should be perceived as important (setting the agenda) and (b) in what terms those problems should be conceptualized. (See Chap. 2, under "State-Directed Communication.") The Reagan administration, with the aid of a compliant media, was able to elevate drug abuse to the status of "Number One domestic issue." Thus DEA man Hector Zuñiga tells Zoyd that "the real threat to America [. . .] is from th'illegal abuse of narcotics" (VL p. 51). Zuñiga is collaborating with Hollywood film magnates—men who seek to "ingratiate themselves with the antidrug hysteria leadership" (VL p. 340)—on a film entitled " 'Drugs—Sacrament of the Sixties, Evil of the Eighties' " (VL p. 342). And the news networks, also serving as channels of government propaganda, dutifully feature reports on the destruction of cannabis harvests (VL pp. 373, 220–21).

It is ironic that Zuñiga, principal mouthpiece for the campaign against drug "abuse," is himself undergoing treatment for "Tubal abuse and other video-related disorders" (VL p. 33). This irony is developed to make the point that television, like some chemical, is "poisoning your brain" (VL p. 336), that it is an addictive and mind-altering toxicant. One comical passage recounts how divorce proceedings—in which Zuñiga's wife names the TV set as correspondent—are finalized on the condition that Zuñiga enters a "Tubal Detoxification Program" (VL p. 348). But the therapy fails absurdly, with Zuñiga "creeping out of his ward at night to lurk anywhere Tubes might be glowing, to bathe in rays, lap and suck at the flow of image" (VL p. 335). Meanwhile, other inmates of the "Tubaldetox" hospital, after lights out, watch TV on smuggled LCD units under their blankets. But this behavior is not far off the norm in Vineland/late-capitalist America, where nearly everyone is seen to be living Under The Influence of TV, obsessively humming TV theme songs (VL pp. 26, 336, 341), acting like, or identifying with, TV stars: " 'Feel like Mildred Pierce's husband, Bert,' is how Zoyd described his inner feelings to Frenesi" (VL p. 57; see also VL p. 60).

However, TV is most often figured as, precisely, a colonizing force, annexing territorial, domestic, and, ultimately, mental space. At the territorial level, Pynchon parodies the expansionism of the cable TV networks as a kind of modern-day range war:

when the cable television companies showed up in the county, [they] got into skirmishes that included exchanges of gunfire between gangs of rival cable riggers, eager to claim souls for their distant principals, fighting it out house by house, with the Board of Supervisors compelled eventually to partition the county into Cable Zones, which in time became political units in their own right as the Tubal entrepreneurs went extending their webs. (VL p. 319)

And, a little later, one of the novel's many songs—"The Tube"—links television's penetration of the private, interior space of the home to its penetration of the most private of interior spaces, namely, the mind: "It sees you in your bedroom /And—on th'toilet too! / [. . .] It knows your ev'ry thought / [. . .] It's plugged right in, to you!" (VL p. 336–37). Television has breached the protective enclosure of the home whence its communication-flows reach deep into the psyche, overrunning its secret spaces, transforming the subject into a terminal. And as if to reinforce the impression of an all-pervasive televisual reality—as eyes start to adjust from print to video pixels—*Vineland,* unusually for a postmodern work, alludes to no more than four or five literary texts or writers. In late-capitalist TV culture, our principal reference points, our koine, are shows such as "Hawaii Five-O" (VL p. 60), "Mod Squad" (VL p. 345), the "4:30 Movie" with Pia Zadora (VL p. 14), the "Eight O'Clock Movie" with Pee-wee Herman (VL p. 370).

One character remarks on the political use of television to crowd out perceptions that "see through" the official ideology (VL pp. 313–14). And, to this end, the excess of television spectacle proves particularly useful. *Vineland* begins with Zoyd performing his annual leap through a plate-glass window in front of a battery of news cameras. (He is observing the terms of a "mental-disability arrangement" forced on him by the federal authorities [VL p. 304].) The venue, a Vineland County roadhouse, has been lit and wired by TV crews for the live transmission of the event. The spectacle is enhanced by Zoyd "obligingly charging at each of the news cameras while making insane faces" (VL p. 12), and by his outfit: an outsize dress in "Day-Glo orange, near ultra-violet purple, some acid green, and a little magenta in a retro-Hawaiian parrots-and-hula-girls print" (VL p. 15). Zoyd's "transfenestration" may be seen as a symptom of that tendency in the news media to turn reality into a series of spectator events (e.g., the obsessive focus on disasters and pageants), to substitute spectacle for information. This tendency has the further advantage of occluding reflection; spectacle, after all, may be seen as a mode of unilateral communication, a non-dialogical form insofar as it renders discussion and critical response redundant. (Cf. Debord 1983, paragraphs 24, 195.) There is no suggestion in the news report that evening that Zoyd's leap had been prearranged and professionally staged: " 'Alerted by a mystery caller, TV 86 Hot Shot News crews were there to record Wheeler's deed' " (VL pp. 14–15).

Pynchon reveals the public as a captive audience for "Tubal fantasies," in particular, "cop shows" plugging "their propaganda message of cops-are-only-human-got-to-do-their-job, turning agents of government repression into sympathetic heroes" (VL p. 345). In other words, prime-time programs like *Hill Street Blues, Mod Squad* and *Miami Vice* provide a public relations service for the intensive and high-profile policing which, as noted earlier, defines endo-colonizing regimes. Perhaps Pynchon sees the public as too passive in its response to television. Michel de Certeau, to take a counterinstance, argues that audiences often recode media messages in terms that subvert their original meanings (De Certeau 1984). Nevertheless, the question of the political effectivity of the mass media remains unresolved (see Chap. 2), and Pynchon is clearly committed to the view that they function as agencies of incorporation. In consequence of a successful appearance on the *Donahue Show,* the members of a motorcycle club, formerly distinguished by their "unqualified hatred of authority," become marketable as characters in profit-spinning movies and mini-series (VL pp. 358–59, 373). As a friend of Zoyd's daughter puts it to Zoyd: " 'Minute the Tube got hold of you folks [i.e., 1960s generation] that was it, that whole alternative America, el deado meato, just like th'Indians, sold it all to your real enemies' " (VL p. 373).

"Vineland the Good"

The demise of "alternative America"—in Vineland, the political radicalisms of the 1960s Left—is a large and complex historical question. Pynchon's own analysis is premised on the thesis of social incorporation, where incorporation is understood as a manifold process: endo-colonialist, economic, cultural, and ideological. Television is given particular prominence as an integrative factor. There is also the massive incorporative power of money, the power which the FBI had exploited to turn college-campus insurgents into hired informers and which, in the novel, Vond cynically exploits to precisely the same end (VL pp. 216, 239); the power which buys off one Ditzah Pisk, former student anarchist, with the luxuries of a consumer culture (VL p. 194), just as it propelled former Yippie leader Jerry Rubin into Wall Street brokerage. And the economic system is seen to have traded on counter-cultural activities, when "revolution went blending into commerce" (VL p. 308) as huge profits were made from drugs and rock-and-roll (VL p. 283).[25]

The incorporation of New Left movements, Pynchon argues, may also have been facilitated by weaknesses inherent in the movements themselves. For example, he observes that "the sixties left" was divided by divergent aims and tactics: "Some wanted to declare war on the Nixon Regime, others to approach it, like any other municipality, on the topic of revenue sharing" (VL p. 210). Formulas as to what may be defined as "politically correct" included anything from Trotsky's analyses to LSD (VL p. 42). Indeed, factionalism had an implosive effect on the New Left as Libertarians, Trotskyists, and Leninists, among others, struggled for leadership. And it was disorganization of this kind that stopped the New Left from building solidly on the momentum and achievements of the Civil Rights and antiwar mass movements (see Buhle 1987, Chap. 7). Pynchon also offers numerous observations on what he sees, unfairly I think, as the immaturity of the student radicals, seeking gurus "like ducklings looking for a mother" (VL p. 229), " 'Still children inside [. . .] waitín for that magic payoff' " (VL p. 28). Finally, Pynchon ventures the hypothesis that these are "children longing for discipline" (VL p. 269); "Brock Vond's genius was to have seen in the activities of the sixties left not threats to order but unacknowledged desires for it [. . .] The deep need only to stay children forever, safe inside some extended national Family" (VL p. 269; cf. Frenesi's "uniform fetish" VL p. 83). Most of these criticisms of the 1960s Left are voiced by characters loyal to the Establishment, like Vond or Zuñiga. It is a feature of the book which reflects Pynchon's own ambivalent attitude to New Left politics. On the one hand, he wants to identify with those movements which actively opposed "War in Vietnam, murder as an instrument of American politics, black neighborhoods torched to ashes and death" (VL p. 38). On the other hand, he is critically alert to what he sees as their defects and vulnerabilities.[26]

By the early 1970s, the emancipatory and insurgent movements of the 1960s had virtually expired: Civil Rights, by 1965; the Student Non-Violent Coordinating Committee (SNCC), by 1966; Students for a Democratic Society (SDS) and Black Panthers, by 1969; the antiwar movement, circa 1972. Moreover, in stark contrast to the New Left radicalisms of the 1960s, the 1970s were distinguished by a "conservative revolution" (Davis 1986), a middle-class insurgency chiefly mobilized around property and income tax revolts and other single issues which helped Reagan to power.[27] Finally, from Pynchon's standpoint (writing in the 1980s), the demobilization of the working class under the harsh disciplinary impact of Reaganomics—with its ruthless unleashing of market forces, its antilabor law reforms—leaves no effective internal opposition to America's late-capitalist order. (Collective action by oppressed working-class communities, in particular, by Afro-Americans and Hispanics—the principal victims of Reaganomics—has been hampered by problems of political organization perhaps greater than at any other time. See Davis 1986, p. 311.) And, perhaps, it is this perceived absence of (left-) revolutionary impetus in the Age of Reagan that has turned Pynchon's attention back to the adversarial currents of the 1960s. (The time-frame of the narrative shifts back and forth between the 1960s and the 1980s.) His view of that tumultuous decade, as he endeavors to understand its strengths and weaknesses, is, as already noted, sympathetic and critical in roughly equal measure; the look back is not simply nostalgic. Yet a crucial element of the 1960s survives in Pynchon and is indeed reproduced in *Vineland*—the spirit of a powerful utopianism. What is the nature of this utopianism?

At the end of the novel, the reality of Reagan's America is, in a curious episode, provisionally displaced by the world of (Yurok) myth. The episode involves the end of Federal Prosecutor Brock Vond, the book's embodiment of state-organized repression. After his mission to abduct Zoyd's daughter, Prairie, has been inexplicably aborted by his seniors (VL p. 376), he attempts to pursue the mission independently but, again, without success. He gets lost in the Vineland forest at night under circumstances that are not just mysterious but positively fantastic. When his car breaks down beside a lighted phonebox, he lifts the receiver only to find Vato (of the tow-truck team, Vato & Blood) already on the line. Of the conversation we learn that "Brock had been vague [. . .] about how he'd started off in a helicopter and ended up in a car. He hadn't been aware of any transition" (VL p. 378). But here "transition" signifies more than just an unaccountable change from one vehicle to another; it recalls an earlier reference to the *Tibetan Book of the Dead* according to which "the soul newly in transition often doesn't like to admit [. . .] that it's really dead" (VL p. 218). Hence, now a passenger in Vato's truck, Vond is soon traveling along a river we recognize as the Yuroks' "river of ghosts" that flows into "Tsorrek, the world of the dead" (VL p. 186). Indeed, the landscape metamorphoses into the mythical Tsorrek, all twisted tree roots and mud. Across the river, a primitive village can be seen where some firelit tribal ritual is in progress. When an old couple approaches him, Vond finds that he is surrounded by human bones. Vato explains that the couple will remove his (Vond's) bones before he is taken across the river to "the land of death" (VL p. 379). Vato concludes: "'Give these third-worlders a chance, you know, they can be a lotta fun'" (VL p. 380). And that is the last we see of Vond.

The fantastic nature of this episode—the transfiguration of the environment, the supernatural events—reads very much like a piece of magic-realist narrative. This mode of writing, closely identified with Third World countries, normally encodes a pre-capitalist scheme of reference. As Fredric Jameson has observed, "magic realism [. . . can] be understood as a kind of narrative raw material derived essentially from peasant society, drawing in sophisticated ways on the world of village or even tribal myth" (Jameson 1986, p. 302). In *Vineland*, Pynchon invokes a pre-Columbian mythos as an ever-present active force. Hence, in the realm of the Yuroks, Vond hears:

Voices, not chanting together but remembering, speculating, arguing, telling tales, uttering curses, singing songs, all the things voices do, but *without ever allowing the briefest breath of silence. All these voices, forever.* (VL p. 379. My emphasis)

The passage suggests the enduring vitality of pre-capitalist narratives. Indeed, if we take this episode as a whole, Vond's abduction to the Land of the Dead may be read metaphorically as Pynchon's belief in the power of such narratives or worldviews (ultimately?) to prevail in the struggle against those narratives or worldviews that sustain the system Vond serves.

The Yurok worldview emerges in some detail in earlier passages. We read how the animistic myths of the Yuroks bind them in a close, sacrosanct relationship to the natural world: "single trees with their own names, springs, pools, meadows, all alive, each with its own spirit" (VL p. 186). Many of the souls of these natural objects are "*woge,* creatures like humans but smaller" who have withdrawn into the features of the landscape "as the generations of Yuroks sat on them, fished from them, rested in their shade, as they learned to love and grow deeper into the nuances of wind and light" (VL p. 186). The Indians could be seen in early photographs posing in the landscape of cliffs and "breathing redwoods, alive forever," photographs which record a pervasive and strangely persistent "light" interpreted as "the call to attend to territories of the spirit" (VL p. 317). The world Pynchon describes has its inclement features too but, nevertheless, it is a world to which the Yurok is spiritually connected, a world in which he/she is at home.

One might charge Pynchon with nostalgia for, or romantic mystification of, pre-Columbian America. Alternatively, one might argue that his invocation of Yurok culture serves the purpose of projecting a vision of home as a "territory of the spirit." It is a utopian image of home in which men and women are figured in a non-alienated relationship to their world. In the context of a nation where space has been militarized (VL pp. 249, 255) and suburbanized (VL pp. 37, 319), and where nature is chiefly understood as a commercially exploitable resource, this utopian use of the past both keeps alive the hope of a better world and provides perspectives which enable a forceful critique of the existing one. *Vineland,* in fact, implies *two* distinct ways of using the past. Early in the book we read that Hollywood (in the 1980s) has

". . . been waitín years for the big Nostalgia Wave to move along to the sixties, which according to [. . .] demographics is the best time most people from back then are ever goín to have in their life—sad for them maybe, but not for the picture business. [. . . The 'dream' is] to make a Film about all those long-ago political wars, the drugs, the sex, the rock an' roll." (VL p. 51)

For the "picture business" such a project will amount to the reification of the past as a visual commodity; Hollywood will create a spectacular pseudo-history of popular liberation movements with which the contemporary public can only connect nostalgically. This is the age of "the spectacle, whose function is to *make history forgotten within culture*" (Debord 1983, paragraph 192). But against this appropriation of the past as spectacle, which effectively strips it of any radical or catalyzing power, we may speak of its appropriation as a Utopian imago which enables a critical rereading of the present and, perhaps, may galvanize mass action for change.

Pynchon's invocation of a past culture that embodies a radical alternative to life under the present system helps to focus current dissent. However, he does not suggest that, at this historical juncture, his utopian appeal to the past could rally the forces for political change. This limitation is implied in the account of the annual reunion of the Traverses and Beckers, four generations of Frenesi's family. They are a "'political family for sure'" (VL p. 372) with a tradition of involvement in working-class struggles, first in the activities of the IWW (VL pp. 75–77) and later in those of the studio unions in Hollywood during the blacklist period (VL pp. 81, 289–90). The festive gathering in the Vineland forest locates this family in the province of Yurok history and myth, that is to say, within the vicinity of sources that Pynchon invests with redemptive potential. Yet, at the same time, they are within the neighborhood of "Thanatoid Village" (VL p. 324), a community of "zombies" who spend "at least part of every waking hour with an eye on the Tube" (VL pp. 170–71). Television viewing is a principal activity at this grand social (VL pp. 324, 370–71), and so we feel that the family with a history of political activism may now be on the Thanatoid path to inertia. Moreover, some suspect that "the light they thought they saw was only coming from millions of Tubes all showing the same bright-colored shadows" (VL p. 371)—lines that seem to allude to others quoted earlier where the "light" in the Yurok's forest is interpreted as "the call to attend to territories of the spirit" (VL p. 317). Here Pynchon implies a false enlightenment, namely, the understanding derived from the Tube's reified images of reality.

The argument of *Vineland* is largely built around what is perceived as this profound displacement: our exile from the "territories of the spirit" into the age of "Tubal Reality." Against the latter domain, in which the spectacle is sovereign, the novel's utopian vocation is to imagine the recovery of the former domain. Intimations of this recovery are felt by Vato and Blood while driving along the Seventh River—the heart of Yurok territory and cosmology:

trails without warning would begin to descend into the earth, toward Tsorrek, the world of the dead. Vato and Blood, who as city guys you would think might get creeped out by all this, instead took to it as if returning from some exile of their own. (VL p. 186)

(This recovery is also anticipated in Frenesi's Dream of the Gentle Flood in which a voice sings of "divers who would [. . .] descend into the Flood and bring back up for us 'whatever has been taken [. . .], whatever has been lost' " [VL p. 256].) However, the notion of the recovery of a domain in which we are spiritually rooted is, above all, figured in the metaphor of "home" repossessed. Thus, early on, we learn that Zoyd and Prairie have been dispossessed of their home (VL pp. 48–49). In the novel's closing line, Prairie, having spent the night in the Yuroks' forest, is wakened by her dog, "wagging his tail, thinking he must be home" (VL p. 385). "Home" is the last word of the book, the final destination of a narrative in terms of which the word acquires a utopian charge, a *promesse de bonheur*. For "home" by now suggests more than a habitation, more than the developers' megalopolis of shopping malls and swept and sanitized suburbs. Rather, Pynchon projects a vision of home held by California's aboriginals, a vision of "Vineland the Good" (VL p. 322). To be sure, there is a suggestion that this repossession is not secured; Prairie, like her mother, is attracted to authority figures; she too has "Brock fantasies" (VL pp. 384–85). Nevertheless, awaking in the ancient forest of redwoods, that is, in the vicinity of Yurok history and myth, Prairie—emblematic of a new generation—has returned, albeit provisionally, from her society's exile.

Concluding Remarks

This current of dissident fiction is not sustained by a political program. While some avant-gardist currents of modernism found hope in communism or fascism, dissident postmodernists express no faith in a redemptive macro-political project. Indeed, any such project with its necessarily totalizing perspective would seem suspect, representing yet one more meaning-system to be deconstructed, to be exposed as a dominative fiction. Yet, in spite of the absence of a basis for political action, we have seen how this writing can still function in a spirited and positive way as a strategic intervention within the domain of late capitalism's prevailing discourses.

The dominant discourses of late capitalism are understood to have colonized all but the margins of our linguistic space—a process facilitated by the broadcasting power of contemporary communications systems. These discourses are looked upon as instruments of integration insofar as they are thought to limit consciousness to modes of intelligence approved by, affirmative of, or innocuous to the social order. A key premise of this fiction is that the dialectical tension between the "centripetal" and "centrifugal" forces in language, which for Bakhtin meant that language can never ossify into a fixed "univocal" system (Bakhtin 1981, p. 272), has wound down. The centripetal tendencies in language are seen to have intensified, the greatest part of our communications now inflected toward the politico-cultural center. The ruling discourses, endorsed, amplified, and propagated with a far greater degree of institutional organization than hitherto, are believed to delimit the mental horizons of the subject, framing his/her reading of the social totality, of history, and rendering alternative readings inconceivable or nonsensical. Dissident postmodernist writers probe this perceived correlation between the conceptual limits of late capitalism's ruling discourses and the limits of consciousness.

Dissident postmodernists (not only Barthelme, Pynchon, and, intermittently, Coover, but also Burroughs and Brautigan, among others) seek a realm of meaning beyond the established universe of discourse. Yet, at the same time, they do not confidently assume that such a realm exists. For insofar as the ruling discourses of late capitalism are thought to monopolize our linguistic space, it is suspected that to speak at all is to be complicitous with the social order, to reproduce its legitimating codes; as Burroughs aphoristically asserts: "To speak is to lie" (Burroughs 1968b, p. 12). Hence, dissident postmodernists, perceiving themselves to be implicated in the language forms of a social order from which they dissent, adopt or innovate techniques that distance them from language while they use it; that subvert the rules by which language normally confers meaning; that lay bare the ideological operations of particular discourses. In other words, perceiving most, if not all, understanding as mediated by the ruling discourses of late capitalism—a perception which does not admit of an assured cognitive standpoint outside of those discourses—dissident postmodernist writers resourcefully exploit their position *within* language to expose and interrogate its workings. They adapt sign-reflective techniques for the purpose of probing and revealing ideological closure, mystification, and mythification—instances, among others, of the *modus operandi* of integration through language. In short, the sign-reflective nature of their fiction enables it to perform a critique of society's privileged and prevailing discourses.

By drawing attention to the ways in which discourses produce signs of the real, the sign-reflective writer is saying: there is no transparent representation of reality; all representations are mediated by signsystems. We think we are apprehending reality when all the time we are, in fact, apprehending others' discourses about reality (cf. Barthes 1974, p. 55). The "real" proves to be *quotation* of the already-written, a point that will help us to understand how pastiche operates in this fiction. Here, pastiche—a mode of writing which flaunts itself as a fabrication of quotations, borrowed motifs, and clichés—performs sign-reflectively to reveal the "real" as the already-written, where it is understood that what is already-written cannot but be those ubiquitous discourses which serve to consolidate, or impede reflection on, the social order.

Dissident postmodernists fashion devices which work to fracture the logic of hegemonic codes. Their texts are distinguished by the incommensurability of their narrative parts. One is struck by the frequency of semantic dislocation and syntactic disruption, of paradox and lacunaè—internal subversions of logic and form which militate against an integrated reading experience. This violation of conventional or "novelistic" narrative order is one of the crucial and conspicuous means by which this fiction fulfills the task which Barthes has assigned to a progressive literature: "to unexpress the expressible," that is, to unsettle and throw into crisis society's prevailing codes (the source of the "expressible") whose truth or validity is assumed or naturalized. Barthes's prescription is advanced in the preface to a collection of essays largely known for their appreciation of the work of Alain Robbe-Grillet, a leading practitioner of the Nouveau Roman (Barthes 1972). There are, indeed, remarkable correspondences between North American dissident postmodernist fiction and the Nouveau Roman. The terms in which Stephen Heath defines the latter's "practice of writing" indicate that the fiction of Robbe-Grillet, Sollers, and others is as radically sign-reflective in its probing of the textual production of meaning as the fiction of the dissident postmodernists. Discussing the shift from a "monologistic realism" to "the practice of writing," Heath remarks:

Its foundation is a profound experience of language and form and the demonstration of that experience in the writing of the novel which, transgressed, is no longer repetition [i.e., "re-presentation" of "Reality"] and self-effacement but work and self-presentation as *text*. Its "realism" is not the mirroring of some "Reality" but an attention to the forms of the intelligibility in which the real is produced, a dramatization of possibilities of language, forms of articulation, limitations, of its own horizon. (Heath 1972, p. 22)

The Nouveaux Romanciers, like the dissident postmodernists, "transgress" the "novelistic" or realist mode of writing. They implicate it, as a force in its own right, in the naturalization of "the *vraisemblable* of a particular society, the generally received picture of what may be regarded as 'realistic'" (p. 20). Hence, their program, as Barthes sees it, is to "unwrite" the world as it is given in realist discourse.

Dissident postmodernist fiction is also engaged in a program of "unwriting," an endeavor to liberate consciousness from entrapment within the dominant language forms of late capitalism. Indeed, it is, in part, this struggle for an alternative order of meaning which induces formal innovation and experiment. Style is the effect of the dissident writer's passage through a centripetal and refractory language; a negotiated route through discourses that embody mystifications, evasions, obfuscations, and simplifications. It is also the discovery and mobilization of new resources within language. This fiction may be postmodern but it is not "post-alienated," "commodified," or in any other way symptomatic of the reified mode of expression which, according to Jameson, Eagleton, and others, distinguishes artistic production in a postmodern culture. Rather, this fiction can be productively read as a powerful source of resistance to the force of late capitalism's hegemonic discourses.

Notes

Chapter One: Constructions of Postmodernism

1. It is the forms and philosophical assumptions of literary realism that, more often than those of modernism, seem to be the prime target of postmodernist deconstruction and parody. Indeed, postmodernist fiction abounds with meta-fictional statements in which authors explicitly question the codes and presuppositions of realism. In *V*, for example, Pynchon speaks of "eyes clear enough to see past the fiction of continuity, the fiction of cause and effect, the fiction of a humanized history endowed with 'reason'" (Pynchon 1975, p. 306). In *Pale Fire*, Nabokov writes: "'reality' is neither the subject nor the object of true art which creates its own special reality having nothing to do with the average 'reality' perceived by the communal eye" (Nabokov 1973, p. 106). Moreover, recall that, from a strictly chronological standpoint, American postmodernist fiction follows a long phase of *non-modernist* literature. (There is an uneven development in the American arts. In painting, for example, the modernist impulse persists well into the 1950s in the form of abstract expressionism against whose "élitism" and "esotericism" the Pop Art of the 1960s may be read as an ironic response. Literary history, however, does not run a parallel course.) By the late 1930s, after Dos Passos and Faulkner had completed their major work, the modernist impulse in American narrative fiction was largely spent. It was outlived and/or followed by a variety of fictional forms (e.g., naturalist or "existentialist") which generally adhered to realist conventions of narrative continuity, story, and plot and focused on problems of self-definition and existential crisis. This moment of American fiction (1940s and 1950s) may be represented by works like Mailer's *The Naked and the Dead*, Bellow's *The Victim*, Ellison's *Invisible Man*, and Salinger's *The Catcher in the Rye*.

2. It has been argued that postmodernism is essentially a continuation of modernist practice and is best understood as "neo-modernism" or late modernism (see Kermode 1968 and Graff 1977). One objection to this view is that those elements of modernist thought and form which can be found in postmodernism, and which suggest to some that postmodernism does not mark a stage beyond modernism, do not necessarily have the same aesthetic and political significance across time—if only because conceptions of aesthetics and politics themselves are not what they were circa 1920.

Chapter Two: Language and Late Capitalism

1. Baudrillard writes: "A genealogy of social relations shows many criteria of domination other than the private ownership of the means of production. Species, race, sex, age, language, culture, signs of either an anthropological or cultural type—all these criteria are criteria of *difference*, of signification and of code. It is a simplistic hypothesis that makes them all 'descendants' in the last instance of economic exploitation" (Baudrillard 1975, p. 142).

2. And, of course, it was evident when, back in the 1940s, Adorno and Horkheimer launched their broadside against the mass media. Perceiving the technology of advertising at work in the "culture industry," they argued that the latter works essentially as "a procedure for manipulating men" (Adorno and Horkheimer 1979, p. 163).

3. The following have been defined as phenomena specific to "late" or "advanced" capitalism: the hypertrophy of the state (Mandel 1978, chap. 15; Miliband 1973, chaps. 1–4; Habermas 1976, part II); technological rationality as the dominant ideology (Mandel 1978, chap. 16; Marcuse 1966, chaps. 1 and 6; Habermas 1971, chap. 6); the dissolution of the "public sphere" (Habermas, *Structurwandel der Offentlichkeit,* Neuwied 1962).

4. Barthes says of the contemporary novel that "it aims to transpose narrative from the purely constative plane, which it has occupied until now, to the performative plane, whereby the meaning of an utterance is the very act by which it is uttered: today, writing is not 'telling' but saying that one is telling and assigning all the referent ('what one says') to this act of locution" (Barthes 1977, p. 114).

Chapter Three: Donald Barthelme

1. In the last paragraph we read: "The balloon [. . .] is a spontaneous autobiographical disclosure having to do with the unease I felt at your absence, and with sexual deprivation" (UPUA p. 29). Not by chance is the meaning finally given to the balloon a psychoanalytic one. The creation of the balloon is seen as a sublimation of repressed sexuality ("spontaneous autobiographical disclosure" suggests a product of the unconscious). Of all contemporary meaning-systems, psychoanalysis is, at least in the view of some of its critics (e.g., H.J. Eysenck and Karl Popper), notorious for its pretensions to an all-embracing significance. Concepts like "Oedipus complex" or "libido" are seen to be formulated at such an abstract level of theory that not only are they unfalsifiable (they are not amenable to empirical testing), but they can be used to explain almost any aspect of human behavior. Accordingly, the allusion to psychoanalytic thought may be read as the culmination of the story's interest in parodying the ease and complacency with which meaning-systems can be used to assimilate the indefinable or abnormal. (Perhaps, more specifically, the Freudian notion of art as a form of displaced sexuality is also parodied here.)

2. Indeed, we are never allowed to forget that we are reading about (capitalist) America. The God-like President looks out of his window across America, aware of "'the falling Dow-Jones index and the screams of the poor. . . .'"He adds: "'I worry about Bill and the boys too [i.e., the dwarves]. Because I am the President. Finally. The President of the whole fucking country. And they are

Americans, Bill, Hubert, Henry, Kevin, Edward, Clem, Dan and Snow White. They are Americans. My Americans'" (SW p. 81).

3. Marcuse (1966, pp. 11–12) notes:

The productive apparatus and the goods and services which it produces 'sell' or impose the social system as a whole. The means of mass transportation and communication, the commodities of lodgings, food, and clothing, the irresistible output of the entertainment and information industry carry with them prescribed attitudes and habits, certain intellectual and emotional reactions which bind the consumers more or less pleasantly to the producers and, through the latter, to the whole. The products indoctrinate and manipulate; they promote a false consciousness which is immune against its falsehood.

Lefebvre (1971, p. 56) speaks of

an *ideology of consumption,* an ideology that has bereft the working classes of their former ideals and values while maintaining the status and the initiative of the bourgeoisie. It has substituted for the image of active man that of the consumer as the possessor of happiness and of perfect rationality. [. . .] In this process of ideological substitutions and displacements man's awareness of his own alienation is repressed.

4. In his essay "Not-Knowing," Barthelme writes:

To turn to the action of contemporary culture on language, and thus on the writer, the first thing to be noticed is a loss of reference. If I want a world of reference to which all possible readers in this country can respond, there is only one universe of discourse available, that in which the Love Boat on seas of passion like a Flying Dutchman of passion and the dedicated men in white of *General Hospital* pursue, with evenhanded diligence, triple bypasses, and the nursing staff. This limits things somewhat. (Barthelme 1985, p. 43)

5. In an interview, Barthelme has observed:

"What I'm most interested in is language and making a kind of music [. . .] What I'm trying to reach is a realm of knowing that cannot be put precisely into words, but must be gotten as music is gotten. Take a piece of music which is not program music, not describing, let's say, 'The Fountains of Rome.' You cannot say precisely what this piece of music means; on the other hand, you cannot say that this piece of music is meaningless. It has a meaning and a very strong meaning, but you cannot say precisely what that meaning is and perhaps should not. It's this kind of thing I would like my writing to do." (Ziegler and Bigsby 1982, p. 45)

6. "Bone Bubbles" in Barthelme 1976, pp. 119–128; "Alice" in Barthelme 1978, pp. 121–131; *Snow White,* Barthelme 1982, e.g., pp. 31, 103.

7. The montage of cut-ups is central to Burroughs' strategy of "Total Resistance" (Burroughs 1968a, p. 104; 1968b, p. 62). Hence,

ODIER: "Is the introduction of what you call 'The message of resistance' the most important thing in the montage?"

BURROUGHS: "Well, yes, I would say it's a very important factor in the montage because it does tend to break down the principal instruments of control which are word and image, and to some extent to nullify them." (Burroughs 1970, p. 19)

8. See note 6, chap. 5.

Chapter Four: Robert Coover

1. The remarks of the police officer in "The Marker" may be read as a statement of this approach. In his view, tradition is not "some malignant evil" to be "rooted out at all costs," because we must recognize that there is a "middle road [where] innovations find their best soil in traditions," and therefore "it is one's constant task to review and revise them" (PD p. 91). Perhaps the old tramp in "The Wayfarer," with his fragments of archaic discourse, may be seen as an embodiment of exhausted narrative traditions, and his execution seen as an *extremist* rejection of those traditions.

2. See, for example, the numerological speculations of the Brunists (Coover 1973) and Nixon's reflections on the "Rosenberg formula": "Courage, Confidence and Perspective" (Coover 1978, p. 172).

3. Cf. Borges, "The Modesty of History" (1952): "Since that time [1792] historic days have been numerous, and one of the tasks of governments (especially in Italy, Germany, and Russia) has been to fabricate them or to simulate them with an abundance of preconditioning propaganda followed by relentless publicity. Such days, which reveal the influence of Cecil B. De Mille, are related less to history than to journalism" (Borges 1973, p. 167).

4. In an interview, Coover has observed: "Our old faith—derived from myths, philosophies, fairy tales, histories, and other fictions which help to explain what happens to us from day to day, why our governments (and institutions) are the way they are, [. . .] why the world turns as it does—has lost its efficacy. Not necessarily is it false; it is just not as efficacious as it was." Similarly, he adds: "Most of society's effort goes into forging the construct, the creative form in which everybody can live—a social contract of sorts. [. . .] Whatever form they set up is necessarily entropic: eventually it runs down and is unable to propel itself past a certain point" (Gado 1973, pp. 142, 157).

5. Cf. *The Origin of the Brunists:* "the affairs of West Condon were compressed into a set of conventionally accepted signs and became, in the shape of the West Condon *Chronicle,* what most folks in town thought of as life, or history" (Coover 1973, p. 145).

6. James Carey has commented on the normally restrictive use of the word "communication": "Substantively, it narrows the scope of study to products explicitly produced by and delivered over the mass media. The study of communication is, therefore, generally isolated from [. . .] the expressive and ritual forms of everyday life—religion, conversation, sport" (Carey 1977, p. 411).

7. For example, LeClair observes: "[Coover's] anthropological perspective suggests history is a fiction, perhaps finer-gauged than most yet without finality. But it is by stretching fact past 'faction' to myth that Coover obviates history and makes *The Public Burning* a major achievement of conscience and imagination" (quoted in Hume 1979, p. 147). And Ramage writes: "Not until the last hundred pages or so of *The Public Burning* does the veneer of history wear away

sufficiently that the pentimento of myth can move into the foreground and make everything 'perfectly clear' " (Ramage 1982, p. 62).

8. It ought to be said that there is nothing in the novel to suggest that Coover believes that overcoming ideology will grant us unmediated access to the truth; he sticks to the position that there is a radical separation between the discursive specification of events and the events themselves; that history is inevitably "received" in textual form.

9. It must be said that Coover's reader learns little about the economic and political motives behind the Cold War. (For a perceptive analysis of these motives, see especially Chomsky 1984, pp. 24–58.) Later, I shall note the role of cold war politics in containing class conflict at home.

10. The problem of *writing history* (the rubric under which the problems of interpreting facts or data, of representing reality, are examined in the novel) wherever it is explicitly addressed, is nearly always expressed as an ideological or political problem; it may be raised within the framework of an analysis of an ideological apparatus such as the press or legal system or else raised in the course of Nixon's reflections on politics. (For example, see PB pp. 110–11, 240–41, 172.)

11. Donald Hall, "Three Million Toothpicks," *National Review*, 30 September, 1977, p. 1118. Paul Gray, "Uncle Sam Takes on the Phantom," *Time*, 8 August, 1977, p. 72. Both quoted in Hume 1979, p. 127.

12. While recognizing that the content of the discourse may alter with historical circumstances, it is worth stressing that many of its key concepts (e.g., America as a nation vulnerable to a conspiracy of subversive forces, America as a nation with a destiny) have persisted with remarkable continuity over generations. Specific examples of this continuity can be found in Hofstadter (1967). See especially chapters 1 and 2. Hofstadter remarks on the historical recurrence, from around 1800 onward, of paranoid and apocalyptic terminology in American political thought.

13. For want of space, I have omitted discussion of a key concept in the discourse of "America" that is closely related to the ideal of free enterprise, that is, the "poor-boy-makes-good-in-America" myth as institutionalized by Horatio Alger (1834–99). Alger's books for boys, which sold in the millions, propagated the myth that, in America, hard work, honesty, and a sense of public duty bring money and success. Nixon sees himself as having had a "genuine Horatio Alger career" (PB p. 321), and there are many more references to Alger in the novel (PB pp. 228, 366, 376, 390, etc.). The myth proved especially useful to the expansion of American industry; it embodied the false promise of Opportunity For All that enticed millions of poor Europeans to the United States as cheap labor.

14. This is the subject explored by Barbara Margolis in her epic documentary *Are We Winning Mommy?* (Margolis 1986). The film examines the domestic side of the First Cold War, seeing it largely as a propaganda campaign secretly organized by government agencies like the CIA with the aim of transforming the postwar mood of pacifism into belligerent anti-Communism. The results, we learn, were decisive. A poll taken in 1945 revealed that, but for a tiny percentage, the American public believed the nation was entering an era of peace. The same poll taken just three years later revealed that 73 percent of the public believed in the imminence or inevitability of war with the Soviet Union. Margolis quotes John Foster Dulles, who remarked in the late 1940s, "We need

to scare our people to bring them up to the level of response to the Soviet threat" (cf. Doctorow 1979, p. 254).

15. Mazurek points out that "In the actual [Checkers] speech, Nixon accused [Adlai] Stevenson of reducing the Communist threat to a matter of 'phantoms among ourselves,' thus providing Coover with a name for the novel's principle of opposition" (Mazurek 1982, p. 39).

16. During the war, American workers were under pressure not to strike; strike action, it was said, would harm the war effort and was, therefore, deemed unpatriotic. The result of workers' compliance was an unprecedented increase in the rate of capital accumulation, a four-fold enlargement of America's industrial capital. America emerged from the War as by far the world's strongest economy. Accordingly, after years of constraint by management, American workers sought a share in the new prosperity. There was a dramatic increase in unionization and popular support for the rash of strikes which followed the armistice. It was a situation which alarmed the big corporations and the Government, and both worked closely together in an effort to suppress union activism.

17. "Anthropological" readings of *The Public Burning* prioritize those passages which suggest the scapegoating of the Rosenbergs is the expression of an atavistic need for cultural regeneration by means of ceremonial sacrifice (Ramage 1982, pp. 63–64; LeClair 1982, pp. 7–8; see also McCaffery 1982, p. 86).

18. Foucault, commenting on the role of prestigious institutions in the production of truth, observes that, today, "'truth' [. . .] is produced and transmitted under the control, dominant if not exclusive, of a few great political and economic apparatuses" (Foucault 1980, pp. 131–32).

19. In several respects, the account of ideology employed here is indebted to Althusser (Althusser 1984). However, I do not wish to lean too heavily on his theory of the relationship between ideology and subjectivity. First, while I would agree that "ideology has the function [. . .] of 'constituting' concrete individuals as subjects" (p. 45), I would not want to go so far as to suggest that all subjectivity is ideologically constituted. Second, Althusser, as his critics have remarked, works with a non-processual, noncontradictory model of the subject; a subject unable to disengage itself from the purely functional identity produced for it by the dominant ideology. Therefore, I shall also make use, albeit schematically, of the (Lacanian) model of the "split subject," a subject whose contradictory nature ensures that it remains always "in-process," always in transition from one identity to the next. (For a fine reading of *Spanking the Maid* that incorporates elements from the work of Lacan, Kristeva, and Deleuze, see Wright 1989.)

20. The sun whose light is repeatedly described as "flooding" the master's room (SM pp. 9, 16, 18, 49, etc.) is, perhaps, an allusion to the title of the famous chapter ("A Flood of Sunshine") in Hawthorne's *The Scarlet Letter* where sunshine is used to extol the liberating power of "wild heathen Nature" against the repression of "human law" (Hawthorne [1850] 1978, chap. 18, p. 220).

Chapter Five: Thomas Pynchon

1. See especially Herzog's last letter (Bellow 1965, p. 347).

2. Pynchon uses the *Tractatus* parodically and with some license (see also *V* pp. 288–89). Strictly speaking, the line quoted means that "the world is every-

thing that is represented by the totality of *true* propositions" (Grayling 1988, p. 34, my emphasis).

3. For a detailed study of the Pentecostal motif in *V* see Lhamon, Jr. 1976.

4. Cf. J.L. Borges's story "Tlön, Uqbar, Orbis Tertius" (1946), in which a possible world (originally the construct of a clique of seventeenth-century metaphysicians) intrudes into material reality and eventually supplants it (Borges 1970, pp. 27–43).

5. Cf. *Gravity's Rainbow* "[Leni] tried to explain to [Franz] about the level you reach, with both feet in, when you lose your fear, you lose it all, you've penetrated the moment, slipping perfectly into its grooves, [. . .], and now the figures are dancing, each pre-choreographed exactly where it is [. . .]" (Pynchon 1978, p. 158). And "Business of all kinds, over the centuries, had atrophied certain sense-receptors and areas of the human brain" (p. 588).

6. Cf. William Burroughs, in an interview given in 1965 (i.e., precisely when Pynchon was writing *Lot 49*): "Yes, it is unfortunately one of the great errors of Western thought, the whole either-or proposition. You remember Korzybski and his idea of non-Aristotelian logic. Either-or thinking just is not accurate thinking. That's not the way things occur, and I feel the Aristotelian construct is one of the great shackles of Western civilization" (Plimpton, ed., 1977, pp. 156–57).

7. One must bear in mind the ideological power of positivism at the time Pynchon was writing. In his introduction to *Habermas and Modernity* (1985), Richard J. Bernstein writes: "By 1968 the positivist tradition, which had its origins in the nineteenth century and was revitalized and refined by the logical positivists, was already under severe attack. But one cannot underestimate the extent to which the positivistic *temper* pervaded and dominated intellectual and cultural life" (pp. 4–5). See also Tom Bottomore, *The Frankfurt School* (1984, pp. 28–33). The influence of positivism can be inferred when Bottomore notes that it was the principal target of Critical Theory right up until "the debate about positivism in 1969" (p. 28).

8. I emphasize "might": Oedipa may, of course, be fantasizing the existence of the Tristero System; nevertheless, real or imagined, it may serve as a symbol of an ideal or alternative order of meaning.

9. We may also speak of the text as having "the secret richness and concealed density of dream" (CL p. 128) that Oedipa ascribes to the Tristero System. Thus, just as Freud recognized that the exposition of the "manifest content" of a dream was exceedingly brief relative to the exposition of its "latent content," so we find that the narrative (or manifest content) of *Lot 49* is notably brief, its signifiers relatively few compared to the volume of commentary required to expound the patterns of meaning "concealed" in them.

10. The historic figure of Wernher von Braun, like the trajectory of his V-2, seems to overarch the narrative of *Gravity's Rainbow*. The first words of the novel are credited to him; the last words describe the descent of a rocket, an offspring of his V-2. (He is referred to by name eight times in the novel.) It is through allusions to the postwar career of von Braun and the subsequent evolution of his rocket that Pynchon is able to project the fascism of the Third Reich (its militarism and imperialism) onto America. Von Braun led the team of scientists that pioneered the development of the V-1 and V-2 rockets. 20,000 slave laborers, imported from Buchenwald, died during the construction of the rockets in the submontane factory at Nordhausen, many thrown live into furnaces when too weak to work, or hanged. At the end of the war, when the

Allies were scrambling for the expertise and hardware of the German rocket program (the theme which connects most of the book's episodes), von Braun was abducted by the CIA and taken to New Mexico. His rehabilitation in the United States was justified on the grounds that "Future scientific importance outweighs present war guilt" (Bower 1987). In 1955, von Braun became a naturalized American citizen. In the 1960s, he led the Apollo space program, a project in which other ex-Nazi scientists, also abducted, played key roles and which culminated, in 1969, with the Apollo XI moon-landing. Thereafter, von Braun was fêted by the media and honored by Nixon's administration. The von Braun affair may be a familiar story to some but there are good reasons for retelling it here. The moon-landing and America's celebration of von Braun occurred while Pynchon was working on *Gravity's Rainbow* (1966–71), and he was evidently alert to the significance of these events. America had become the principal beneficiary of Hitler's pet project, the V-2, whose advanced technology would guarantee her military supremacy in the postwar era. What surely disturbed Pynchon was the link between Hitler's rocket program and America's, the *continuity* in missile development.

11. For Burroughs, "war is absolutely essential to the maintenance of modern society" (1970, p. 69). In his work, from *The Naked Lunch* to recent publications like *Cities of the Red Night* (which chronicles the development of weaponry from eighteenth-century firearms to germ and nuclear warfare), society is essentially defined by perpetual war and conflict.

12. It is the logic of a rationalized total system which informs the thought of Wimpe, sales representative of the pharmaceutical cartel I.G. Farben. He understands addiction to pain-killing drugs not as a medical problem but as a problem of economic dysfunction: " 'A demand like 'addiction,' having nothing to do with [. . .] real economic needs, unrelated to production or labor [. . .] A rational economy cannot depend on psychological quirks. We could not *plan'* " (GR 348–49).

13. See Peter Hamilton, *Talcott Parsons* (1983), chapter 3. The work of Parsons, criticized, among other things, for defining social structures essentially in terms of integration and consensus rather than "constraint, conflict and change" (Ralf Dahrendorf, quoted in Hamilton), remains the locus classicus of systems theory. Moreover, the writing of *Gravity's Rainbow* (1966–71) coincided with the emergence of "world-system theory," notably in the writings of Immanuel Wallerstein. Paul Buhle remarks: "Wallerstein's *The Modern World System* (1974) [. . .], has arguably been the most influential single book of the post-New Left era. Critics have shrewdly noted that Parsonian functionalism, disguised in the thicket of Marxist political convictions, has returned suspiciously to the essential interpretation. All sub-systems resemble each other and fit into a single, overarching system; transformation of the system piecemeal ultimately serves as readjustment of integration *grosso modo*" (Buhle 1987, p. 265).

14. Cf. GR 521, "We have to look for power sources here, and distribution networks we were never taught, routes of power our teachers never imagined, or were encouraged to avoid . . . we have to find meters whose scales are unknown in the world, draw our own schematics, getting feedback, making connections, reducing the error, trying to learn the real function . . . zeroing in on what incalculable plot?"

15. It might seem that Pynchon is shooting at a straw target in citing Pavlov's thought as an intellectual force to be reckoned with. After all, even by the

1940s (the principal time frame of the novel), Pavlov's stimulus-response model of the human subject had been decisively rejected as succeeding generations of psychologists (e.g., Clark Hull, Edward Tolman) found it necessary to introduce mediating processes ("intervening variables") in order to account for the complexities of behavior. However, if the fundamental tenets of Pavlovian or "classical" behaviorism have not survived, its methodology prevails to this day and is evident in the search for empirical relationships between observable variables which characterizes most laboratory work. In the postwar period, behaviorist research into conditioning and motivation has been of service to military institutions in providing techniques of discipline, indoctrination, and interrogation, and to industrial management in providing techniques of worker-control (e.g., in the forms of ergonomics or incentive schemes). Such examples seem to support the view that the science of behaviorism embodies a logic of domination.

16. Foucault has proposed that the "human sciences" embody a "disciplinary" logic, that is, they are oriented toward practices which control or manipulate the subject. He has argued that behind the scientific dream of the "knowable man" lies an "effort in discipline and normalization" (Foucault 1980, p. 61).

17. There are, in the novel, just two direct references to Marxist theory (GR pp. 317, 701); in both cases they are criticisms which are perfunctory and prematurely dismissive.

18. Adorno and Horkheimer 1979, p. 28. Insofar as they understood the Enlightenment as a project to establish total mastery over the natural world, they perceived a radical change in man's relationship to it: "domination is paid for by the alienation of men from the objects dominated" (p. 28). Enlightenment "extirpated" animism and, in its place, demanded that men take a purely objective, scientific view of the natural world (p. 5).

19. Pynchon's menu was surely inspired by Burroughs' concoctions: "The Clear Camel Piss Soup," "The After-Birth Suprême de Boeuf," "The Limburger Cheese sugar cured in diabetic urine," all on the menu Chez Robert in The Naked Lunch (Burroughs 1982a, p. 150).

20. The title originally planned for Gravity's Rainbow was "Mindless Pleasures" (see Levine and Leverenz 1976, p. 3). This title, or variations of it (GR pp. 270, 681, 177, 367), is one of Pynchon's recurrent phrases and it refers us to those orders of meaning which, he believes, are uncorrupted by "rationalization."

21. Compare the account of the bus ride (GR pp. 412–13) proceeding from the lines "Living inside the System is like riding across the country in a bus driven by a maniac bent on suicide," and the account of "Albatross Nosology" (GR p. 712) proceeding from the line "[Slothrop] has become one plucked albatross."

22. Discontinuities of narrative structure are, of course, the norm in several currents of modernist and postmodernist writing. Indeed, an exhaustive inventory of syntactic and semantic discontinuities would reveal a surprisingly wide range of forms. Eliot's "dislocated discourse," Joyce's "stream of consciousness," Breton's "automatic writing," Gass's individually titled paragraphs (Gass 1981, pp. 172–206) are all examples of narrative discontinuity. However, even if identical instances of Pynchon's techniques of discontinuity can be found in modernist or postmodernist texts, their meanings would be different, either because the text originated in another historical context (modernity) or,

if contemporaneous, because it does not participate in the same schema of oppositions which define the polemics of Pynchon's book. As I have argued, Pynchon's narrative techniques acquire meaning chiefly as an adversarial discourse which negates the logic of a historically specific ideology, that is, the technological rationality of late capitalism.

23. In affirming the value of a preverbal, intuitive mode of consciousness as a source of resistance to the established system of meaning, Pynchon may be compared with Burroughs or Kathy Acker: "That part of our being (mentality, feeling, physicality) which is free of all control let's call our 'unconscious.' Since it's free of control, it's our only defence against institutionalised meaning, institutionalised language, control, fixation, judgment, prison" (Acker 1988, pp. 133–34). Furthermore, I have read Pynchon as suggesting that the limited use of this mode of consciousness is a historical, not an ontological, condition: "Business of all kinds, over the centuries, had atrophied certain sense-receptors and areas of the human brain" (GR p. 588).

24. Cf. Virilio and Lotringer: "Reaganism is already endo-colonization applied to America" (1983, p. 98).

25. Rock and roll is represented as a potent countercultural force. It is valued in just the same way as the "Jes Grew" dance craze of the 1920s, invoked in Reed's *Mumbo Jumbo*, namely, as subversive of the routinized and instrumental mind-set of a (white) capitalist culture. One chapter recounts the history of a "nation" of revolutionary students that secedes from California and which is named "after the one constant they knew they could count on never to die. The People's Republic of Rock and Roll" (VL p. 209). But rock and roll is, like so much else, seen as susceptible to incorporation as, for example, "background shopping music [. . .], perky and up-tempo, originally rock and roll but here reformatted into unthreatening wimped-out effluent" (VL p. 328; see also p. 314). (There is a fully articulated politics of popular music running through *Vineland* which deserves attention as a topic in its own right.)

26. A similarly ambivalent attitude to the 1960s Left can be found in two other notable postmodernist works: Doctorow's *The Book of Daniel* and Mailer's *The Armies of the Night*. Doctorow's doubts about the redemptive powers of the New Left are suggested, for example, by the mock-apocalyptic account of the student "liberation" of Columbia University (Doctorow [1971] 1979, p. 318) and by the implied contrast between the "new consciousness" of libertarian student-leader Artie Sternlicht who seeks liberation through spontaneous action—"A revolution *happens*. It's a happening!"—and the organizational and party discipline of the Old Left (pp. 152–53). And Mailer describes the New Left/hippy revolution as "revolution by theater and without a script" (Mailer 1968, p. 249), alternating, as a "Left Conservative," between sympathy for and cynicism toward the shamanistic and psychedelic features of this "theatrical" revolution (pp. 142–43).

27. Mike Davis writes "Grassroots political mobilization during the 1970s was on the whole an inverse mirror-image of that of the 1960s. If the latter decade was dominated by the mass civil rights movement, followed by the new student left and various cognate liberation currents, then the 1970s were, without quite so much sound and fury, the decade of the revanchist middle strata" (Davis 1986, p. 222).

Bibliography

Abernethy, Peter (1972). "Entropy in Pynchon's *The Crying of Lot 49*." *Critique* 14, 2: 18–33.

Acker, Kathy (1988). *Empire of the Senseless*. London: Pan/Picador.

Adorno, T., and M. Horkheimer (1979). *Dialectic of Enlightenment*. Trans. John Cumming. London: Verso. Orig. pub. 1944.

Althusser, Louis (1984). "Ideology and Ideological State Apparatuses." In *Essays on Ideology*. London: Verso, pp. 1–60. Orig. pub. 1970.

Armstrong, P., A. Glyn, and J. Harrison (1984). *Capitalism Since World War II*. London: Fontana.

Ashbery, John (1971). "They Dream Only of America." In *Penguin Modern Poets 19*. Harmondsworth: Penguin, p. 23. Orig. pub. 1962.

Bakhtin, Mikhail M. (1981). *The Dialogic Imagination*. Ed. Michael Holquist, trans. Michael Holquist and Caryl Emerson. Austin: University of Texas Press. Essays originally published in the 1930s.

Barth, John (1969). *Lost in the Funhouse, Fiction for Print, Tape, Live Voice*. London: Secker and Warburg. Orig. pub. 1968.

Barthelme, Donald (1964). *Come Back, Dr. Caligari*. Boston: Little, Brown.

—— (1976). *City Life*. New York: Pocket Books. Orig. pub. 1970.

—— (1978). *Unspeakable Practices, Unnatural Acts*. New York: Pocket Books. Orig. pub. 1968.

—— (1981). *Sixty Stories*. New York: Putnam.

—— (1982). *Snow White*. New York: Atheneum. Orig. pub. 1967.

—— (1985). "Not-Knowing." In *Voice-Lust: Eight Contemporary Fiction Writers on Style*. Ed. Allen Wier and Don Hendrie, Jr. Lincoln: University of Nebraska Press, pp. 37–50.

Barthes, Roland (1972). *Critical Essays*. Trans. Richard Howard. Evanston, Ill.: Northwestern University Press. Orig. pub. 1964.

—— (1973). *Mythologies*. Trans. Annette Lavers. London: Granada. Orig. pub. 1957.

—— (1974). *S/Z*. Trans. Richard Miller. New York: Hill and Wang. Orig. pub. 1970.

—— (1975). *The Pleasure of the Text*. Trans. Richard Miller. New York: Hill and Wang. Orig. pub. 1973.

—— (1977). *Image-Music-Text*. Trans. and ed. Stephen Heath. London: Fontana.

Baudrillard, Jean (1975). *The Mirror of Production*. Trans. Mark Poster. St. Louis: Telos Press. Orig. pub. 1973.

—— (1983a). "The Ecstasy of Communication." Trans. John Johnston. In *The Anti-Aesthetic*. Ed. H. Foster. Washington: Bay Press, pp. 126–34.

—— (1983b). *In the Shadow of the Silent Majorities*. Trans. P. Foss, P. Patton, and J. Johnston. New York: Semiotext(e).

—— (1983c). *Simulations*. Trans. P. Foss, P. Patton and P. Beitchman. New York: Semiotext(e).

—— (1988). *Selected Writings*. Ed. M. Poster. Cambridge, Mass.: Polity Press.

Bellow, Saul (1965). *Herzog*. Harmondsworth: Penguin. Orig. pub. 1964.

Berman, Neil (1978). "Coover's *Universal Baseball Association:* Play As Personalized Myth." *Modern Fiction Studies* 24: 209–22.

Bernstein, Richard J., ed. (1985). *Habermas and Modernity*. Cambridge: Polity Press.

Bhabha, Homi (1986). "The other question: difference, discrimination and the discourse of colonialism." In *Literature, Politics and Theory*. Ed. Francis Barker, Peter Hulme, Margaret Iverson, and Diana Loxley. London: Methuen, pp. 148–72.

Borges, Jorge Luis (1970). *Labyrinths: Selected Stories and Other Writings*. Ed. Donald A. Yates and James E. Irby. Harmondsworth: Penguin. Orig. pub. 1964.

—— (1973). *Other Inquisitions, 1937–52*. Trans. Ruth L.C. Simms. London: Souvenir Press, pp. 167–70.

Bottomore, Tom (1984). *The Frankfurt School*. Chichester: Ellis Horwood.

Bower, Tom (1987). *The Paperclip Conspiracy*. London: Michael Joseph.

Bradbury, Malcolm (1983). *The Modern American Novel*. Oxford University Press.

Brown, John (1966). "Information Theory." In *New Horizons in Psychology 1*. Ed. Brian M. Foss. Harmondsworth: Penguin, pp. 118–34.

Brummer, Alex (1986). "U.S. 'cuts loose' in July 4 patriotic orgy." *The Guardian*, July 5, 1986.

Buhle, Paul (1987). *Marxism in the USA*. London: Verso.

Burroughs, William (1968a). *The Ticket That Exploded*. London: Calder and Boyars. Orig. pub. 1962.

—— (1968b). *Nova Express*. London: Granada. Orig. pub. 1964.

—— (1970). *The Job*. London: Jonathan Cape.

—— (1982a). *The Naked Lunch*. London: John Calder. Orig. pub. 1959.

—— (1982b). *Cities of the Red Night*. London: Pan/Picador. Orig. pub. 1981.

Carey, James (1977). "Mass Communication Research and Cultural Studies: an American View." In *Mass Communication and Society*. Ed. James Curran, Michael Gurevitch, and Janet Woollacott. London: Edward Arnold, pp. 409–25.

Caute, David (1978). *The Great Fear*. London: Secker and Warburg.

Chomsky, Noam (1984). "The United States: From Greece to El Salvador." In Noam Chomsky, Jonathan Steele, and John Gittings, *Superpowers in Collision*. Harmondsworth: Penguin.

—— (1988). *The Chomsky Reader*. Ed. J. Peck. London: Serpent's Tail.

Coover, Robert (1970). *Pricksongs and Descants*. New York: Plume. Orig. pub. 1969.

—— (1971). *The Universal Baseball Association, Inc., J. Henry Waugh, Prop.* New York: Plume. Orig. pub. 1968.

—— (1973). *The Origin of the Brunists*. London: Panther. Orig. pub. 1965.

—— (1978). *The Public Burning*. Harmondsworth: Penguin. Orig. pub. 1977.

—— (1980). *A Political Fable.* New York: Viking Press. Orig. pub. 1968.

—— (1988). *Spanking the Maid.* London: Paladin. Orig. pub. 1982.

Cope, Jackson I. (1986). *Robert Coover's Fictions.* Baltimore: Johns Hopkins University Press.

Couturier, M., and R. Durand (1982). *Donald Barthelme.* London: Methuen.

Davis, Mike (1986). *Prisoners of the American Dream.* London: Verso.

—— (1988). "Los Angeles: Civil Liberties between the Hammer and the Rock." *New Left Review* 170 (July/August 1988): 37–60.

Debord, Guy (1983). *Society of the Spectacle.* Detroit: Black and Red. Orig. pub. 1967.

De Certeau, Michel (1984). *The Practice of Everyday Life.* Trans. Steven Rendell. Berkeley: University of California Press.

Derrida, Jacques (1977). "Signature Event Context." *Glyph* 1: 172–97.

Doctorow, E. L. (1979). *The Book of Daniel.* New York: Bantam Books. Orig. pub. 1971.

Eagleton, Terry (1985). "Capitalism, Modernism and Postmodernism." *New Left Review* 152 (July/August 1985): 60–72.

Ehrlich, H.J. (1971). "Social Conflict in America: the 1960s." *Sociological Quarterly* (Summer 1971).

Engels, Friedrich (1977). "Letter to Margaret Harkness." In *Marxists on Literature.* Ed. D. Craig. Harmondsworth: Penguin, pp. 269–71. Orig. pub. 1888.

Fiedler, Leslie (1968). "The New Mutants." In *Innovations.* Ed. B. Bergonzi. London: Macmillan.

—— (1975). "Cross the Border-Close that Gap: Postmodernism." In *American Literature Since 1900.* Ed. M. Cunliffe. London: Barrie and Jenkins, pp. 344–66. Orig. pub. 1968.

Fokkema, Douwe (1986). "The Semantic and Syntactic Organization of Postmodernist Texts." In *Approaching Postmodernism.* Ed. Bertens and Fokkema. Amsterdam and Philadelphia: John Benjamins, pp. 81–95.

Foster, Hal (1985). *Recodings.* Washington: Bay Press.

——, ed. (1983). *The Anti-Aesthetic.* Washington: Bay Press.

Foucault, Michel (1980). *Power/Knowledge: Selected Interviews and Other Writings 1972–77.* Ed. C. Gordon. New York: Pantheon Books.

—— (1981). "The Order of Discourse." In *Untying the Text.* Ed. R. Young. London: Routledge and Kegan Paul, pp. 48–78. Orig. pub. 1970.

Foulkes, A.P. (1983). *Literature and Propaganda.* London: Methuen.

Gado, Frank, ed. (1973). *First Person: Conversations on Writers and Writing.* Schenectady, N.Y.: Union College Press.

Gass, William (1978). *The World within the Word.* New York: Knopf.

—— (1980). *Fiction and the Figures of Life.* Boston: Godine. Orig. pub. 1970.

—— (1981). *In the Heart of the Heart of the Country.* Boston: Godine. Orig. pub. 1968.

Gott, Richard (1986). "The Crisis of Contemporary Culture." *The Guardian,* December 1, 1986: 10.

Graff, Gerald (1977). "The Myth of the Postmodernist Breakthrough." In *The Novel Today.* Ed. M. Bradbury. London: Fontana, pp. 217–49. Orig. pub. 1973.

Gramsci, Antonio (1971). *Selections from Prison Notebooks.* Trans. Quintin Hoare and Geoffrey Nowell Smith. London: Lawrence and Wishart. Originally written between 1929 and 1935.

Grayling, Anthony (1988). *Wittgenstein.* Oxford: Oxford University Press.

Green, Pete (1985). "The Contradictions of the American Boom." *International Socialism,* no. 26 (Spring 1985): 3–53.

Guerard, A.J. (1974). "Notes on the rhetoric of anti-realist fiction." *TriQuarterly,* no. 30 (Spring 1974): 3–50.

Habermas, Jürgen (1971). *Toward a Rational Society.* Trans. Jeremy J. Shapiro. London: Heinemann. Essays originally published 1968, 1969.

—— (1974). "The Public Sphere." *New German Critique,* no. 3 (1974): 49–55. Orig. pub. 1964.

—— (1976). *Legitimation Crisis.* Trans. Thomas McCarthy. London: Heinemann. Orig. pub. 1973.

—— (1983). "Modernity—An Incomplete Project." Trans. Seyla Ben-Habib. In *The Anti-Aesthetic.* Ed. H. Foster. Washington: Bay Press. Orig. pub. 1981.

—— (1985). "A Philosophico-Political Profile." Interview in *New Left Review* 151 (May/June 1985): 75–105.

Hamilton, Peter (1983). *Talcott Parsons.* Chichester: Ellis Horwood.

Harman, Chris (1982). "State capitalism, armaments and the general form of the current crisis." *International Socialism* no. 16 (Spring 1982): 37–88.

Hassan, Ihab (1971). "POSTmodernISM." *New Literary History* III, no. 1 (Autumn 1971): 5–30.

—— (1980). "The Question of Postmodernism." In *Romanticism, Modernism, Postmodernism.* Ed. H.R. Garvin. Lewisberg, Pa.: Bucknell University Press, pp. 117–26.

Haug, W.F. (1986). *Critique of Commodity Aesthetics.* Trans. Robert Bock. Cambridge: Polity Press. Orig. pub. 1971.

Hawthorne, Nathaniel (1978). *The Scarlet Letter.* Harmondsworth: Penguin. Orig. pub. 1850.

Heath, Stephen (1972). *The Nouveau Roman.* London: Elek.

Hebdige, Dick (1979). *Subculture.* London: Methuen.

Heckard, Margaret (1976). "Robert Coover, Metafiction, and Freedom." *Twentieth Century Literature* 22: 210–27.

Herr, Michael (1978). *Dispatches.* London: Pan/Picador.

Hite, Molly (1983). *Ideas of Order in the Novels of Thomas Pynchon.* Columbus: Ohio State University Press.

Hofstadter, Richard (1967). *The Paranoid Style in American Politics.* New York: Vintage Books.

Hume, Kathryn (1979). "Robert Coover's Fictions: The Naked and the Mythic." *Novel* (Winter 1979): 127–48.

Hutcheon, Linda (1987). "Beginning to theorize postmodernism." *Textual Practice* 1, no. 1 (Spring 1987): 10–31.

—— (1989). *The Politics of Postmodernism.* London: Routledge.

Huyssen, Andreas (1984). "Mapping the Postmodern." *New German Critique* 33 (Fall 1984): 5–52.

Jameson, Fredric (1971). *Marxism and Form.* Princeton, N.J.: Princeton University Press.

—— (1981). *The Political Unconscious.* London: Methuen.

—— (1984a). "Postmodernism, or the Cultural Logic of Late Capitalism." *New Left Review* 146 (July/August 1984): 53–92.

—— (1984b). "The Politics of Theory." *New German Critique* 33 (Fall 1984): 53–65.

—— (1986). "On Magic Realism in Film." *Critical Inquiry* 12 (Winter 1986): 301–25.

Jones, Barry (1982). *Sleepers, Wake!* Sussex: Wheatsheaf Books.

Joyce, James (1960). *A Portrait of the Artist as a Young Man.* Harmondsworth: Penguin. Orig. pub. 1916.

Kellner, Douglas (1988). "Postmodernism as Social Theory: Some Challenges and Problems." *Theory, Culture and Society* 5, nos. 2–3 (June 1988): 239–69.

Kermode, Frank (1968). "Modernisms." In *Innovations.* Ed. B. Bergonzi. London: Macmillan, pp. 66–92.

Klinkowitz, Jerome (1980). *Literary Disruptions.* Urbana: University of Illinois Press.

Laclau, E., and C. Mouffe (1985). *Hegemony and Socialist Strategy.* Trans. Winston Moore and Paul Cammack. London: Verso.

LeClair, Thomas (1982). "Robert Coover, *The Public Burning,* and the Art of Excess." *Critique* 23, no. 3 (Spring 1982): 5–27.

LeClair, Thomas, and Larry McCaffery, eds. (1983). *Anything Can Happen: Interviews with Contemporary American Novelists.* Urbana: University of Illinois Press.

Lefebvre, Henri (1971). *Everyday Life in the Modern World.* Trans. Sacha Rabinovitch. London: Allen Lane. Orig. pub. 1968.

Levine, G., and D. Leverenz, eds. (1976). *Mindful Pleasures: Essays on Thomas Pynchon.* Boston: Little, Brown.

Lhamon, Jr., W. T. (1976). "Pentecost, Promiscuity, and Pynchon's *V:* From the Scaffold to the Impulsive." In *Mindful Pleasures: Essays on Thomas Pynchon.* Ed. G. Levine and D. Leverenz. Boston: Little, Brown, pp. 69–86.

Lodge, David (1977). "Modernism, Antimodernism and Postmodernism." *New Review* 4, no. 38 (May 1977): 39–44.

London, Jack (1984). *The Iron Heel.* London: Journeyman Press. Orig. pub. 1907.

Lovell, Terry (1980). "The Social Relations of Cultural Production." In *One-Dimensional Marxism.* Ed. S. Clark, T. Lovell, K. McDonnell, K. Robins, and V.J. Seidler. London: Allison and Busby, pp. 232–56.

Lyotard, J.F. (1984a). *The Postmodern Condition.* Trans. Geoff Bennington and Brian Massumi. Manchester: Manchester University Press. Orig. pub. 1979.

——— (1984b). "Answering the Question: What Is Postmodernism?" Appendix to Lyotard 1984a, pp. 71–82.

McCaffery, Larry (1981). "Robert Coover on His Own and Other Fictions: An Interview." In *Novel vs. Fiction: The Contemporary Reformation.* Ed. J.I. Cope and G. Green. Norman, Ok.: Pilgrim Books.

——— (1982). *The Metafictional Muse.* University of Pittsburgh Press.

McHale, Brian (1987). *Postmodernist Fiction.* London: Methuen.

McLuhan, Marshall (1967). *Understanding Media.* London: Sphere. Orig. pub. 1964.

McQuail, Denis (1983). "The Influence and Effects of Mass Media." In *Mass Communication and Society.* Ed. J. Curran, M. Gurevitch, and J. Woollacott. London: Edward Arnold, pp. 70–94. Orig. pub. 1977.

Mailer, Norman (1968). *The Armies of the Night.* New York: Signet.

——— (1973). *Marilyn: A Biography.* London: Hodder and Stoughton.

——— (1976). *The Presidential Papers.* St. Albans: Panther. Orig. pub. 1963.

Mandel, Ernest (1978). *Late Capitalism.* Trans. Joris De Bres. London: Verso. Orig. pub. 1972.

Mangel, Anne (1976). "Maxwell's Demon, Entropy, Information: *The Crying of*

Lot 49." In *Mindful Pleasures: Essays on Thomas Pynchon.* Ed. G. Levine and D. Leverenz. Boston: Little, Brown, pp. 87–100. Orig. pub. 1971.

Marcuse, Herbert (1966). *One-Dimensional Man.* Boston: Beacon Press. Orig. pub. 1964.

——— (1969). *An Essay on Liberation.* London: Allen Lane.

——— (1979). *The Aesthetic Dimension.* London: Macmillan. Orig. pub. 1977.

Margolis, Barbara (1986). *Are We Winning Mommy?* National Film Board of Canada. Broadcast on Channel 4 ("The Eleventh Hour"), 10 August 1987.

Marx, Karl (1976). *Capital.* Vol. 1. Trans. Ben Fowkes. Harmondsworth: Penguin. Orig. pub. 1867.

Mattelart, Armand (1980). *Multinational Corporations and the Control of Culture.* Sussex: Harvester Press.

Mazurek, Raymond (1982). "Metafiction, the Historical Novel, and Coover's *The Public Burning.*" *Critique* 23, no. 3 (Spring 1982): 29–41.

Miliband, Ralph (1973). *The State in Capitalist Society.* London: Quartet Books. Orig. pub. 1969.

Mendelson, Edward (1976). "Gravity's Encyclopaedia." In *Mindful Pleasures: Essays on Thomas Pynchon.* Ed. G. Levine and D. Leverenz. Boston: Little, Brown, pp. 161–95.

Morris-Suzuki, Tessa (1986). "Capitalism in the Computer Age." *New Left Review* 160 (November/December 1986): 81–91.

Nabokov, Vladimir (1973). *Pale Fire.* Harmondsworth: Penguin. Orig. pub. 1962.

Ngũgĩ wa Thiong'o (1985). "The Language of African Literature." *New Left Review* 150 (March/April 1985): 109–27.

Philo, Greg (1990). *Seeing and Believing: The Influence of Television.* London: Routledge.

Plater, William (1978). *The Grim Phoenix.* Bloomington: Indiana University Press.

Plimpton, George, ed. (1977). *Writers at Work.* 3rd Series. Harmondsworth: Penguin, pp. 141–74.

Podhoretz, Norman (1977). "Uncle Sam and the Phantom." *Saturday Review* (17 September 1977): 27–28, 34.

Pynchon, Thomas (1975). *V.* London: Pan/Picador. Orig. pub. 1963.

——— (1976). *The Crying of Lot 49.* Philadelphia: Bantam. Orig. pub. 1966.

——— (1978). *Gravity's Rainbow.* London: Pan/Picador. Orig. pub. 1973.

——— (1985). *Slow Learner.* London: Pan/Picador. "Entropy." Orig. pub. 1960.

——— (1990). *Vineland.* London: Secker and Warburg.

Ramage, John (1982). "Myth and Monomyth in Coover's *The Public Burning.*" *Critique* 23, no. 3 (Spring 1982): 29–41.

Reed, Ishmael (1988). *Mumbo Jumbo.* London: Allison and Busby. Orig. pub. 1972.

Roszak, Theodore (1970). *The Making of a Counter Culture.* London: Faber and Faber.

Russell, Charles (1985). *Poets, Prophets and Revolutionaries.* New York: Oxford University Press.

Rustin, Michael (1989). "Post-Kleinian Psychoanalysis and the Post-Modern." *New Left Review* 173 (January/February 1989): 109–28.

Schiller, Herbert (1981). *Who Knows? Information in the Age of the Fortune 500.* Norwood, N.J.: Ablex Publishing Corporation.

Scholes, Robert (1975). *Structural Fabulation*. Notre Dame, Ind.: University of Notre Dame Press.

—— (1979). *Fabulation and Metafiction*. Urbana: University of Illinois Press.

Schwartz, Walter (1985). "Fellow travelling with the loony right." *The Guardian*, 22 March 1985.

—— (1987). "Ayatollahs of the Sunbelt." *The Guardian*, 6, 7, 8 April 1987.

Shils, Edward (1970). "Centre and Periphery." In *Modern Sociology*. Ed. P. Worsley. Harmondsworth: Penguin, pp. 415–27. Orig. pub. 1961.

Sinclair, Upton (1965). *The Jungle*. Harmondsworth: Penguin. Orig. pub. 1906.

Sontag, Susan (1983). "The Aesthetics of Silence." In *A Susan Sontag Reader*. Harmondsworth: Penguin, pp. 181–204. Orig. pub. 1967.

Stevick, Philip (1977). "Scheherezade runs out of plots, goes on talking; the king, puzzled, listens: an Essay on New Fiction." In *The Novel Today*. Ed. M. Bradbury. London: Fontana, pp. 186–216.

Sukenick, Ronald (1972). "The New Tradition." *Partisan Review* 39 (1972): 580–88.

Tanner, Tony (1971). *City of Words: American Fiction 1950–1970*. London: Jonathan Cape.

—— (1982). *Thomas Pynchon*. London: Methuen.

Therborn, Göran (1982). *The Ideology of Power and the Power of Ideology*. London: Verso.

—— (1984). "New Questions of Subjectivity." *New Left Review* 143 (January/February 1984): 97–107.

Vidal, Gore (1987). *Armageddon?: Essays 1983–1987*. London: Andre Deutsch.

Virilio, Paul, and Sylvere Lotringer (1983). *Pure War*. New York: Semiotext(e).

Vološinov, V.N. (1973). *Marxism and the Philosophy of Language*. Trans. L. Matejka and I.R. Titunik. New York: Seminar Press. Orig. pub. 1929.

Waterhouse, Roger (1974). "The Scapegoat." *Radical Philosophy*, no. 7 (Spring 1974): 21, 24–27, 33.

Waugh, Patricia (1984). *Metafiction*. London: Methuen.

White, Allon (1984). "Bakhtin, Sociolinguistics and Deconstruction." In *The Theory of Reading*. Ed. F. Gloversmith. Brighton: Harvester Press, pp. 123–46.

White, Hayden (1975). *Metahistory: The Historical Imagination in Nineteenth-Century Europe*. Baltimore: Johns Hopkins University Press. Orig. pub. 1973.

—— (1978a). *Tropics of Discourse*. Baltimore: Johns Hopkins University Press.

—— (1978b). "The Historical Text as Literary Artifact." In *The Writing of History*. Ed. R. Canary and H. Kozicki. University of Wisconsin Press, pp. 41–62.

White, Michael (1987). "A candidate who could be in with a prayer." *The Guardian*, 24 November 1987.

Wilde, Alan (1976). "Barthelme Unfair to Kierkegaard." *Boundary 2*. 5, no. 1 (Fall 1976): 45–70.

—— (1987). *Middle Grounds*. Philadelphia: University of Pennsylvania Press.

Wohlforth, Tim (1989). "The Sixties in America." *New Left Review* 178 (November/ December 1989): 105–23.

Wright, Elizabeth (1989). "Inscribing the Body Politic: Robert Coover's *Spanking the Maid*." *Textual Practice* 3, no. 3 (Winter 1989): 397–410.

Zavarzadeh, Mas'ud (1976). *The Mythopoeic Reality.* Urbana: University of Illinois Press.

Ziegler, Heide and Christopher Bigsby, eds. (1982). *The Radical Imagination and the Liberal Tradition: Interviews with English and American Novelists.* London: Junction Books.

Index

Borges, Jorge Luis, 39, 163; "The Library of Babel," 38; "The Modesty of History" (essay), 192 n. 3; "Tlön, Uqbar, Orbis Tertius," 195 n. 4
Bottomore, Tom, 195 n. 7
Bourdieu, Pierre, 26
Bradbury, Malcolm, 15–16, 23
Brautigan, Richard, 185
Brecht, Bertolt, 12
Breton, André, 15, 197 n. 22
Bricolage, 29
Brooke-Rose, Christine, 19
Buhle, Paul, 137, 138, 180, 196 n. 13
Burroughs, William, 10, 17, 21, 37, 40, 54, 75, 79, 131, 150, 152, 171, 185, 198 n. 23; in interview, 75, 191–92 n. 7, 195 n. 6, see also *The Job*; *Cities of the Red Night*, 196 n. 11; *The Job*, 35, 196 n. 11; *The Naked Lunch*, 196 n. 11, 197 n. 19; *Nova Express*, 10–11, 40–41, 75, 186; *The Ticket That Exploded*, 35, 75

Calvinism, 151
Carey, James, 192 n. 6
Caute, David, 115
Central Intelligence Agency, 115, 117, 193 n. 14, 196 n. 10
Cervantes Saaverdra, Miguel de, 20
Chomsky, Noam, 32, 33, 106–7, 193 n. 9
Christian fundamentalism, 103, 110, 116–17
Class, 7, 9, 12, 13, 18–19, 24, 25, 26, 120–21, 151, 162, 166, 180, 183, 194 n. 16
Cold War, 33, 98, 100, 102, 104, 106–7, 109–110, 117, 121, 156, 193 n. 9, 193 n. 14, 194 n. 15
Collage, 74–75, 77
Commodity: commodity aesthetics, 4, 11, 12, 21, 133; commodity fetishism, 8, 11, 12, 14, 22, 71, 73, 133, 183; commodity production, 4, 28, 34, 45, 54, 58, 68, 145, 157, 164. *See also* Consumerism
Communication: intersubjective communication, 141–42; mass communication, 1, 7, 26, 28–29, 30, 31–32, 33, 37, 68, 88, 121, 138–39, 154, 177–79, 185, 192 n. 6; temporal communication, 133–34, 135–36; transcendent

communication, 134, 136; underground communication, 136, 138, 149. *See also* Ideal speech situation
Communism, 25, 99, 107, 108, 110, 185
Computers, 7, 27–28, 55, 87, 142–43
Consumerism, 22, 58, 61, 64, 68, 78, 131, 133, 145, 179, 191 n. 3. *See also* Commodity
Coover, Robert, 15, 18, 20, 21, 22, 37, 40, 82–130, 185, 192 n. 7, 193 nn. 8, 9, 194 n. 15; in interview, 101, 103, 192 n. 4; "Dedicatoria y Prólogo a don Miguel de Cervantes Saavedra," 9–10, 90; "The Elevator," 89; "The Marker," 192 n. 1; "Morris in Chains," 86–88; *The Origin of the Brunists*, 89, 97, 192 n. 5; "Panel Game," 82–84; "A Pedestrian Accident," 89; *A Political Fable*, 97; *Pricksongs and Descants*, 9–10, 18, 82, 126; *The Public Burning*, 97–126, 192 n. 7, 193 nn. 8, 9, 10, 13, 194 nn. 15, 17; *Spanking the Maid*, 126–30, 194 nn. 19, 20; *The Universal Baseball Association, Inc., J. Henry Waugh, Prop.*, 88–97; "The Wayfarer," 84–86, 192 n. 1
Cope, Jackson I., 126
Counterculture, 17, 25, 137, 138, 166, 179–180, 198 nn. 25, 26
Counter-pastoral, 86
Couturier, Maurice, 43, 52
Critical distance, 13–14, 40–42, 45–46, 47–48, 50–55, 56, 61, 64, 66–67, 99, 152, 153

Davis, Mike, 28, 33, 174, 175, 180, 198 n. 27
Debord, Guy, 178, 183
Decentered subject, 5
De Certeau, Michel, 26, 179
Deconstruction, 6
Deictics, 169
DeLillo, Don, 37, 40
Democracy, 6–7, 137
Derrida, Jacques, 6, 97
Depthlessness, 11–12, 74, 77
Descartes, René, 5, 131
Detective fiction, 136, 146, 147
Dialectic, 6, 13, 95–96, 148, 151, 166
Différance, 6
Discourse: discourse of "America," 103–20, 122, 123, 193 nn. 12, 13; "primacy

This book was set in Baskerville and Eras typefaces. Baskerville was designed by John Baskerville at his private press in Birmingham, England, in the eighteenth-century. The first typeface to depart from oldstyle typeface design, Baskerville has more variation between thick and thin strokes. In an effort to insure that the thick and thin strokes of his typeface reproduced well on paper, John Baskerville developed the first wove paper, the surface of which was much smoother than the laid paper of the time. The development of wove paper was partly responsible for the introduction of typefaces classified as modern, which have even more contrast between thick and thin strokes.

Eras was designed in 1969 by Studio Hollenstein in Paris for the Wagner Typefoundry. A contemporary script-like version of a sans-serif typeface, the letters of Eras have a monotone stroke and are slightly inclined.

Printed on acid-free paper.